The ABCs of
Online Banking
with Quicken®

The ABCs of
Online Banking
with Quicken®

Michael Meadhra

SYBEX®

San Francisco - Paris- Düsseldorf - Soest

Associate Publisher: Carrie Lavine
Acquisitions Manager: Kristine Plachy
Developmental Editor: Dan Brodnitz
Editor: Julie Powell
Project Editor: Bonnie Bills
Technical Editor: Juli Geiser
Book Designer: Tracy Dean
Book Design Director: Catalin Dulfu
Technical Artists: Kris Warrenburg, Catalin Dulfu
Desktop Publisher: Kris Warrenburg
Production Coordinator: Kim Wimpsett
Indexer: Ted Laux
Cover Designer: Design Site
Cover Illustrator/Photographer: Jim Krantz and Sergie Loobkoff

Screen reproductions produced with Collage Complete.

Collage Complete is a trademark of Inner Media Inc.

SYBEX is a registered trademark of SYBEX Inc.

TRADEMARKS: SYBEX has attempted throughout this book to distinguish proprietary trademarks from descriptive terms by following the capitalization style used by the manufacturer.

Every effort has been made to supply complete and accurate information. However, neither SYBEX nor the author assumes responsibility for its use, nor for any infringement of the intellectual property rights of third parties which would result from such use.

Library of Congress Card Number: 96-67497
ISBN: 0-7821-1886-0

Manufactured in the United States of America

10 9 8 7 6 5 4 3 2

Acknowledgments

A book such as this is a team effort, and I've had the pleasure of working with a great team: the people at Sybex. My thanks to Acquisitions Manager Kristine Plachy, Manager of Developmental Editors Richard Mills, and Developmental Editor Dan Brodnitz for helping me develop the concept of this book and bring it to completion. Project Editor Bonnie Bills and Editor Julie Powell have been a joy to work with. Thanks also to Associate Publisher Carrie Lavine; Technical Editor Juli Geiser; Desktop Publisher Kris Warrenburg; Line Artist and Book Design Director Catalin Dulfu; Production Coordinator Kim Wimpsett; and Indexer Ted Laux.

Thanks also go to Brent Prouty at Intuit, Inc. for his assistance in answering my many questions, and to Ravi Bellur and Rebecca Tsou in Intuit's beta test department. In addition, I'd like to offer my thanks and compliments to the customer support staff at Centura Bank. They were unfailingly cheerful as they helped me recover from the mistakes I made while exploring the limits of a new system.

Contents at a Glance

Table of Contents

PART 4: FINANCIAL INFORMATION & OTHER SERVICES 227

Chapter 13: Portfolio Price Update .229

Chapter 14: Investor Insight 251

Introduction

It's been said that we're in the midst of a revolution—the network revolution—as stand-alone personal computers gain the benefits of connectivity with other computer systems. You see the effects of this revolution everywhere you turn. Suddenly, everyone at the office is using e-mail; some workers telecommute from home; and then there's the explosive growth of the Internet.

Banking and personal finance have now become a part of the network revolution. With a personal computer, a modem, and the appropriate software, you can check your current bank balance, pay bills, transfer funds between accounts, receive e-mail from your bank, and download stock prices. The links between your computer and the financial institutions participating in a banking network are transforming personal finance into *online* personal finance.

The Purpose of This Book

This book is intended to serve as an introduction to online personal finance. Its purpose is to provide you with the information you need to get comfortable with the technology of using online connections to banks, bill payment services, and stock quote services. Specifically, this book shows you how to use the online personal finance features available in the leading personal finance software—Quicken.

We expect that most readers are already using their computer to help manage their personal finances. Perhaps you are using Quicken, or maybe you're using another personal finance program. Either way, you're probably already familiar with the basics of using such a program. So we didn't attempt to create a comprehensive reference or tutorial for Quicken. Instead, we focused on the realm of online personal finance—the expansion of the personal finance field made possible by linking your personal computer to a network of banks and other providers of financial services.

If you're truly new to personal finance software and are looking for a complete guide to the features of Quicken, I recommend *Mastering Quicken 5,* also published by Sybex. It complements this volume nicely.

How This Book Is Organized

This book is divided into four parts, plus a collection of appendices at the back. The first part is an overview of online personal finance: what it is and who provides the services. The second part covers downloading account balances from your bank and the other components of what Quicken defines as Online Banking. Paying bills online is the subject of the third part. The fourth part talks about using online connections to help you track securities and also presents a brief profile of the other online services and options that are available.

Part 1: Overview of Online Personal Finance

- Chapter 1 asks (and answers) the question "What Is Online Personal Finance?" It defines the terms and lays out what you can expect from the current state of the art of online personal finance.
- Chapter 2, "Getting to Know the Players," introduces the team members that work together to provide online personal finance services to Quicken users.
- Chapter 3, "Selecting a Banking Partner," explores some of the new facets that online access adds to your relationship with your bank—especially as it applies to selecting a new bank.
- Chapter 4, "The Question of Security," helps you understand the steps Intuit takes to keep your personal finances private and secure when you conduct your banking business online.

Part 2: Online Banking

- Chapter 5 is titled "The First Step: Setting Up Your Intuit Membership." As the name implies, it takes you through the process of establishing your Intuit membership, which is your point of access for most of Quicken's online personal finance features.
- Chapter 6, "Setting Up an Account for Online Banking," explains how to get an account ready for online access, both at the bank and in your Quicken software.
- Chapter 7, "Using Online Banking," shows you how to get an online bank statement and how to enter the downloaded transaction information into your Quicken account register.
- Chapter 8, "Exploring Other Online Banking Features," covers such topics as accessing a credit card account, reconciling your account register, and using e-mail to communicate with your bank.

Part 3: Online BillPay

- Chapter 9, "Writing Electronic Checks," describes how the online bill payment process works to get a payment from your computer screen to your payee.
- Chapter 10, "Getting Ready for Online BillPay," shows you how to sign up for the bill payment service and set up your Quicken account for Online BillPay.
- Chapter 11, "Making Online Bill Payments," gives you step-by-step instructions for creating and sending online payments in Quicken.
- Chapter 12, "More Online BillPay Techniques," shows you how to generate payment inquiries and stop-payment orders and how to use e-mail to communicate with the payment processing center.

Part 4: Financial Information & Other Services

- Chapter 13, "Portfolio Price Update," tells you how to use this built-in Quicken feature to download stock and mutual fund prices and update your Quicken investment portfolio.
- Chapter 14, " Investor Insight," introduces you to this tool for serious investors. You'll learn how to download and review stock prices, financial news, and detailed company profiles.
- Chapter 15, "Other Online Services," profiles the Quicken Financial Network and other sources of online personal finance information.

Appendices and Glossary

- Appendix A, "Where to Find Help," will help you get in touch with the right source of assistance when you have a problem.
- Appendix B, "CheckFree and Quicken," shows you how to use this alternative online bill payment service.
- Appendix C, "Member Bank Offerings," summarizes in table form the basic services offered by some of the participating financial institutions in Intuit's online banking network.
- The Glossary is a handy reference where you can find definitions for the terms and buzzwords you'll find in this book.

Oh, By the Way...

A note about terminology is in order here. When most people say *online banking*, they mean any banking transaction that is conducted online (over a modem or network). The term in this context covers getting bank statements, paying bills, and more. However, Intuit adopted *Online Banking* as the name of a specific group of features and services available in the Quicken software. It includes getting online statements, but not paying bills—that's a separate service called Online BillPay.

In this book, the generic term *online banking* appears in lowercase, and the name of the Quicken feature is capitalized (*Online Banking*). To reduce confusion, we've chosen the term *online personal finance* to encompass the complete spectrum of Quicken's online features, which includes downloading stock quotes and financial advice as well as conducting banking and bill payment operations.

On another note, you should be aware that we've altered many of the screens that appear in the figures and illustrations in this book. We've replaced real bank names and logos with those of a fictitious bank and substituted bogus information for account numbers and other personal data.

Part 1

Overview of Online Personal Finance

Chapter 1

WHAT IS ONLINE PERSONAL FINANCE?

Your relationship with your bank—and the way you handle your personal finances—is changing, evolving, and adapting to new technology. You used to go into a bank branch to conduct business at a teller's window; you balanced your checkbook with a pen and a calculator. Then you began using an automated teller machine (ATM) and tracking your personal finances with your computer. Now you're ready to take the next step: going online with a connection between your computer software—Quicken—and your bank.

The online aspect of personal finance is a whole new realm, just now coming into its own thanks to a convergence of technologies and market factors. You're poised to begin your exploration of this new world of online personal finance. So let's get started with a brief overview of online personal finance and the capabilities of Quicken.

Taking Advantage of an Emerging Technology

Online personal finance lets you conduct your banking business from the comfort and privacy of your own home and on your own schedule. You don't have to visit a bank branch during business hours, or even make a trip to the nearest ATM. All you need is your personal computer, the appropriate software (such as Quicken), and a modem to allow your computer to connect to your chosen financial institution. You can check account balances, see what transactions have cleared your bank, transfer funds between accounts, pay bills, and even check stock prices.

In retrospect, it's a little surprising that online personal finance has taken so long to develop. The fundamental technology has been around for about a decade, but it hasn't caught on with large numbers of people until recently.

There have been several attempts to popularize banking online. For the past few years, the leading personal finance software programs have included provisions for electronic bill payment, but the feature has attracted relatively few users. Similarly, software that lets investors get stock prices online has yet to develop a broad user base. Some banks tried their own online personal finance programs, with only limited success. Widespread acceptance of banks' own online systems was hampered by awkward, propriety software and expensive fees for the service. Add security concerns to the picture, and you can see why demand for online personal finance has grown so slowly in the past.

Now, however, the time has come for online personal finance. This previously limited market has finally reached the critical mass needed to attract intense interest from software developers, banks, and consumers alike.

Several factors have converged to set the stage for rapid growth of online personal finance. Among them:

- Personal computers (PCs) have become a household appliance. No longer the exclusive province of computer nerds, they have found their way into a significant percentage (some say almost half) of all U.S. households.
- Banks are aggressively cutting costs by shutting down expensive branches and teller windows and are looking for alternative ways to deliver their services.
- Consumers are demanding more convenience and flexibility in all things, including their banking and personal finance.
- Encryption technologies have developed to address security concerns.
- More software programs—notably Quicken—include easy-to-use online personal finance features.
- More banks, brokerages, and credit card companies are offering their services online, thus making online personal finance available to more people.

As a result, the experts project explosive growth in the online personal finance arena. They estimate that the 100,000 users of online personal finance in 1995 will have grown to more than one million users in just a year or so.

More services available from more financial institutions, lower fees, easier access to online services through enhanced software—it all adds up to more convenience and time savings for online personal finance users like you.

Online Options

Online personal finance isn't just one piece of software or one service. It's a whole category of activities that encompasses any personal finance operation (banking, paying bills, getting stock market quotes) that you perform online—that is, by connecting your computer to a financial institution's computer via a modem and phone line or via a network. There are several different ways to access online personal finance features, including:

- Proprietary software
- Online services
- The Internet
- Personal finance software

Proprietary Software

Proprietary software provides dedicated access to a financial institution (bank, credit card company, or brokerage) or to a specialty service provider such as CheckFree. Such software may allow you to access your bank accounts, download lists of transactions, initiate stock transactions, or pay bills. The limited, specialized nature of the software usually prevents you from using any one product to get a consolidated picture of your finances without duplicating the information in yet another piece of software.

Online Services

Online services such as Prodigy, America Online, and CompuServe all offer some sort of online personal finance capability. All provide their subscribers with access to stock prices. Prodigy was the first to offer limited online banking. More recently, America Online (AOL) announced a collaboration with Intuit (the makers of Quicken) to make more extensive online personal finance available to AOL subscribers. You can expect all the major online services to expand their online personal finance features in the near future. Of course, you must subscribe to a service in order to use them.

The Internet

Online personal finance on the Internet is still in its infancy, but it's drawing a lot of attention. A few pioneering banks (such as Security First Network Bank) offer online banking via World Wide Web sites. Others (such as Mark Twain Bank) are exploring methods to facilitate cash and credit transactions on the Net. Intuit has announced its intention to expand its Quicken Financial Network (Intuit's own Web site) to include more online personal finance features. This is an exciting area that bears watching, but it's still in the experimental stage of development, and many consumers aren't yet comfortable with the solutions to the various security issues.

Personal Finance Software

For most people, using online personal finance means working with the built-in features of personal finance software such as Quicken and Microsoft Money. The latest versions of these programs include online access to bank balances, online bill paying, and online stock price updates, among other features. Both programs are continuing to build and expand their feature sets, and other software developers are sure to follow. This book will focus on the overwhelming market leader—Quicken.

What Can You Do Online?

These days, you can conduct almost any routine personal finance transaction online. That includes nearly all the options available at an ATM, and more:

- Check account balances

- See what transactions have cleared the bank
- Download transaction details
- Pay bills
- Transfer funds
- Check stock prices
- Research public companies and stock offerings
- Buy and sell securities

NOTE Quicken lets you do everything on this list except buy and sell securities. For that, you'll need specialized software from your broker (assuming that your brokerage supports online stock trades).

About the only common transaction you can't handle from your computer is a deposit. Even that can be done electronically if your employer offers direct deposit; you just can't initiate it from your system. Additionally, some banks support their online customers with telephone customer service representatives who can help you open accounts and apply for loans over the phone. As a result, you may not need to visit a bank branch unless you must get some papers from your safe-deposit box—or you simply miss the distinctive decor and chatting with the teller.

Getting Your Bank Statement via Modem

What's the current balance in my bank account? Has a specific check cleared the bank yet? Did I forget to record an ATM transaction last week?

No doubt you've found yourself asking similar questions. Thanks to Quicken's Online Banking feature, you no longer have to wait until your bank statement arrives in the mail to get the answers. Online Banking gives you instant access to this information and more—provided you bank with one of the participating financial institutions that have joined with Intuit to provide the service to their customers.

Online Banking lets you contact your bank from Quicken and get an electronic version of your bank statement. An online statement, such as the one shown in Figure 1.1, is even more powerful than the paper version that arrives in the mail. Like a paper account statement, it allows you to:

- Check your current account balance
- See a list of transactions that have cleared the bank since the previous statement

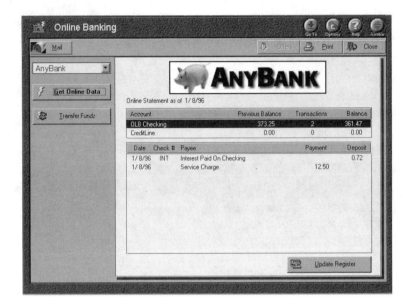

FIGURE 1.1:
Get an up-to-date bank statement anytime you want with Quicken's Online Banking feature.

In addition, Online Banking lets you do more. You can:

- Download transaction details and transfer them to your Quicken account register. (Entering transactions in your register automatically saves time and reduces errors.)
- Transfer funds between accounts at the same bank (provided the bank allows you to do so)
- Reconcile your register balance to your online bank statement

NOTE   See Chapter 6, "Setting Up an Account for Online Banking," for instructions on getting started with Online Banking. See also Chapter 7, "Using Online Banking," for information on basic Online Banking operations. See Chapter 8, "Exploring Other Online Banking Features," for information on reconciling your account and transferring funds.

Paying Bills Online

Nobody likes to pay bills. It's bad enough to see all that money draining out of your checking account, without the process itself being such a hassle. First you must make sure you have enough funds to cover the needed payments, then you must write the checks, sign them, stuff envelopes with checks and payment stubs, lick, stick, and stamp the envelopes, and finally, take them to the post office. And you have to repeat the process several times every month. Whew!

If you use Quicken, you already know how the program can help you with the first part—keeping track of the funds in your accounts—and it can even print checks for you, which helps a little. But there's still room for improvement. Now, Online BillPay lets you completely skip the paper check and all the handling that goes with it.

Instead of printing (or handwriting) checks, you send your payments electronically. Quicken gathers your electronic payments (see Figure 1.2) and lets you send them on their way with a click of your mouse. Intuit Services Corporation (or CheckFree) will process the payments for you and send them to your vendors according to your specifications. Some bills are paid by check. Others are paid by electronic funds transfers (like the automatic payments to insurance companies and utilities). Either way, it's all handled for you—and the cost is about what you'd pay for stamps.

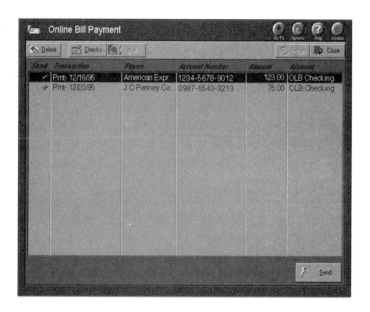

FIGURE 1.2:
Instead of printing checks, send them electronically with a click of your mouse.

NOTE   See Chapter 9, "Writing Electronic Checks," for general information on Online BillPay. See Chapter 10, "Getting Ready for Online BillPay," for instructions on setting up your accounts to pay bills electronically. See also Chapter 11, "Making Simple Online Bill Payments," and Chapter 12, "More Online BillPay Techniques," for the detailed procedures involved in Online BillPay.

Communicating with Your Financial Institution by E-Mail

The electronic connection between Quicken and your financial institution can carry more than online bank statements and bill payments. As a bonus, along with the other Online Banking and Online BillPay features, you get the ability to exchange electronic messages—e-mail—with your bank. With e-mail, you can:

- Inquire about the status of Online BillPay payments
- Send a message about a specific transaction
- Communicate with the bank regarding your account

E-mail can be more convenient than calling your bank's customer service department on the phone, because it's available at any time. There are no special hours; no long waits on hold; no misunderstood voice messages; no telephone tag; and no calls returned at inconvenient times. You simply type a short message, as shown in Figure 1.3, and send it just like any other online transaction. Later, after the bank has had time to respond, you can log on to collect the reply. It all happens on your schedule, and without leaving Quicken.

NOTE   See Chapter 8, "Exploring Other Online Banking Features," for details on exchanging e-mail with your bank. See also Chapter 12, "More Online BillPay Techniques," for instructions on using e-mail for payment inquiries.

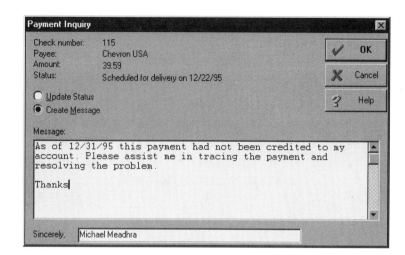

FIGURE 1.3:
E-mail is a convenient way to communicate with your bank online.

Accessing Financial Market Information and Updates

With the volatile nature of the securities markets, how do you know the true value of your investment portfolio? You could search the newspaper for yesterday's prices on the stocks you own and meticulously enter them into Quicken, but that's time-consuming and error-prone.

Portfolio Price Update supplies a better alternative. This Quicken feature can update your portfolio automatically with just a few mouse clicks. Once you sign up for the service, Portfolio Price Update will let you go online and get the current prices for the stocks and mutual funds in your Quicken investment accounts. It's a fast, easy way to keep your stock portfolio up-to-date.

For the more serious investor, Quicken 5 Deluxe for Windows offers a separate program called Investor Insight. It includes the capabilities of Portfolio Price Update, plus other additional features. Investor Insight lets you track securities you don't own, and it collects much more information, including:

- Current stock prices
- Historical performance
- Company profiles
- Financial news related to selected stocks

Although Quicken doesn't provide the means to buy and sell securities online, it does include features to help you track the performance of your investments and other securities, as shown in Figure 1.4. Using these features will help you make more informed decisions about buying and selling securities.

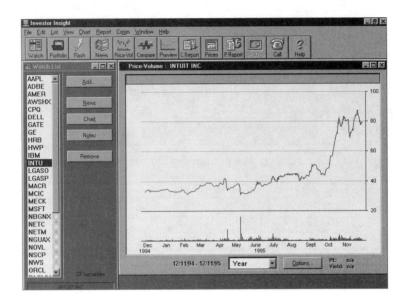

FIGURE 1.4: Investor Insight gives you a historical perspective on a security as well as the current price.

In addition to Portfolio Price Update and Investor Insight, Quicken provides access to more information about stocks and mutual funds. Some of this information is included on the Quicken Deluxe CD-ROM; more is available on the Quicken Financial Network (which is accessible from within Quicken or from the Internet).

NOTE See Chapter 13, "Portfolio Price Update," for detailed information on using this handy feature. See also Chapter 14, "Investor Insight," to learn more about the Investor Insight program.

What Do You Need?

To use Quicken's online personal finance features, you'll obviously need the Quicken software. Many of the features discussed in this book are new to Quicken 5 for Windows and Quicken 6 for Macintosh. (These are the "New for '96" versions of the product that were released in the fall of 1995.) Previous versions of Quicken for Windows, Macintosh, and DOS don't offer Online Banking or other more advanced features. They do, however, support online bill payment through CheckFree and have limited capabilities for importing register transactions and stock prices that you can download with separate utilities.

To run Quicken 5 for Windows, you must have a computer that meets or exceeds the following requirements:
- 386-based (or higher) PC
- Windows 3.1 or Windows 95
- 4 MB RAM (minimum)
- 14 MB available hard-disk space
- Windows-compatible VGA or higher monitor
- 3.5-inch floppy disk and/or CD-ROM drive
- Any printer supported by Windows (optional)

Quicken 6 for Macintosh requires:
- Any Apple Macintosh or Power Macintosh computer with a hard disk (68020 or better processor recommended)
- 4 MB RAM for System 7; 8 MB RAM for System 7.5
- 4 MB available hard-disk space
- Printer (optional)

In addition, an online connection for either system requires:
- 2400-baud modem (9600-baud or faster recommended)
- Access to a phone line

The Quicken software provides the basic online personal finance features, but the nature of an online communication requires a compatible system on the other end of the connection. For each online personal finance feature, there's a financial institution or other service provider involved. You must purchase individual online services from those providers. You'll need some, or all, of the following:
- An Intuit membership account with Intuit Services Corporation, which acts as gate-keeper for several online services (see Chapter 5)
- Online Banking, which requires an account with a participating financial institution and registration for the service (see Chapter 6 and Appendix C)
- Online BillPay, which requires a checking account at a U.S. bank plus the service from Intuit Services Corporation or CheckFree (see Chapters 9 and 10)
- Portfolio Price Update, which goes through Intuit Services Corporation but requires a separate sign-up and monthly fee (see Chapter 13)
- An Investor Insight account, which is a separate service that you can subscribe to regardless of the other services you use (see Chapter 14)
- The Quicken Financial Network and other services, which are separate and are described in the respective portions of this book

You can order a la carte to assemble the package of services you need.

What Does It Cost?

The prices for all these online personal finance services will vary, depending on the service and the financial institution. If you use only the basic Online Banking, you might get the service free (included in the normal monthly service charge for your bank account). On the other hand, for a heavy user who pays lots of bills and checks stock prices hourly, the fees for online personal finance might be more than $100 per month.

Here's a brief listing of typical charges for the base services:

- Intuit membership is free.
- Quicken Financial Network (Intuit's World Wide Web site) is free.
- Online Banking fees range from $3 to $10 a month for about eight online statements (which is usually enough). The fee is often included in the monthly service charge for the bank account.
- Online BillPay typically costs $5.95 per month for up to 20 payment transactions.

NOTE See Appendix C, "Member Bank Offerings," for a table of the fees charged by participating financial institutions.

- Portfolio Price Update costs $2.95 per month for six updates.
- Investor Insight is more expensive at $9.95 per month, but it supplies more information.

NOTE You'll find a more detailed discussion of the fees associated with each online personal finance service in the appropriate sections of this book.

Chapter 2

GETTING TO KNOW THE PLAYERS

FEATURING

- **Intuit and the Quicken software**
- **Intuit Services Corporation**
- **What about CheckFree?**
- **Participating financial institutions**
- **Credit cards**
- **Your local bank**
- **Sources of investment information**
- **The Quicken Financial Network**
- **America Online and the Internet**
- **Sorting through your options**

Online personal finance encompasses a variety of products and services provided by several different suppliers. Delivering online personal finance features to your personal computer requires the cooperative effort of software developers, financial institutions, communications networks, and other specialty services.

If you want to understand how your online personal finance transactions work, you need to get to know the players in the game and the roles they each play. But like a spectator at the big game, you may find it difficult to identify the players without a program. That's what this chapter is all about.

It's Not Just You and Your Bank

Simply installing some software on your computer isn't enough to let you enter the world of online personal finance—that's just the beginning. There must be a participating financial institution at the other end of the online connection.

So far you have three parties involved in making online personal finance work: you, your financial institution, and Intuit, the company that created the Quicken software you use. But wait, there's more. There are other banks as well as brokerages and credit card companies that provide similar, but slightly different, services. Now things are starting to get complicated.

You *could* connect to each separate financial institution directly, but you'd probably need a different software program, or at least a different (and possibly incompatible) setup, to access each one. Also, each financial institution would have to independently develop the technology and security measures to allow customers to connect to their computer systems. This is exactly how things worked until recently, when Intuit set up a subsidiary company, Intuit Services Corporation, and added Online Banking capabilities to Quicken.

Adding another player to the game has actually simplified things. The presence of an intermediary between you (and your personal finance software) and the financial institutions makes it possible to standardize the connections. The intermediary—Intuit Services Corporation—facilitates online connections, provides security, and handles the most common online transactions, thus relieving banks of many of the burdens of setting up online banking for their customers. The large number of established Quicken users gave Intuit the necessary clout to establish practical standards and make it attractive for leading banks to adopt those standards.

But online personal finance goes beyond standard financial transactions with a bank. In addition to Quicken's Online Banking, you can, for example, check stock prices and peruse the Internet for financial information. While these services require separate connections to separate suppliers, Quicken and its related software make the process of connecting to them relatively simple.

Intuit and the Quicken Software

Let's start with the component of the online personal finance system with which you are probably most familiar, the Quicken personal finance software. Intuit, Inc. is the company that develops, sells, and supports this popular program.

Quicken is available for both Windows (version 3.1 and Windows 95) and Macintosh platforms. There are even versions of Quicken for DOS and for Personal Digital Assistants (PDAs) and other handheld computers. Intuit has also developed add-on programs for Quicken (such as QuickInvoice and QuickPay), business accounting software (QuickBooks), and tax preparation software (TurboTax). In addition, Intuit sells checks and other supplies for use with its programs.

This book focuses on the online personal finance capabilities of the most popular version of the Quicken program, Quicken 5 for Windows (shown in Figure 2.1). However, most of the same features are also available in the Macintosh version (Quicken 6 for Macintosh).

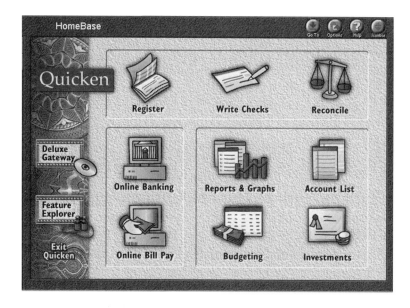

FIGURE 2.1:
The Quicken software is your doorway to the world of online banking.

Quicken offers you the ability to perform a wide variety of personal finance functions. For example, you can:

- Track expenses
- Write checks
- Track bank balances
- Reconcile bank accounts
- Track credit card balances
- Create budgets
- Generate reports
- Track investments
- Estimate taxes
- Analyze loans
- Create charts to visualize your finances

In the fall of 1995, Intuit added several new online personal finance features to Quicken. These features include the ability to:

- Get account statements electronically
- Check current account balances
- See what transactions have cleared the bank
- Download transactions and post them to your account registers
- Pay bills online with electronic checks
- Get stock price updates online
- Contact financial institutions with e-mail
- Connect to the Internet for financial information

Most of Quicken's online personal finance capabilities are available in the basic version of the program. The Deluxe version (and the Quicken Financial Suite) adds some more features. The Macintosh version of Quicken offers most of the same online personal finance features, but it implements some features differently.

The Quicken software is your starting point for entering the world of online personal finance. You'll conduct nearly all your online personal finance activities from within Quicken, but there's more going on behind the scenes. Quicken also reaches out across the phone lines to interact with other online personal finance players, making many of their features available to you.

Intuit Services Corporation

Intuit Services Corporation (ISC) is a subsidiary of Intuit Inc., located halfway across the country (Illinois as opposed to California) from the company that produces the Quicken software. ISC exists to provide online services—such as Online Banking and Online BillPay—for Quicken users and others.

> **NOTE**   In the Quicken documentation you'll see references to Intuit Online Services and Automated Financial Services (AFS). Although there are subtle differences, these terms generally refer to Intuit Services Corporation and the services you get from the Quicken software and ISC. For simplicity, I'll just refer to ISC in this book.

For Online Banking, ISC is the intermediary providing the connection between your Quicken software and your bank. ISC furnishes a communications conduit from your computer, through their facility, to the bank's system. It's a private communications network that employs advanced encryption technology to keep your financial transactions secure.

ICS provides you with dial-up access to its system, handles communications with your computer software, establishes your user identity, and forges a trusted connection to the bank's computers. It can accommodate thousands of users and dozens of banks simultaneously.

For Online BillPay, ISC serves another purpose. Using the same private, secure communications network, ISC accepts bill payment requests from your Quicken software, processes each request, and sends a payment to the payee you specify. ISC can make payments by printing and mailing paper checks on your behalf or by initiating electronic funds transfers (EFTs). ISC offers this service for any account that has checking privileges—not only for accounts at banks connected to Intuit's online network, but for accounts at almost any financial institution in the country.

You'll need to sign up for an Intuit membership if you want to use Quicken's online services: Online Banking, Online BillPay, and Portfolio Price Update. The membership itself is free. You'll pay a fee directly to ISC only if you subscribe to Portfolio Price Update or use Online BillPay from an account at a bank that isn't a member of Intuit's online banking network. For Online Banking and Online BillPay from a member bank, ISC gets paid by the financial institution; there's no separate charge by ISC to you.

NOTE See Chapter 5, "Setting Up Your Intuit Membership," for more on establishing your connection to Intuit Services Corporation.

What about CheckFree?

If you've used previous versions of Quicken, you've probably heard of (and may have used) CheckFree for paying bills electronically. CheckFree is an independent company located in Columbus, Ohio, that has been affiliated with Intuit for several years.

CheckFree is set up to process electronic bill payments for large corporate clients, but also makes the service available to individual users. You can send bill payment instructions to CheckFree electronically from your computer using either Quicken or CheckFree's own software. CheckFree will process the payment for you, contact your payee, and send payment by EFT, bank draft, or paper check.

Despite the fact that CheckFree is a separate company, the service has been so transparently integrated into Quicken that some users may not have realized that CheckFree is not part of Intuit. Now, however, the relationship between Intuit and CheckFree is changing. Intuit Services Corporation can now serve the same purpose, and it has become the default provider of Online BillPay service from Quicken for Windows. (Online BillPay from Quicken for Macintosh will continue to go through CheckFree.)

Quicken for Windows still allows you to pay your bills with CheckFree. If you previously used CheckFree for your online bill payments, you can continue to do so after upgrading to Quicken 5 for Windows, or you can switch to ISC. The choice is yours.

NOTE See Appendix B for more on working with CheckFree.

Participating Financial Institutions

Quicken can't work its Online Banking magic with just any bank or financial institution. To use Online Banking, you must have an account with a financial institution that has a prearranged affiliation with Intuit Services Corporation. You *can* set up Online BillPay with other banks, but only member banks offer full online banking (downloading current balances and cleared transactions).

NOTE If you plan to take advantage of Quicken's Online Banking features, you must have an account with one of the participating financial institutions.

Most banks don't offer online services to their customers—yet. Some financial institutions may offer limited online services through proprietary software or through another software package, but only a limited (albeit growing) number of financial institutions offer online banking services through Quicken.

For Quicken's Online Banking system to work, the financial institution must establish computer connections with ISC and arrange for all the details of responding to user requests. There are security procedures and lots of technical considerations to be worked out before a financial institution can go online.

ISC signed up 19 major financial institutions to launch their new online banking service in the fall of 1995. The list included banks from across the country, plus brokerages and credit card companies. More financial institutions are joining the list as time goes by. As this book goes to press, the list is up to more than 35 financial institutions and growing.

TIP The original participating financial institutions show up on lists in dialog boxes when you're setting up accounts for Online Banking. Later arrivals may not appear on the list, but the software will still support access to accounts at those banks if you enter the correct identifying numbers.

Unless you already have an account at one of the member banks, you'll need to choose a new bank for your online relationship if you plan to take advantage of Quicken's Online Banking features. Note that even among member banks, the range of online services available and the bank fee for each service varies widely. It's best to shop around.

> **NOTE**   Each participating bank will charge fees for online banking services on your account according to its own policies. The bank then contracts with ISC to provide access from Quicken for its customers. See Chapter 3, "Selecting a Banking Partner," for more on choosing a financial institution for online banking.

Credit Cards

It's not hard to see how online banking works with checking and savings accounts, or even with similar accounts at a brokerage house. But what about credit cards? Can you get access to credit card accounts online as well?

The answer is yes, no, and maybe. Yes, it's possible to access some credit card accounts. No, you can't use Online BillPay with credit card accounts. And if you have a credit card account at a participating financial institution, maybe you'll be able to access it with Quicken's Online Banking feature.

American Express

When you look at the list of participating financial institutions, you'll notice American Express near the top. Although American Express is not really a bank, it offers some key online banking features for its cardholders. You can use Quicken's Online Banking to get account balances and cleared transactions for your American Express and Optima accounts (as shown in Figure 2.2), just like getting an online statement from your checking account.

Intuit IntelliCharge/Quicken Credit Card

For the past few years, Intuit has offered Quicken users the ability to retrieve account balances on a credit card—a special Intuit-sponsored Visa or MasterCard. You could get your credit card account statement via a disk in the mail or downloaded via modem. Then, once you had the account balance and transaction information in electronic form, you could import the information into your Quicken account register.

The new version of Quicken updates the process. Now, with one of these accounts, you can get your account information via the Online Banking feature. No more waiting for disks or making other calls with your modem.

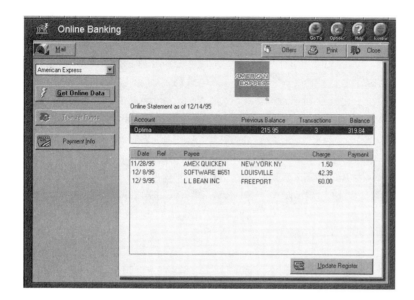

FIGURE 2.2:
Online Banking isn't just for checking accounts; you can download credit card statements too.

Other Credit Cards

Most Visa and MasterCard accounts are set up through a bank—often the same bank where you have your checking and savings accounts. If you have a Visa or MasterCard account at one of the member banks, you'll be able to access your credit card account just like any other account at the bank—provided the bank supports that feature. Some do; some don't.

You won't be able to access Visa or MasterCard accounts at other banks from within Quicken—not until those banks join Intuit Services Corporation as participating financial institutions. The same goes for other credit cards, such as Discover. As this book goes to press, none of the other credit card companies have signed up with ISC. But that may change.

Your Local Bank

OK, suppose your local bank isn't one of the participating financial institutions in the Intuit online banking network. Does that mean you can't use any of Quicken's online personal finance features? Not at all!

If a bank or financial institution isn't part of the Intuit network, you can't get online statements and check on cleared transactions, because there's no way to get information from the non-member bank into Quicken. However, you can still use Online BillPay to pay bills electronically from Quicken.

The Online BillPay feature works with any bank account in the United States that has checking privileges. You contract with Intuit Services Corporation (or CheckFree) for the Online BillPay service from your account at a non-member bank. Then you can create and send online bill payments normally. When you send the payments from Quicken, the payment requests go to ISC rather than to your bank. ISC handles the electronic paperwork to print a check or initiate an electronic funds transfer (EFT).

Your bank gets EFT requests through the federal banking system's Automated Clearing House, just like an electronic payment request for an automatic payment to a utility or insurance company. A check is even simpler. The paper check goes to your payee, who deposits it at their bank. The check then gets presented to your bank for payment just like any other check.

As a result, your local bank conducts business as usual, with no special arrangements required to handle your online bill payments. The difference is that you didn't have to write the check, stuff it in an envelope, and lick the stamp.

Investment Information

Quicken's online personal finance features extend to your investments as well. With Portfolio Price Update and Investor Insight, you can get invaluable investment information such as current stock prices, historical data, and more. There's even more investment information and advice available on the Quicken Deluxe CD. In addition, NetWorth, available on the Quicken Financial Network, is an online source of information about mutual funds.

Portfolio Price Update

Portfolio Price Update is built into Quicken. It lets you get stock price updates online and update the value of your investment accounts. You can check current prices on stocks, mutual funds, and market indexes from the New York Stock Exchange, American Stock Exchange, and NASDAQ.

When you access Portfolio Price Update, it dials Intuit Services Corporation and automatically downloads current prices (delayed by 20 minutes) for the securities in your investment accounts; it then automatically updates prices in Quicken to show the current value of your investments. After three free updates, the service incurs a monthly fee and a small charge for each update that exceeds the monthly allotment.

NOTE See Chapter 13 for more information about Portfolio Price Update.

Investor Insight

Need more investment information than a quick check of current prices? Then you should check out Investor Insight, a separate program available in Quicken Deluxe for Windows. It includes more elaborate features for the serious investor. You get access to some of the same information sources used by professional stock analysts and brokers.

Investor Insight lets you track stocks and mutual funds. Unlike Portfolio Price Update, which tracks prices of stocks in your Quicken investment portfolio, Investor Insight lets you track stocks you don't own and get a wealth of information for making buying and selling decisions. Along with current prices, you can also get price history, financial news, and even company profiles.

Investor Insight operates independently of Quicken. It doesn't go through a connection to Intuit Services Corporation, and it costs more than Portfolio Price Update, but it provides much more information in exchange. Although it's a separate program, Investor Insight can pass price updates to Quicken to update your investment accounts.

NOTE See Chapter 14, "Investor Insight," for more information about this feature.

Quicken Financial Network

The Quicken Financial Network (QFN) is Intuit's home on the Internet, part of the highly publicized World Wide Web. It provides a convenient source of news, information, and advice about Quicken and other Intuit products. On QFN, you can find answers to questions and make suggestions about the software and various personal finance issues. QFN also provides access to financial information such as NetWorth (which supplies data on mutual funds).

Installing Quicken installs the software you need for convenient, free access to QFN from within Quicken. The software will automatically configure itself to use your modem and dial the nearest node of the network with which ISC has contracted to provide Internet access to Quicken users. A special personal edition of Netscape Navigator Web browser software allows you to view Quicken's Web page (shown in Figure 2.3).

WARNING Although access to the Quicken Financial Network from within Quicken is usually free, long-distance telephone charges may apply in some (typically rural) areas.

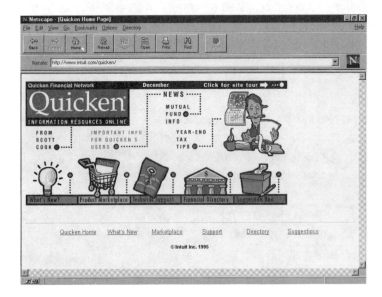

FIGURE 2.3:
The Quicken Financial Network is Intuit's home on the Internet.

While the Quicken Financial Network is on the Internet, Net access from Quicken is normally restricted to QFN. However, Intuit, through its Internet service provider, offers you the option of expanding this service to include full, unrestricted Internet access at very competitive rates.

If you already have Internet access, you can use your favorite Web browser to access the Quicken Financial Network at **http://www.intuit.com**.

NOTE See Chapter 15, "Other Online Services," for more on the Quicken Financial Network.

> **TIP** In addition to QFN, Intuit maintains a presence on the major online services such as CompuServe (GO INTUIT), America Online (Keyword: Intuit), and Prodigy (JUMP INTUIT).

Coming Attractions:
America Online and the Internet

Coming soon, to a computer screen near you...

Intuit has announced two major new online personal finance initiatives—online banking on America Online (AOL) and on the Internet. As this book goes to press, neither one is working yet, and there are no details available about what features will be included or how they will be implemented. We can make some educated guesses, though.

First of all, the online personal finance features Intuit provides on the Internet or AOL are likely to be a subset of those available from within Quicken. So if you have and use the latest version of Quicken, you probably won't find much in the way of additional capabilities available on the Internet or AOL. Don't expect the Internet or AOL to replace your Quicken software or Intuit Services Corporation and your Intuit membership—at least not initially.

Intuit will probably offer AOL subscribers and Internet users accessing Intuit's Quicken Financial Network (QFN) Web site similar capabilities. I expect to see the ability to check account balances and view an online statement. There might even be a limited bill payment capability. If Intuit's offering is similar to what some individual banks are doing, everything will happen online. This means you won't need separate software (beyond your AOL access program or Internet Web browser) on your PC in order to use the service, but you won't have data on your accounts and transactions on your PC either.

How Intuit will provide security for online banking on these new venues is going to be interesting to see. Undoubtedly, there will be some kind of sign-up required, and users will get an ID and password similar to the Intuit membership. I suppose Quicken will use the security features of the Netscape Web browser to keep Internet communications private. We'll have to wait and see what other security measures Intuit takes.

Only time will tell how close my speculations are to reality. By the time you read this, the service may be available. Check out Intuit's area on AOL (keyword **Intuit**) or QFN (**http://www.intuit.com/**) for the latest information.

Sorting through Your Options

As you have seen, Quicken offers numerous options for online personal finance. You can decide which online services you want to use. You might use one service and ignore the rest, or sign up for everything and go for the total online experience—or at least as close as today's systems and technology will allow. In order to reach out with your Quicken software and join the online world beyond your personal computer, you'll need to deal with one or more players in the online personal finance game. Which players you deal with will depend on the online personal finance services you choose.

The main online personal finance areas are:

Online Banking	Requires an account at a participating financial institution
Online BillPay	Available for any bank account with checking privileges
E-mail to banks	Included with Online Banking and Online BillPay
Stock quotes	Available from Portfolio Price Update or Investor Insight

To get started using Quicken's online personal finance features, you'll need to:
- Sign up for an Intuit membership with Intuit Services Corporation
- Contact a participating financial institution for Online Banking and Online BillPay
- Contact Intuit Services Corporation for Online BillPay at a non-member bank
- Start using Portfolio Price Update or Investor Insight for stock price updates—sign-up is automatic

You can also get financial information from the Quicken Financial Network (QFN) and the Internet, which is accessible from within Quicken or from your own Internet connection.

Chapter 3

SELECTING A BANKING PARTNER

- **What are your choices?**
- **What makes a good online banking partner?**
- **Comparing banking services**
- **Reading the fine print**

A chapter on selecting a bank may seem unusual in a book about a specific software program. But the Quicken software can't deliver on the promise of Online Banking without a partnership with a participating financial institution. Consequently, your selection of a banking partner will have a significant impact on your experience with online personal finance.

You can arrange online bill-paying service from almost any bank account. However, for full-fledged online banking, you'll need an account at one of the financial institutions that have joined Intuit's online banking network.

If you already bank with one of the member banks, you've got it made. You can probably get the Online Banking feature added to your existing account very easily. It may take only a phone call to the bank's customer service department. In that case, you can just skim this chapter, or skip it completely.

The rest of us, on the other hand, must select a member bank and establish a new banking relationship before taking advantage of the Online Banking features in Quicken. This chapter outlines the major factors you should consider as you choose a new bank—especially those that affect your online relationship. Some of these factors may be familiar, but since most people don't change banks often, a thoughtful review is in order. Even if you're comfortable with the ins and outs of forming a new banking relationship, I encourage you to at least skim this chapter for insight into the online angle.

What Are Your Choices?

If you want to download current account balances into Quicken and see what transactions have cleared in your account, you need to establish two-way communication with your bank. You can't do that with just any bank. The financial institution must be set up to exchange information with your software. When you use Quicken, that information exchange takes place through the facilities of Intuit Services Corporation (ISC). Consequently, Quicken's Online Banking features are available only for accounts at financial institutions that are connected to Intuit's network.

Intuit has assembled a network of major financial institutions from around the country. Most of the participating financial institutions are large regional banks, although credit card companies and brokerage houses are also represented. As this book goes to press, the list of active member banks includes the following:

- American Express
- Bank of Boston
- Centura Bank
- Chase Manhattan Bank
- Chemical Bank
- Citibank
- Compass Bank
- CoreStates Bank
- Crestar Bank
- First Chicago
- First Interstate Bank
- Home Savings of America
- M & T Bank

- Marquette Banks
- Michigan National Bank
- Sanwa Bank California
- Smith Barney
- SunTrust Bank
- Texas Commercial Bank
- Union Bank
- U.S. Bank
- Wells Fargo

In addition to the financial institutions listed above, Intuit has announced that many more are making preparations to support Online Banking from Quicken. Most of the new financial institutions will be operational by the time this book is printed; others will be joining the network over the next few months. The list of new participating financial institutions includes the following:

- Alex. Brown & Sons
- BankAtlantic
- Bank of Stockton
- Charles Schwab & Co. Inc.
- Commerce Bancshares
- Commercial Federal Bank
- Dreyfus Services Corp.
- Fidelity Investments
- First Hawaiian Bank
- First Union National Bank
- Laredo National Bank
- Mellon Bank
- PNC Bank
- Republic National Bank of New York
- Signet Bank

You'll find a partial list of participating banks in the *Quicken User's Guide* and also in the program's Help file. If you have the Deluxe CD, you can run the Deluxe Gateway and click on Financial Directory. This will open the dialog box shown in Figure 3.1. Just click on a button to see more information about a financial institution. Some banks have special offers for Quicken users.

FIGURE 3.1: Quicken's Deluxe CD provides push-button access to information about some of the participating banks.

The list of participating financial institutions is constantly growing as more join Intuit's online banking network. Before you pick a bank, you'll want to check the most recent list. If you have Internet access, you can get an updated list of member banks at the Quicken Financial Network World Wide Web site (**http://www.intuit.com/quicken/**). Just click on Financial Directory in the initial screen and then follow the links to the latest list of banks.

Selecting a Financial Institution

If you find your current bank on the list of participating financial institutions, your choice is obvious. If not, you'll want to do some research before choosing your new bank. It's an important, long-term decision, and you should invest some time in shopping for the financial institution that best meets your needs.

It's unlikely that you have the time or the desire to thoroughly investigate every participating financial institution. On the other hand, you don't want to make a hasty decision. While all of the financial institutions on the list are good, they're not all the same. For instance, some don't serve all parts of the country. And the banks operating in your area will, no doubt, offer several different packages of services at different prices.

You'll probably recognize the banks that are active in your area. Those will be a good place to start your research. You can also refer to Appendix C in this book for more information about them. The best strategy is to choose a few likely candidates and then contact them for general information. Most of the participating financial institutions have toll-free phone lines staffed by customer service representatives who can answer your questions. Ask for brochures; then read and compare the offerings. Call back with more questions if necessary.

The rest of this chapter discusses some of the factors you should consider when choosing an online bank. Generally, they are the same factors that you would consider when choosing any bank, but the online aspect adds a little different spin. Once you make your choice, the bank's customer service staff will help you establish an account and sign up for online banking. Then you can set up the account in Quicken and begin using the Online Banking features.

What Makes a Good Online Banking Partner?

All financial institutions are *not* created equal. Some are set up to handle customers located anywhere in the country; others serve a limited geographic region. Some offer a full range of services; others offer more limited choices. There are similarities, to be sure, but each of the participating financial institutions in the Intuit online network has its own "personality."

Your challenge is to find a financial institution that offers the combination of services you need and want at an attractive price. This is a case where bigger isn't necessarily better, but it isn't necessarily bad either. There's no one perfect combination of size, location, and services to look for in a bank. After all, a traveling corporate executive, a self-employed small businessman, an investor, and a retired couple will all have different needs and expectations. What's important is the best possible *match* between you and your bank.

Safety

Of course, your first priority in selecting a financial institution is to be confident that your money will be safe and secure. Given the stature of the banks that have joined with ISC to support Quicken, the safety of your deposits isn't a major concern. (The security of your online transactions as they travel from your computer to the bank is a separate issue and the topic of the next chapter.)

NOTE See Chapter 4, "The Question of Security," for information on keeping your financial transactions secure and private.

Before opening any account at a financial institution, you should make sure you understand which deposits are insured and the relative risk of various investments. The fact that you'll be dealing with the financial institution online doesn't change that. You might also want to inquire about bank policies regarding privacy issues, such as what information the bank will release to credit agencies and the like.

Location

Location, location, location! It's said those are the three most important things about a piece of real estate. The same used to be true of banks. When every banking transaction had to be conducted on the bank premises, the location of the local branch was probably the most important factor in selecting a bank (assuming, of course, that you were choosing between equally sound institutions).

The introduction of banking by mail and by phone started weaning bank customers away from the teller window. ATMs have accelerated the process to the point that many bank customers seldom see the inside of a bank branch anymore.

With the advent of online banking, you don't even need to stick a card in an ATM to connect to your bank. Once your modem connects your computer to Intuit's network, you can communicate with any of the participating financial institutions with equal ease. It no longer matters whether the bank's headquarters are located across town or across the country. You might expect this development to completely eliminate physical location as a factor in choosing a bank. But that's not the case.

Not all banks can or will serve customers in all areas. There is a complex web of federal and state banking laws that restrict the options available to financial institutions. A combination of these regulations and the bank's business policies restricts most banks to serving a certain geographic area. Often, the financial institution's service area will be confined to an individual state or county, although it may extend to a region of several states. Only a few banks serve customers nationwide. As a result, your choice of an online banking partner is limited to those financial institutions that serve your area.

WARNING Don't be fooled by the word "National" in the name of the bank. It doesn't mean the bank can do business nationwide. In fact, even small local banks can, and often do, have names such as "First National Bank of Smallville."

Obviously, then, when selecting a financial institution, the first thing you need to determine is whether you are within the bank's service area. The problem isn't any limitation on your ability to connect to the bank from Quicken; it's the rules the bank must follow when setting up new accounts. For instance, the bank may require a verifiable address within the states it serves. Normally, that's a pretty clear-cut issue. However, the specific rules for each bank vary, so if you really want to do business with a specific financial institution, it might pay to explore the options. For example, your home address may not matter if you can open the account in person at one of the bank's branches, where you can show a picture ID and sign forms in the presence of a bank officer.

Once you establish a relationship with a financial institution, you can usually continue that relationship even if you move outside the bank's normal service area. However, the specific rules vary, so it's a good idea to check if you anticipate relocating.

NOTE If you travel, you don't have to worry about losing contact with your bank if you leave its service area. You can still use Quicken to conduct Online Banking transactions normally when you're on the road. Location is an issue only when establishing your relationship with the bank.

Local Banks

Local banks are those that operate exclusively within a small geographic area, such as a county. It's unusual to find a local bank that offers any sort of online banking unless it is a subsidiary of one of the larger regional banks. Most people select a local bank for its convenient branches located close to home, work, or shopping areas. Increasingly, ATMs in convenient locations are more important than branch locations. If you travel out of town, it's important to consider whether the bank's ATM card will work in other networked ATMs locally, regionally, and nationally.

Regional Banks

Many of the participating financial institutions in the Intuit network are regional banks. Online banking gives them the opportunity to serve customers from a centralized facility instead of building expensive new branches. The area served by a regional bank is larger than that of a local bank—it may encompass several states—but it's usually still limited. You need to make sure the bank you're considering operates in *your* area. If the bank has a major presence in your locale, that'll be easy—you'll see the bank's logo everywhere you turn. But that's not always the case. Some regional banks may not blanket their entire potential service area with local branches, but their services are available in the area nevertheless. Also, a formerly independent local bank may have merged with a larger regional bank but continues to operate under its old name. As a result, you may not be aware of the local bank's affiliation with a larger regional bank unless you ask.

Using online banking will reduce your need to have convenient physical access to your bank, but there are still times when having a bank branch (or at least one of the bank's own ATMs) close by is a definite plus.

Banks with National Scope

As yet, no truly nationwide banks have emerged. However, several of the regional banks, such as Wells Fargo and Citibank, have managed to break free of the constraints of geographic boundaries to offer online banking to anyone in the country. You'll get the greatest benefit from a relationship with one of these banks if you live and work within their home territory. You'll have all the advantages of convenient local branches and ubiquitous ATMs as well as online banking. But it is possible to establish and operate a long-distance relationship with these banks. The key to making this kind of banking work is good accessibility—not to a physical location, but via phone, mail, and modem.

Accessibility

In the past, accessibility to your bank was a simple matter of branch locations and hours of operation. Now, however, with so many more ways to conduct banking transactions, there are numerous factors to consider when evaluating a bank's accessibility:

Physical access	It's becoming less important, but there are times when proximity to a branch is handy, especially if you need to deposit cash or take advantage of other services such as safe-deposit boxes, notary services, certified checks, and the like.
Phone and Mail	Look for toll-free customer service phone numbers available during extended hours, provisions for handling deposits by mail, and other accommodations for long-distance banking customers.
ATMs	You'll want to make sure the bank's ATM card will work in local machines (via networks such as Cirrus, Honors, and Plus System).
Paper checks	The old stand-by still works.
Debit cards	They look like a credit card, but work like a check; the funds are deducted from your checking account immediately. A debit card with the Visa or MasterCard symbol may be more welcome at local stores than checks from an out-of-town bank.
Online	This is where your Quicken software comes in. However, not all banks support all of Quicken's online features.

When evaluating a bank's online accessibility, check for these features:

Online Banking	Downloading your bank statement with information on cleared transactions and your current balance. All the participating banks support this feature, but you'll want to compare fees.
Online BillPay	Does the bank support writing electronic checks on the account you want to open?
Access to all accounts	If you have more than one account at the same bank, will the bank allow you to access all of those accounts online?
Access to credit card accounts	Some banks support online access to credit card accounts at their bank as well as regular checking and savings accounts.
Transfers between accounts	Although Quicken will allow you to transfer funds electronically between different accounts at the same bank, some financial institutions don't support this feature.

Banking Services

Banks and financial institutions offer a bewildering array of accounts and services. These include:

- Checking accounts
- Interest-bearing checking accounts
- Savings accounts
- Money market accounts
- Brokerage accounts
- Credit cards
- Debit cards
- ATM cards
- Retirement accounts
- Traveler's checks
- Cashier's checks

Banks package various combinations of accounts and services at different prices to appeal to different customers. There's no magic formula for finding the package that's best for you. You must assess your needs and then go shopping for a package that offers the best balance of the features you want at a reasonable cost.

If you're dealing with an out-of-town bank, remember that you won't be able to take advantage of many of the bonus features (such as a free safe-deposit box or notary services) that the bank might add to some packages to make them more attractive to their local customers.

Cost

There's no free lunch—or free checking account. There are all sorts of fees and conditions attached to banking services that affect their true cost. They include:

- Account service charges
- Minimum balance requirements to avoid monthly service charges or to earn interest on your account
- Check-processing fees
- ATM transaction fees
- Handling charges for mailing you your canceled checks or printing copies of canceled checks from the bank's microfilm files

ATM Fees

More and more we seem to be moving away from the teller window and toward automated teller machines as our primary way of dealing with our banks. As a result, the fees that a bank charges for ATM transactions will have a greater impact on the cost of doing business with a bank.

ATM transactions at the bank's own machines are often free. In contrast, using your ATM card at another bank's machine can incur a charge for each transaction. The fees for "foreign" ATM transactions are typically about $1, but some banks charge more than twice that amount. If you sign up for online banking with an out-of-town bank, you're likely to use your ATM card even more than you would if you banked with a local bank. As a result, the ATM transaction fees could be the most expensive part of maintaining an account.

ATM transaction fees and the rules for imposing those fees vary widely from bank to bank. For instance, some banks consider point-of-sale transactions that you make with an ATM/debit card to be the same as a foreign ATM transaction and charge a fee accordingly. Other banks would consider the same transaction to be the electronic equivalent of a check and charge a smaller fee (or no fee at all).

Check out a prospective bank's ATM fees. It could save you some money.

Besides the standard fees associated with your bank accounts, you can expect to pay additional fees for online banking services. Most participating banks charge fees for:

- Online Banking access to an account—usually a flat monthly fee of $3 to $10 that allows you to download statement information a certain number of times (typically eight) each month. Some banks include Online Banking access in an account's standard monthly service charge.
- Additional statement updates (beyond the fixed number of downloads covered by the monthly fee). The average is about $.50 per statement.
- Online BillPay service (usually includes an allotment of about 20 electronic payments). The standard price is $5.95, but several banks include Online BillPay for free when you sign up for Online Banking.
- Additional electronic payments (about $.40 each) if you exceed the allotment.

WARNING If your bank charges a fee for each check it processes, you might think you can reduce your costs by using Online BillPay. However, since Intuit Services Corporation pays most of your bills with checks rather than electronic funds transfers, you may still wind up paying those check-processing fees—even on the bills you pay online.

Making Deposits

Most of us spend more time making withdrawals from our bank accounts by writing checks, getting cash at the ATM, or making online payments than we do making deposits. Consequently, it's easy to overlook the importance of being able to make deposits conveniently. But remember that you have to deposit funds in your account before you make any withdrawals—and you must keep making timely deposits to replenish those funds.

When you depend on the income from a salary, a business, investments, or other source, getting it deposited at a local bank isn't much of a concern. On the other hand, making deposits can be the biggest problem you're likely to encounter when dealing with an out-of-town bank.

Making a Deposit at a Local Bank Branch

If you need to deposit funds in your account at the local bank, you have plenty of options. You can:

- Go to the teller window in the bank
- Go to the drive-through window
- Drop an envelope into the night deposit slot
- Make a deposit into the bank's ATM
- Send your deposit by mail
- Arrange for your paycheck to be deposited directly into your account

Making a Deposit at an Out-of-Town Bank

Making a deposit into an account at an out-of-town bank can be more troublesome. You have only two choices:

- Direct deposit
- Mail

With an out-of-town bank, you have no local access, so the teller, drive-through, and night deposit are not available. Using an ATM for your deposit seems like an option, but it's not. Although you can get cash from your own bank's ATMs and also from any other ATM that will recognize and honor your card, you can't send deposits back in the same way. You can make deposits only at your bank's own ATMs, and the closest one may be hundreds of miles away. This may change eventually, but as I write this, you can't make deposits at a "foreign" ATM.

Direct deposit works great for depositing your paycheck, provided your employer gives you that option. The problem is that direct deposit isn't available to everyone, or for all checks. That means that some, if not all, of your deposits must go to your out-of-town bank through the mail.

Sending deposits through the regular U.S. Postal Service mail is inexpensive, and the banks are set up to accept and process your deposit this way. The problem is that while the mail is reasonably reliable, it's certainly not guaranteed, and it's difficult to predict how long the deposit will take in transit. Sometimes a first-class envelope will make it to its destination in two days; sometimes it takes ten. That makes it hard to manage your account because you don't know when the funds will be available.

> **TIP** To make mail deposits a little easier, select a regional bank instead of one on the other side of the country. And consider using Priority Mail at a cost of $2.85 for fairly predictable two-day delivery.

Once the deposit arrives at the bank and gets processed, you'll be able to use the Online Banking feature to confirm when the deposit was credited to your account. However, tracking deposits with Online Banking still has its drawbacks. You can monitor, but not control, the arrival of the deposit; and getting frequent online statements could add to the fees you must pay.

Direct Deposit

If you're like most people, you take your paycheck directly to the bank and deposit it into your account. Payday means an extra errand to run at lunchtime or on the way home. It's the same routine every time.

Direct deposit allows you to instruct your employer to deposit your paycheck directly into your bank account. It happens automatically. The money moves by electronic funds transfer (EFT) from your employer's bank account to yours. You get paid as usual, but you skip the hassle of handling a paper check and making the trip to the bank to deposit it.

Direct deposit is faster and more reliable than a paper check that can get lost or stolen before you can get it to the bank. There's no problem if you're out of town on payday; the money still gets to your bank on time. Perhaps the best thing is that the funds are credited to your account immediately—you don't have to wait for the check to clear before your bank will let you access the funds. While direct deposit is convenient when you bank locally, it's by far the best way to deposit funds if you bank out of town.

Unfortunately, direct deposit isn't available just for the asking. Since it relies on EFT, it's available only from payers that can initiate EFT transactions, such as large corporations and government agencies. Direct deposit also requires some setup, so it's generally limited to regular payments such as payroll, pensions, government checks, and so on. Direct deposit doesn't lend itself to one-time payments, although the IRS will use it for tax refunds.

If you're offered the option of being paid by direct deposit, I recommend that you take it. If the option isn't offered, ask for it.

Don't Forget the Fine Print

When you're looking over a bank's brochures, reading about the packages of services it offers, be sure to read the fine print too. You might be tempted to skip the disclosure statements and bank policies, thinking that they're all the same. However, some potentially crucial details do differ from bank to bank.

One area where banks have different policies is on the availability of deposits. If one bank takes significantly longer to make your deposits available, that could affect the minimum balance needed to assure that your checks will be covered even if a deposit is delayed. Also be alert to differences in the availability of deposits made at a bank branch versus those sent through the mail. This is especially important with an out-of-town bank.

Availability of Deposits

Just because you make a deposit into your account doesn't mean you can use those funds immediately. You usually can't deposit a check and withdraw the funds as cash the same day—or even the next day. Banks can and do delay the availability of funds you deposit to allow time for checks to clear and funds to be transferred between banks and into your account.

The system for clearing checks is still based largely on moving pieces of paper, sometimes long distances. There's a significant amount of time required for handling paper, posting transactions, requesting and getting confirmation, and so on. Although some aspects of this process are covered by banking regulations, individual banks have some discretion in establishing specific rules on the availability of deposits.

For example, a bank might make funds from a small check drawn on a local bank available the next business day; a larger local check might be available in two days. Out-of-town checks might take five days or more. One bank might define small checks as under $500; another might impose the strictest standards only on checks over $5,000. Then there's the question of what constitutes a local check. Some banks define local checks as those drawn on a bank headquartered in the same town; others will consider all the banks in the same Federal Reserve banking region (which can cover parts of several states) as local.

Another section of fine print that deserves scrutiny is the one covering miscellaneous fees. These fees can vary dramatically from bank to bank, and, if they are high, can make a real difference in the cost of doing business with a bank if you incur them often. Miscellaneous fees include overdraft charges, stop-payment fees, and wire-transfer fees.

If you're contemplating signing up with an out-of-town bank, you'll want to pay attention to the fees for wire transfers. Most people don't use wire transfers often and may not be aware of them. However, they can be a valuable tool. Wire transfers enable you to move funds quickly and reliably between banks. They can be the answer if you absolutely must get money transferred from an account at a local bank to your account at an out-of-town bank as fast as possible. Unfortunately, the fees are often steep, with charges applied at both the sending and the receiving ends of the transaction.

Chapter 4

THE QUESTION OF SECURITY

- **Why the concern?**
- **System security**
- **Who goes there—passwords and PINs**
- **Data encryption**
- **Protecting your privacy**
- **Commonsense security precautions**

The security at your local bank branch is easy to see. There are surveillance cameras and a vault with a huge door and formidable locks. These and other clues give you confidence that the bank is taking appropriate precautions to ensure that your money and your financial transactions with the bank will remain safe and secure.

Security measures aren't as apparent on a computer system. Just by looking, you can't distinguish a computer and software system that employs significant security measures from a system with little or no security. That might leave you feeling a little uneasy.

In an effort to remedy that situation, this chapter will point out some of the computer counterparts of surveillance cameras and vault doors that Intuit has incorporated into the Quicken software and the Intuit Services Corporation network.

Why the Concern?

You've heard the stories, seen the movies, read the books and newspaper articles. Tales abound about computer crackers who break into computer systems, intercept messages, and monitor activity.

No doubt, you've been told that the Internet lacks security. The Internet is, after all, a network of many interlinked computer systems—some of which have few, if any, security controls. The Internet works by relaying messages from one computer system to the next until the message finally reaches its destination. As a result, messages traveling on the Internet might be intercepted and read at any of the intermediate steps along the way.

Not all computer systems and networks operate this way. Some systems are inherently more secure than others. Despite all the media hype surrounding the Internet, it's just one part of the total world of computer networks and communications. Furthermore, there are very effective technologies available to enhance the security of important data traveling on any kind of network.

If you're sending a chatty e-mail note to a friend, security isn't a serious issue anyway. So what if someone else reads the message—it doesn't really make any difference. However, your personal financial transactions are a different matter. You probably don't want any unauthorized person knowing details of your personal business. Even if you were willing to broadcast your online personal finances to the world, you'd still have to take measures to keep things like credit card and bank account numbers secret to protect yourself from fraud and theft.

Online personal finance opens up a new world of convenience for computer users. However, the very things that make online activities convenient also create serious questions and concerns about security. Before you can become comfortable using online personal finance, you must be confident that your online information and transactions are safe, secure, and private.

System Security

Online personal finance isn't a single product or service. It's a complex series of activities taking place at different times and on different computer systems and networks. Some online personal finance activities are confined to your personal computer; some occur on Intuit Services Corporation's network. The Quicken Financial Network operates on the Internet. By the time you read this, Intuit may be offering online personal finance through America Online and other online services as well. Each of these networks and computer systems have different security provisions.

Intuit Services Corporation

Intuit Services Corporation (ISC) has set up a private computer network to provide online personal finance services to Quicken users. This network incorporates leased telephone lines that allow users to connect directly to ISC's computer system. When Quicken connects to ISC for an online session, your transactions do *not* travel across the Internet.

NOTE **Your online personal finance transactions go straight from Quicken to Intuit Services Corporation via private phone lines. They aren't traveling on the Internet.**

ISC is, in turn, connected to the participating financial institutions via trusted, private links to these banks' computers. ISC hired leading computer security experts to design a system with the same level of security employed by commercial banks and the Federal Reserve.

Since the ISC network is a private system with considerable internal security controls, it is actually quite safe. ISC is merely a conduit for communications with your financial institution. Ultimately, your money and your financial transactions are handled by your bank. In the unlikely event that the bank itself is successfully attacked online, your deposits enjoy the same protections that they have from other forms of bank robbery and embezzlement.

Quicken Financial Network

The Quicken Financial Network (QFN) is very different from the private, controlled world of the Intuit Services Corporation network. QFN is Intuit's entry into the Internet and the World Wide Web. It's an open system linked to thousands of computers around the world—definitely *not* a secure system.

The inherent lack of security on the Internet isn't a problem for QFN, however. QFN is primarily a source of information about Intuit, the Quicken software, and financial information such as profiles of various mutual funds—none of which is sensitive, private information. All your online personal finance transactions from Quicken go through the ISC network, not the Quicken Financial Network.

Intuit is working on encryption and other techniques to provide sufficient security that would allow users to conduct at least some online personal finance on the Internet—and do so safely. As this book goes to press, those capabilities are not in place yet. If you're interested, check QFN for the latest developments.

Intuit contracts with an Internet service provider (ISP) to furnish free access to the Quicken Financial Network from within Quicken. In addition, you have the option of upgrading the dedicated QFN access to a full-fledged Internet access account. However, when you do, you're asked to supply a credit card number for billing. You might have some very legitimate concerns about sending your credit card number out over the Internet.

To allay your fears, Intuit and its ISP have taken steps to protect your credit card number. When you elect to upgrade from free QFN access to complete Internet access, Quicken dials a toll-free phone number for a direct connection to a special computer server for registration. Quicken encrypts your credit card data before sending it, and the ISP stores your credit card data and other account information on a computer that is *not* linked to the Internet. Only after you complete your registration do you connect to the full Internet.

Your Own System

Quite possibly, the weakest security of all is found on your own personal computer system. Very few PC users employ any meaningful security, even if it's available.

If your PC sits at home where it's available only to family members, you probably don't need much security. Your biggest concern isn't protecting your data from access by an unauthorized person; it's protecting it from accidental erasure by your spouse or child. (The best defense is to keep a current backup of your Quicken data file.)

If, on the other hand, you work with Quicken on a computer at your office or on a notebook computer that you carry to work and on trips, then your Quicken data are more vulnerable. If your system is in a network or connected to the Internet, your files might be exposed to even more risk. Someone could use your computer to run your copy of Quicken while you're away, or even copy your Quicken data files and all the financial information they contain.

Your computer operating system and network system probably contain some basic security features that you can use to reduce your risk. For instance, you might disable file sharing for the directories containing your Quicken data to thwart casual access over a network. In addition, Quicken offers password protection for Quicken data files.

Who Goes There – Passwords and PINs

Passwords and personal identification numbers (PINs) are intended to ensure that you, and only you, can access your online accounts and issue payment instructions. Passwords and PINs act like keys to a door; they let you unlock access to your online accounts.

When you use any of Quicken's online personal finance features, you'll usually need to supply a password, a PIN, or both. This allows the computer system to verify that you are, indeed, authorized to access certain accounts.

Passwords and PINs are effective security devices *only* if they are kept secret. Your name and address may be widely known, but your password or PIN should be known only to you and the computer system you're contacting. By entering the correct password, you prove to the online computer that you are who you say you are. However, if anyone else knows your password, they can impersonate you and gain access to your accounts on the computer system.

Passwords

The password you'll use most as you work with Quicken's online personal finance features is your Intuit membership password. You create it when you first register for membership with Intuit Services Corporation. You'll need to supply the password each time you access any of the services that go through ISC; that includes Online Banking, Online BillPay, and Portfolio Price Update.

Only you know your password, and you should keep it a closely guarded secret. Quicken displays asterisks when you type your password (see Figure 4.1 on the following page) so no one can look over your shoulder as you type and read your password from the screen.

FIGURE 4.1:
To keep your password secret, Quicken hides it as you type.

Quicken also lets you add password protection to your Quicken data file, requiring you to enter the password before opening the file. This can prevent unauthorized access to your data. Similarly, you can create passwords for certain transactions to provide additional security. See the *Quicken Users Guide* for instruction on assigning passwords.

Storing Passwords

For convenience, you can have Quicken store your Intuit membership password. Quicken will enter the stored password automatically when you need to log on to the ISC network. Storing your password saves you a step by eliminating the need to type your password, but it also significantly reduces security. It's like leaving the key in the lock; an unauthorized person could log on to your Intuit membership without having to know your secret password.

PINs

A PIN (personal identification number) is a form of password. You're probably familiar with PINs from using ATM cards. You must enter the correct PIN into the ATM to show that you are the authorized user of the card. PINs serve the same purpose in Quicken. They provide an added level of security for online banking—over and above the password required for access to Intuit Services Corporation. If your password is like a key to the lock in the doorknob, your PIN is like your key to the deadbolt.

When you sign up for Online Banking or Online BillPay, your financial institution will assign you a PIN to be used for access to online services from that bank. Normally, you can't get your PIN over the phone. Instead, it's sent to your mailing address. For added security, the financial institution sends your online banking PIN separately from any other account information. This prevents a thief from getting all the information necessary to access your account by stealing a single piece of mail. Normally, you'll use the bank-assigned PIN only for your initial access to your online account. Then you must change your PIN to a number of your choice.

Mother's Maiden Name

Your personal information file at Intuit Services Corporation includes your mother's maiden name. That may seem like strange information for ISC to need—it's totally unrelated to online personal finance.

The reason for asking for your mother's maiden name is that it's a bit of information about you that isn't included in commonly available references, such as phone books and driver's license records. And, unlike arbitrary passwords, your mother's maiden name is something you're not likely to forget—even months later. ISC personnel can use this information to confirm that you are who you say you are when you call for assistance. ISC staff will ask you questions and compare your answers to the data in your personal information file. An impersonator might know your name, address, and phone, but they are not likely to know your mother's maiden name.

Data Encryption

All the data transferred between Quicken and Intuit Services Corporation is encrypted—scrambled with secret codes. Encryption protects your data by rendering it unintelligible until it's deciphered by the intended recipient, as shown in Figure 4.2.

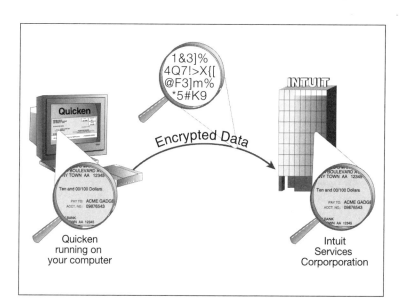

FIGURE 4.2:
Encryption makes your online transactions unintelligible to prying eyes.

Quicken uses encryption from RSA Data Security for your online personal finance transactions. The RSA logo appears in some dialog boxes (see Figure 4.3) as a reminder that your online session is being protected by RSA data encryption.

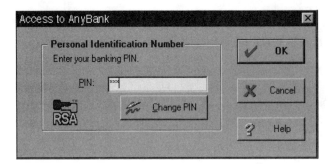

FIGURE 4.3:
Intuit licenses powerful encryption software from RSA Data Security. Notice the RSA logo.

The RSA encryption scheme uses an individualized, two-part key to scramble data in such a way that it can only be unscrambled by the party with the other part of the key. The system works so well it's considered practically unbreakable. (In fact, the U.S. government considers RSA encryption a weapon and restricts its export.) The larger the key used to encrypt a message, the harder it is to break the encryption and read the message. Some programs use 40-bit RSA encryption keys. Intuit, on the other hand, has licensed 1024-bit keys to protect Quicken's online personal finance communications.

Protecting Your Privacy

It doesn't do much good to take elaborate security precautions to protect your data if the information eventually gets released to others. The privacy of your personal financial information is controlled to some extent by laws and banking regulations, but mostly, it's a matter of policy.

Intuit Services Corporation has pledged to keep your personal financial information confidential. The details of your financial transactions are shared only with the relevant financial institutions. ISC *does* make its mailing list available to some direct marketers; however, the company will remove your name from the mailing list if you request it.

Intuit, Inc. (the software company) also supplies its mailing list of registered Quicken users to other companies. If you don't want your name on this list, simply check the appropriate option on the registration form.

Each financial institution has its own policies concerning customer privacy. You should check with your financial institution to find out what information it will supply to credit reporting agencies and other parties. Typically, a financial institution will release details of your financial transactions only to legal authorities, but it may acknowledge that you have an account to anyone who asks.

Commonsense Security Precautions

Even the most elaborate security system can't protect your valuable information if you don't use it properly. What good is a lock if you leave the door standing open?

Here are a few commonsense precautions you can take to help preserve the integrity of Quicken's security system:

- Treat passwords and PINs like keys. Don't leave them lying around where an unauthorized person will have access to them. Writing a password on a note stuck on your computer is asking for trouble. Hiding it somewhere close by is only slightly better. Written records of your passwords are a good idea, but they should be for emergency access only. Store passwords in a secure location away from your computer system.
- Select your passwords carefully. A good password should be easy for you to remember, but hard for someone else to guess.
    - Don't use your name or the name of a person or pet in your family.
    - Don't use common words as passwords.
    - Passwords should be at least eight characters long.
    - The best passwords use a combination of letters and numbers or letters and symbols. One good tactic is to use two uncommon words joined or surrounded by numbers or symbols. For example: pallid%perch#
- Don't keep your Quicken data files on a network server or on a shared drive that is accessible by other network users.
- Before giving out any personal information, know who you're giving it to. The personal information you enter into Quicken is safe, but you need to be cautious when dealing with vendors on the phone and such. Be especially careful with your credit card numbers and bank account numbers.
- Don't supply personal information in open forums such as Internet e-mail, or in the forums and bulletin boards of online services such as CompuServe and America Online.

Part 2

Online Banking

Chapter 5

THE FIRST STEP:

SETTING UP YOUR INTUIT MEMBERSHIP

FEATURING

- Joining the club
- Setting up your modem
- Establishing your Intuit membership
- Getting a member ID number
- Changing your membership information
- Storing passwords
- Maintaining more than one Intuit membership

Before you can use Quicken's online personal finance features such as Online Banking, Online BillPay, or Portfolio Price Update, you must register with Intuit Services Corporation and obtain a user ID number and password. Your Intuit membership then opens the doorway to the online communications that make online personal finance possible. This chapter describes how to set up and maintain that all-important Intuit membership.

Joining the Club

Your Intuit membership is a master account with Intuit Services Corporation (ISC), the subsidiary of Intuit, Inc. that handles online services from your Quicken software.

An Intuit membership serves several purposes, including:

- Establishing your identity as a registered member of the Intuit online personal finance community
- Providing security by checking that you have entered the correct password and PIN and by handling the encryption process
- Furnishing links to online services such as Portfolio Price Update and ISC's own Online BillPay service
- Affording access to member banks for Online Banking

Setting up your Intuit membership is quick and easy. All you need is the proper version of Quicken software, a Hayes-compatible modem installed in your computer, and, of course, access to a phone line for the modem.

> **TIP** You can use almost any modem speed to connect to Intuit Services Corporation. Even 1200- and 2400-baud modems will work, although the connection will be slow. Intuit Services Corporation recommends that you use at least a 9600-baud modem.

Setting up an Intuit membership is similar to getting a membership card for a club or being issued a name badge at a large corporation. Initially, you go through a sign-up procedure, supplying personal information to obtain your membership. Once you complete the sign-up process, your membership information is saved in your Quicken file. Subsequently, when you want to use Quicken's online personal finance features, your software will log on automatically using your Intuit membership number. You just supply the password (and perhaps a PIN) for security, and you're in. ISC keeps track of which bank and accounts you've registered to use and links you to those accounts automatically.

Why Is Intuit Membership Necessary?

Intuit membership is *required* for most of Quicken's online personal finance services, including Online Banking, Online BillPay, and Portfolio Price Update. It isn't possible to implement any of these features solely with software installed on a stand-alone personal computer. They all require a connection between your software and a financial institution or online service provider. If you use Quicken, that connection is provided by Intuit Services Corporation. As a result, if you plan to use any of these online personal finance features, you must first get an Intuit membership. Quicken will even lead you through the sign-up procedure automatically if you try to use any of these online features without first setting up your membership.

> **TIP** If Quicken asks you to set up an Intuit membership despite the fact that you've already done so, it's probably because you are using a different Quicken file. You don't need to set up a separate Intuit membership for each file. See the section titled "Using an Existing Intuit Membership" later in this chapter for instructions on linking a new Quicken file to an Intuit membership you've already established.

What Does It Cost?

Intuit membership is free. There is no sign-up fee and no monthly maintenance fee. It costs nothing to become a *potential* online personal finance user. Some services you access with your Intuit membership (Online Banking, Online BillPay, and Portfolio Price Update) have costs associated with them, which help Intuit Services Corporation cover the cost of maintaining the network, but there is no direct cost for the Intuit membership itself. If you sign up for an Intuit membership and don't use any of the fee-based services, you won't be billed.

Setting Up Your Modem

Before you can use any computer communications feature, you must set up (or configure) your modem. However, you may be able to skip this sometimes frustrating step, since Quicken will attempt to take care of it automatically. Modem setup happens automatically when you first attempt to use any of these features:
- Online Banking
- Online BillPay
- Portfolio Price Update

- Online software registration
- Product orders from the Intuit Marketplace

In addition, the Quicken Financial Network and Investor Insight include modem setup during the sign-up process for those services.

If you try to use any of these online features without first setting up your modem, Quicken alerts you and attempts to auto-configure your modem. Once you confirm the settings established by the software, Quicken will dial out with your modem and proceed with the sign-up process for the online feature you selected.

You're likely to need to set up your modem manually only in the following circumstances:

- The software failed to automatically configure your modem
- You have an unusual modem that requires manual configuration for optimal operation
- You need to set up special dialing instructions in order to access an outside line or disable a telephone company custom-calling feature
- You just want to step through the process deliberately

You shouldn't minimize the importance of the last point. It can be a little distracting to have to deal with setting up your modem *and* signing up for your Intuit membership and Online Banking or other service at the same time. You may find it easier to handle modem setup as a discrete step instead of combining it with your first online access attempt.

If you do decide to set up your modem manually, follow these steps:

1. Choose Set Up Modem from Quicken's Online menu. This opens the Set Up Modem dialog box, as shown in Figure 5.1.

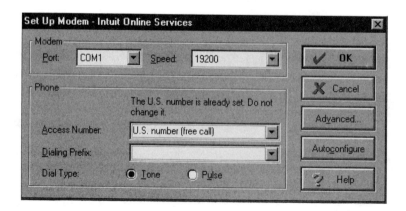

FIGURE 5.1:
The Set Up Modem dialog box lets you control your modem setup.

2. Start by clicking on the Autoconfigure button to let Quicken try to configure your modem for you. You can then customize the configuration if necessary.

   Quicken displays status messages as it scans your system, attempting to locate and identify your modem and determine the appropriate settings. Once the automatic configuration process is complete, you should see the message shown in Figure 5.2. Click on the OK button to return to the Set Up Modem dialog box and check the automatic settings.

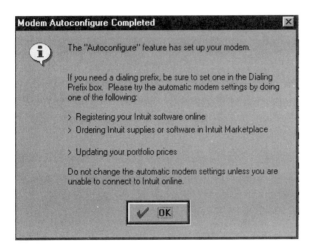

FIGURE 5.2:
After automatically configuring your modem, Quicken gives you a few extra words of advice.

3. Make sure the Port setting reflects the communications port where your modem is installed. If necessary, select the correct port from the Port drop-down list box.

4. In the Speed drop-down list box, select the communications speed that matches (or exceeds) your modem. In most cases, you can leave this at the default setting of 19200.

TIP

If you have trouble getting Quicken to communicate reliably, you might need to use a lower speed setting, even if your modem is capable of much faster speeds. Slower modem connections are less susceptible to noise interference on the phone lines. Try using 9600.

5. You can probably skip the Access Number setting. It's preconfigured, and you normally don't need to change it unless instructed to do so by Intuit's technical support staff.

The default Access Number is 950-1288, the number for the AT&T data network. It's a toll-free number that works from most areas. However, there may be a charge for the call if you are charged for other local calls. If you get a recording when you dial this number or will incur charges for the call, you can substitute AT&T's toll-free long-distance number: 800-328-2427.

6. If you need to dial numbers or codes to access an outside line, enter them in the Dialing Prefix text box. If you need to wait for a second dial tone, add a comma to instruct the modem to pause for 2 seconds. For example, if you need to dial 9 and then wait 4 seconds for a dial tone before dialing an outside number, you'd enter **9,,** in the Dialing Prefix field.

> **TIP**
>
> **If you have call-waiting service from your phone company, the signal indicating an incoming call can disrupt your online session, causing it to abort. Fortunately, most phone companies let you disable the call-waiting feature for the duration of a given call by dialing a special code before dialing the number. Adding *70, to the Dialing Prefix field will usually do the trick. However, the code will be different in some areas; check the front of your phone book or call your phone company representative for instructions.**

7. For the Dial Type setting, choose Tone (if you have touch-tone phone service) or Pulse (if you have a rotary phone line).
8. You shouldn't need to adjust the modem initialization string, but if you do, click on the Advanced button to open the Advanced Modem Setup dialog box, shown in Figure 5.3.

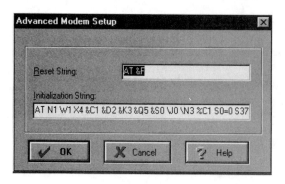

FIGURE 5.3:
The Advanced Modem Setup dialog box lets you adjust the modem initialization string. Fortunately, it's rarely necessary.

This dialog box lets you customize the reset string and initialization string for your modem. The initialization string is a complex series of codes that configure various options and parameters in your modem. You'll need to consult your modem documentation for the specific codes supported by your modem and their meanings.

TIP If you have trouble connecting to ISC, check the modem initialization string. If you find N1 in the string, change it to N0 (zero) and try again. This fixes the problem for many users.

Quicken's Autoconfigure process can create a workable initialization string for most modems. You shouldn't need to change it. However, if you do, you can simply highlight the text you want to change and type in the replacement. The text will scroll within the text boxes to accommodate longer lines of text. Then click on the OK button to return to the Set Up Modem dialog box.

TIP If you suspect that there's a problem with your modem initialization string, try using *ATZ* in place of the long series of codes. This will reset most modems to the default settings.

9. After checking all the settings in the Set Up Modem dialog box, click on the OK button. Now Quicken is ready to use your modem.

WARNING *Quicken can't share your modem with other programs.* You must exit or disable other communications software before using Quicken's modem setup or any of the online features. Attempting simultaneous modem access from more than one program could cause your computer to lock up. In particular, be sure you disable any fax or communications program that is configured to automatically answer your modem phone line. This includes Microsoft Fax and other TAPI-compliant communications programs running in Windows 95.

Disabling Microsoft Fax

If you use Microsoft Fax in Windows 95 and have it configured to automatically answer your fax modem to receive fax transmissions, the software's Auto Answer feature will conflict with Quicken's online services.

Luckily, you can quickly disable the Auto Answer feature to allow Quicken to access your modem. Click on the Microsoft Fax icon in the tray at the right end of the Task Bar to open the Microsoft Fax Status dialog box. Next, open the Fax Modem Properties dialog box by selecting Modem Properties from the Options menu. Click on the Don't answer option and then click on the OK button to close the dialog box. Quicken will now be able to use the modem.

Later, you can return to the Fax Modem Properties dialog box and reinstate the Auto Answer feature by specifying what ring you want the fax program to answer on. Once you set the answer ring, be sure to click on the Answer Now button in the Microsoft Fax Status dialog box to reinitialize the modem. After initializing the modem, click on the Hang Up button to release the phone line and close the dialog box. Microsoft Fax will now answer the fax modem and receive faxes normally.

Membership Setup

Before you can use any of Quicken's online personal finance features, you must register with Intuit Services Corporation to establish your Intuit membership. You might as well take care of that little chore as soon as you decide you want to use any of the online services. If you try to sign up for an online service, such as Online Banking, without first setting up your Intuit membership, the software will divert you to the Membership Setup procedure. You could wait and get your Intuit membership when you sign up for the first service you want to use, but setting up your Intuit membership ahead of time lets you make sure your modem and communications with Intuit Services Corporation are working properly.

Establishing a New Intuit Membership

To establish a new Intuit membership, follow these steps:

1. Pull down the Online menu, click on Intuit Membership, and then choose Set up... from the cascading menu that appears.

- If the About Intuit Membership dialog box appears (see Figure 5.4), click on the Set up new Intuit Membership… button to continue.

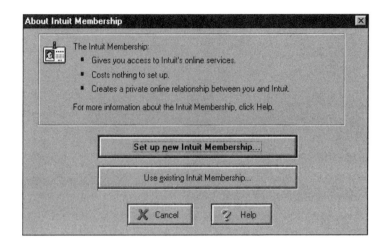

FIGURE 5.4:
Choose to use an existing Intuit membership or set up a new one for this file.

- If you already have an Intuit membership, you can use it with the current Quicken file. (See the section "Using an Existing Intuit Membership" later in this chapter.)

2. When the Intuit Membership Setup dialog box appears, as shown in Figure 5.5, fill in your name, address, and phone numbers where requested. Click on the OK button to proceed.

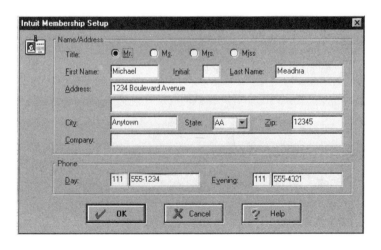

FIGURE 5.5:
To sign up for your Intuit membership, you need to tell Intuit Services Corporation a little about yourself.

3. Next, Quicken opens the Set Intuit Membership Password dialog box, as shown in Figure 5.6.

FIGURE 5.6:
You choose your own password in the Set Intuit Membership Password dialog box.

- Type a password in the first text box. To keep your password private, it appears as a series of asterisks. This is so no one looking over your shoulder will be able to read your password from the screen.
- Type your password a second time in the Re-enter password box. Since the password doesn't appear on-screen, typing it twice is a way to check that you entered it correctly. If you make a typing error and the two password entries don't match, Quicken will display a message asking you to enter the password again.

WARNING *Don't forget your password!* No one, not even Intuit Services Corporation technical support staff, can tell you what it is. If you forget your password, you'll be locked out of your account—at least temporarily. It's possible to have ISC reset your account so that you can create a new password, but it's a hassle and may delay your access to online services.

- Enter your mother's maiden name in the bottom text box.

NOTE *Why does Intuit Services Corporation need to know my mother's maiden name?* It's a security device, a bit of personal information that's not readily available to someone who may try to impersonate you. You may forget a made-up password, but you're not likely to forget your mother's maiden name, even months later. If you need to call ISC for help with your account, they may ask your mother's maiden name (along with other questions) to verify your identity before discussing details of your financial transactions. Actually, you could enter another name instead of your mother's maiden name. Just be sure it's something you'll remember and be able to supply on request.

4. After entering the password information, click on the Connect button. Quicken will dial up Intuit Services Corporation, connect with its computer system, and exchange information. During this process, Quicken will keep you informed of its progress with a message similar to the following:

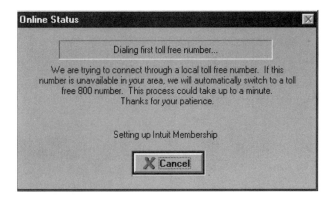

5. Quicken will take care of signing you up; you won't need to enter any information online. When the setup is complete, Quicken displays the Setup Confirmation dialog box, as shown in Figure 5.7. The dialog box includes your Intuit membership number. It's a good idea to jot the number down and keep it with your financial records. Click on the OK button to close the dialog box.

FIGURE 5.7:
The Setup
Confirmation
dialog box con-
firms your new
Intuit membership.

NOTE

If you can't successfully connect to Intuit Services Corporation, there are several possible explanations. Your modem setup could be wrong, but the problem might be that Intuit's system is busy or has shut down for maintenance. (ISC shuts down its network for routine maintenance each day from 2 a.m. to 6 p.m. central time so don't expect to conduct online sessions during these hours.) After a failed attempt to connect, Quicken displays an error message. Normally, the dialog box contains a Help button that you can click on to get suggestions for solving the problem. Often, the best solution is to just call back later.

Using an Existing Intuit Membership

If you already have an Intuit membership set up for use with another Quicken file, you can use it with your current Quicken file by taking the following steps:

1. Pull down the Online menu, click on Intuit Membership, and then choose the Set Up… command; the About Intuit Membership dialog box will appear, as shown earlier in Figure 5.4.

2. Click on the Use existing Intuit Membership… button to open the Existing Intuit Membership dialog box, as shown in Figure 5.8.

FIGURE 5.8:
Select which
membership you
want to access
with the current
Quicken file.

3. To specify the Intuit membership you wish to use, simply type in or select the number in the Intuit Membership Number text box. You'll also need to enter the correct password for the selected membership in the Password text box.

4. Click on the OK button; Quicken verifies your membership and saves the information in your Quicken file. The program displays the following dialog box to confirm that the Intuit membership is linked to your current Quicken file.

Your Member ID Number

Your Intuit membership number is your primary form of identification as a subscriber to Intuit's online services. The number first appears in the Setup Confirmation dialog box (see Figure 5.7) when you sign up for your Intuit membership. It's a good idea to make a note of the number for future reference.

You can also display your Intuit membership number by following these steps:

1. Pull down Quicken's Online menu and click on Intuit Membership. When the cascading menu appears, choose View Detail to display the Intuit Membership Detail dialog box, as shown in Figure 5.9.

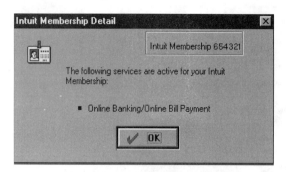

FIGURE 5.9:
Check your Intuit
membership
number by dis-
playing the Intuit
Membership
Detail dialog box.

The dialog box shows your Intuit membership Number and also lists what online services you've signed up for.

2. Click on the OK button to close the dialog box.

Changing Your Membership Information

Suppose you move, change phone numbers, or change your name. Then you'll need to update the personal information on file as part of your Intuit membership.

It's important to keep the information up-to-date. First of all, Intuit Services Corporation needs the information in order to contact you if there are any questions about your account, and to send you information about updates and changes in the services. More importantly, if you need to contact ISC about a problem with your account or a payment you made, the support staff will use items from the personal information to help verify your identity.

You can change your personal information easily from within Quicken. However, it's important to remember that any change you make updates *only* your personal information on file at ISC. The information is *not* passed on to any bank or financial institution. You must contact your bank separately.

Changing Your Personal Information

To change your name, address, or other personal information on file at Intuit Services Corporation, follow these steps:

1. Pull down the Online menu, click on Intuit Membership, and choose Change. This opens the Change Intuit Membership dialog box, as shown in Figure 5.10.

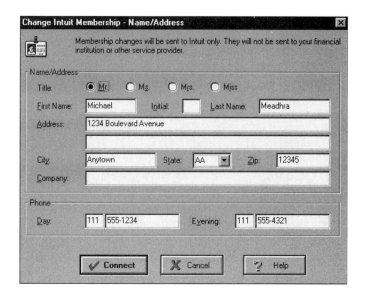

FIGURE 5.10:
Keep your personal information up-to-date in the Change Intuit Membership dialog box.

2.   Edit the information in the dialog box as needed, and then click on the Connect button. Quicken will open the Enter Password dialog box shown in Figure 5.11.

FIGURE 5.11:
You must enter your password before Quicken will change your personal information.

3.   Type in your Intuit membership password and then click on the OK button.
     Quicken calls Intuit Services Corporation, logs on, updates your personal information, and then logs off. The program displays status messages during this process and a confirmation message when the update is complete.

4.   Click on the OK button to close the dialog box. Your Intuit membership information has been changed as you requested.

Changing Your Password

From time to time, you'll need to change your Intuit membership password. To protect the security of your transactions, you should change your password any time there is any possibility that the password has been compromised. In addition, security experts recommend changing passwords periodically, just in case.

Changing your Intuit membership password is easy when you follow these steps:

1. Pull down the Online menu, click on Membership Password, and then choose Change from the cascading menu. Quicken opens the Change Intuit Membership Password dialog box, as shown in Figure 5.12.

FIGURE 5.12: For security, change your password occasionally using the Change Intuit Membership Password dialog box.

2. Enter your current password in the first text box. As always, the password appears on-screen as a string of asterisks.
3. In the middle text box, type your new Intuit membership password.
4. Type your new password a second time in the bottom text box, to confirm that you've entered it correctly.
5. After entering the password, click on the Connect button.

   Quicken calls Intuit Services Corporation, logs on, registers the new password for you, and then disconnects. You'll see the usual status messages during the call. When the process is complete, Quicken displays the confirmation message shown here.

6. Click on the OK button to close the dialog box.

If You Forget Your Password

No one has access to your Intuit membership password but you. If you forget it, you won't be able to access your account and use Quicken's online personal finance features.

Intuit Services Corporation can't tell you your password—but the support staff can help if you forget what it is. Here's the process you'll need go through to regain access to your account if you forget that all-important password:

1. Call Intuit Services Corporation (708-585-8500) and explain your problem.
2. The customer service representative will ask for details from your personal information file to confirm your identity. (This is where your mother's maiden name comes in.)
3. After confirming your identity, the representative can reset your password and instruct you how to create a new password.
4. You can now change your password by following the steps outlined in the preceding section. Once you do that, you can access your account as usual using your new password.

Storing Passwords

Typing in your Intuit membership password every time you need to access one of the online personal finance features can become a bit tiresome. It's an important element of Quicken's security system, but it's inconvenient nonetheless.

To make things easier, Quicken offers you the option of storing your password. The program will then enter your stored password automatically when you log into your Intuit account. This eliminates the need for you to type the password into the Enter Password dialog box for each online session. It makes online access faster and more convenient. If your computer and your Quicken files are well protected from unauthorized use, you may be able to forgo the added security the password provides.

WARNING Storing your password is convenient, but it removes a level of security for some transactions. Anyone with access to your computer will be able to use it to access your Intuit membership. Use this option only if you are confident that no one else can use your computer or access your Quicken files.

Even if you choose to store your Intuit membership password and let the software enter it automatically, you'll still have to enter your PIN (personal identification number) to initiate bank transactions such as Online Banking and Online BillPay. For obvious security reasons, PINs are never stored.

NOTE

If you store your password, you won't be using it regularly. This increases the likelihood that you will forget your password. Protect yourself by recording the password and keeping it safely away from your computer.

Follow these steps to store your Intuit membership password:

1. Pull down the Online menu, click on Membership Password, and then choose Store. Quicken opens the Store Password dialog box as shown in Figure 5.13.

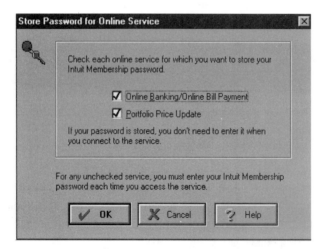

FIGURE 5.13:
Select the online services for which you want Quicken to store your password.

2. Click on the checkbox next to each online service for which you want to store your password. You can store the password for Quicken's banking features (Online Banking and Online BillPay), for Portfolio Price Update, or for both.
    *   A check in the checkbox means that Quicken will enter the password for you automatically when you access the feature.
    *   A blank checkbox means that Quicken will present the Enter Password dialog box and require you to type in your password before accessing the feature.

TIP   A good password storage strategy is to store your password for online banking features but not for Portfolio Price Update. The banking features will remain protected by requiring a PIN for access. By not using a stored password for Portfolio Price Update, you can prevent unauthorized accesses that might run up your bill.

3. After making your choices, click on the OK button. Quicken asks for your password in the dialog box shown in Figure 5.14.

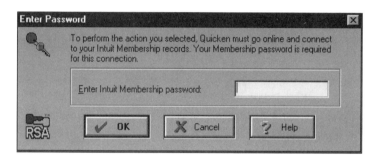

FIGURE 5.14:
You must enter your password before Quicken will store it for automatic use.

4. Enter your password and click on the OK button. Quicken logs onto Intuit's system to record your change and then logs off. The program displays the usual status dialog box during your brief online session and the following confirmation when the process is complete.

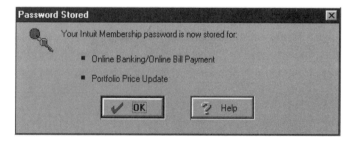

5. Click on the OK button to close the dialog box. The next time you access your Intuit membership, Quicken will automatically enter your stored password for you. You won't need to type your password into the Enter Password dialog box before you log on.

Removing Your Password from Storage

At some point after storing your Intuit membership password, you may find that you want to reverse your decision and reinstate the extra measure of security the password provides. Perhaps you're going on a trip, and your trusty laptop computer will leave the relative safety of your home office for the riskier environs of airports and motel rooms.

Whatever the reason, the procedure for removing your password from storage is essentially the same as storing it:

1. Click on Membership Password in the Online menu and then choose Store. When you do, Quicken opens the Store Password dialog box (refer back to Figure 5.13).

2. Click on the checkbox to remove the check mark next to the online service for which you want to stop storing your password. To eliminate stored passwords completely, clear both checkboxes.

3. After making your choices, click on the OK button.

    If you just cleared password storage options, Quicken won't need to log on to Intuit's system to implement your request. Quicken will display the following confirmation message.

4. Click on the OK button to close the dialog box. The next time you access your Intuit membership, Quicken will display the Enter Password dialog box requiring you to enter your password manually before using each online feature.

Maintaining More Than One Membership

You can access multiple Intuit online services—such as Online Banking, Online BillPay, and Portfolio Price Update—from the same Intuit membership. As a result, there's usually no need for more than one membership. There are a few exceptions to this rule, however. For instance, you might want more than one Intuit membership if you need separate billing for business and personal services, or need to use Portfolio Price Update to update prices on more than 200 securities.

The way the Quicken software stores information about your Intuit membership restricts the system to only one membership per Quicken data file. Therefore, multiple Intuit memberships require multiple Quicken files. That may not be a problem if you're establishing multiple accounts to keep business and personal finances separate. However, it's a major inconvenience if you need to work with more than 200 securities and want to consolidate your investment portfolio into one place.

Each Intuit membership is separate; one membership can't share services with another Intuit membership. For instance, if you want to use Portfolio Price Update in two different Quicken files with two different Intuit memberships, you must sign up for (and pay for) the service twice.

Chapter 6

SETTING UP AN ACCOUNT FOR ONLINE BANKING

- **Establishing an Online Banking account**
- **Setting up a Quicken account for Online Banking**
- **Making the first online contact**
- **Opting out—how to discontinue the service**

Quicken's Online Banking feature lets you download your bank statement, check your current balance, and see what transactions have cleared the bank—all from your computer screen. You can even download transaction details and add the information to your Quicken account register. But all this good stuff doesn't happen by magic. First, you must properly configure your Quicken software and make arrangements with both the bank and Intuit Services Corporation to provide the service.

Online Banking requires the following elements working together:

- An Intuit membership
- A suitable account at a member bank
- A link between your bank account and your Intuit membership
- A corresponding Quicken account with the Online Banking feature enabled

Setting up your Intuit membership was covered in Chapter 5. This chapter describes the other steps you'll need to take: contacting the bank, establishing an account, activating online access to the account, and setting up a Quicken account for Online Banking services.

Establishing an Online Banking Account

As you know by now, Quicken's Online Banking feature isn't available with just any bank. Online Banking requires two-way communication between your Quicken software and the bank. That's only possible if you have an account at one of the more than 35 financial institutions that allow Quicken users to access their account information via the Intuit Services Corporation network. Intuit Services Corporation (ISC) is the intermediary between you (and thousands of other Quicken users) and the bank. You go through ISC to get your account information, but ultimately, your banking relationship is with the financial institution, not Intuit.

Even after you establish an account at a member bank, you can't just fire up Quicken, log on, and tap into your account. The bank must activate the Online Banking feature and link your account to ISC. Then the bank will send you a personal identification number (PIN) to ensure that only you can access your account.

What Accounts Are Eligible for Online Banking?

To use Online Banking, you not only need an account at a participating financial institution—it must be an account for which the bank supports Online Banking access.

Some banks offer Online Banking only with selected types of accounts. For instance, you can probably get Online Banking access to a checking account and even a savings account, but you may not be able to access a credit card account or line of credit. Or a bank might allow Online Banking with personal accounts, but not with corporate accounts. Some banks allow you to access multiple accounts at the same bank and may even let you transfer funds between different accounts at the same bank.

NOTE Some credit card companies—American Express and Quicken's Intellicharge—also support Online Banking with Quicken. Like regular banks, they let you check your credit card account balance and download transaction information with online statements.

You can have Online Banking active for multiple accounts at the same bank, and even access accounts at separate financial institutions from the same Quicken file and Intuit membership.

NOTE Initially, Quicken users were limited to an online banking relationship with only one member bank from each Quicken file and Intuit membership. Furthermore, each online banking relationship needed to be keyed to a different Social Security number. The only exception to the "one member bank" rule was the credit card companies. You could set up Online Banking with both a member bank and a credit card company without any conflict between the two. However, as this book goes to press, ISC is in the process of implementing changes that will remove the one-bank restriction. By the time you read this, there should be no problem accessing accounts at two or three different participating financial institutions with the same Intuit membership.

Opening a New Account

Unless you already bank with one of the participating financial institutions, your next step is opening a new account with a member bank in order to use Online Banking.

NOTE Refer back to Chapter 3 for guidelines on selecting a banking partner for Online Banking. Also see Appendix C for a comparison of the services offered by participating financial institutions.

Opening a new account for Online Banking is just like opening any bank account. Start the process by selecting a bank and contacting its customer service department. Nearly all of the participating financial institutions have toll-free phone numbers to make contacting them easy. Then select the kind of account that suits your needs (make sure Online Banking is available for that account), fill out the required forms, and make it official by depositing some funds.

You may be able to supply most of the information the bank needs to open your account over the phone. You can expect at least the paperwork, though—signature cards, federal tax reporting forms, and so on. If you don't live close to a bank branch, you can probably handle the paperwork by mail and maybe even fax the necessary forms to the bank. On the other hand, a few banks may require that you live within a certain area and may even request that you visit a branch to complete the paperwork. It all depends on a combination of state and federal banking regulations and the bank's own policies.

For a checking or savings account, you'll normally need to deposit funds in the account when you open it. Don't forget to check how large the initial deposit must be and how soon those funds will be available.

> **TIP**
>
> You can expedite your opening deposit in a new bank account by sending a certified check for the deposit amount. That way, you won't have to wait for the regular check to clear both banks before being able to use your new account. Getting a certified check will probably require a trip to your local bank branch and incur a small fee, but it could be worth it if you're in a hurry to get started with Online Banking.

When you apply for your new account, tell the customer service representative that you want to use Quicken's Online Banking features with the account. The bank must set up the connection between your account and Intuit Services Corporation before you'll be able to access it. Usually, the bank can take care of online access at the same time it opens your account, but you have to ask for the service, and there will probably be an additional form you'll need to sign.

> **WARNING**
>
> You must have your bank activate your account for online access. This is separate from your Intuit membership and anything you set up in your Quicken software.

After you open your new account, you'll get all the usual banking paraphernalia: checks, ATM card, and a handful of paperwork covering disclaimers and regulations. In addition, you'll get a welcome kit for Online Banking containing the following:

- A supplemental Quicken manual covering the Online Banking features
- A letter with the information (the bank's routing number and your account number) that you'll need to enable your Quicken account for Online Banking
- A personal identification number (PIN) that you'll need to unlock access to your account
- A disk that will update your Quicken software to include your bank in the Financial Institution drop-down list (you won't receive this if your bank is already in the list)

For security reasons, the PIN is mailed separately, timed to arrive a couple of days before or after the rest of the online welcome kit. You need both the account information and the PIN in order to access your account from Quicken. Of course, you can write checks and use your ATM card for access to your Online Banking account, just like any other account.

WARNING Don't confuse your Online Banking PIN with the PIN for your ATM card. If you open a new account, both PINs may arrive at about the same time and look similar.

Activating Online Banking for an Existing Account

If you already have an account with one of the financial institutions participating in Intuit's banking network, you're lucky. The hard part of setting up an Online Banking account is done. Now, all you need to do is make arrangements to access your existing account with Quicken.

The bank must activate the Online Banking feature for each account you wish to access. To start the ball rolling, call the bank's customer service department and tell them that you want to use Quicken to access your account. The customer service representative will explain the bank's procedures for activating Online Banking. The details will vary from bank to bank. You may be able to initiate the process by phone, or you may need to get some forms by mail or fax and then sign and return them to the bank.

Once you complete the sign-up process, the bank activates Online Banking for your account and links it to Intuit Services Corporation's banking network. You will be sent an Online Banking welcome kit containing the following:

- A supplemental Quicken manual covering the Online Banking features

- A letter with the information (the bank's routing number and your account number) that you'll need to enable your Quicken account for Online Banking
- A personal identification number (PIN) that you'll need to unlock access to your account
- A disk that will update your Quicken software to include your bank in the Financial Institution drop-down list (you won't receive this if your bank is already in the list)

For security reasons, the PIN is mailed separately, just like the PIN for an ATM card. You need both the account information and the PIN in order to access your account from Quicken. While you're waiting for online access to your account, you can continue to write checks and use your ATM card as usual.

> **TIP**
>
> **If your Online Banking PIN arrives before the rest of the welcome kit, you can probably go ahead and get started with Online Banking right away. The account information you need to set up your Quicken account is usually available on your checks and bank statement.**

What Does Online Banking Cost?

Banks vary significantly in what they charge for Online Banking. Several banks offer Online Banking free—which really means it's included at no extra charge when you sign up for a package of services. There is, however, usually a monthly service charge or minimum balance required for the package of services that includes Online Banking. When Online Banking is charged separately, the fee typically ranges from $3 to $10 a month. Sometimes, the fee will differ from one account type to another at the same bank.

> **NOTE**
>
> **See Appendix C for a comparison of the Online Banking fees at participating financial institutions.**

Online Banking isn't usually like an "all-you-can-eat" buffet. You don't get an unlimited number of online account statements for one low price. At most banks, subscribing to the Online Banking service entitles you to download a certain number of account statements (eight seems to be a common number) each month. If you check your account more frequently, expect to pay for the extra accesses—$.50 per additional statement is typical.

Eight statements a month doesn't sound like much, but that averages out to getting a current bank statement twice a week. It's a big difference from getting a paper bank statement only once a month—especially when you consider that the paper bank statement is several days out of date by the time it arrives in your mailbox.

Your Intuit membership provides the connection between you and your bank, but there's no cost to you for this service. The bank pays Intuit Services Corporation to provide the service for its customers. Of course, you pay for the service indirectly by paying your bank a monthly fee (or by maintaining a minimum balance) for Online Banking.

Setting Up a Quicken Account for Online Banking

OK, you have your Intuit membership, you have a bank account with a participating financial institution, and you've signed up for Online Banking access to your account. Now you're ready to set up an account in your Quicken data file for the bank account and configure Quicken to enable the Online Banking features for that account. You can either

- Enable Online Banking when you set up a new account
- Add the Online Banking feature to an existing account

You'll need your account number and the bank's routing number in order to set up Online Banking in Quicken. This information will be in the welcome kit you receive from the bank after signing up for the service. You'll also need a PIN supplied by the bank in order to log on for the first time.

Setting Up a New Account

You can create a new Quicken account and enable the Online Banking feature for that account by following these steps:

1. Open your Quicken data file and display the Account List (click on the Account List icon in the Home Base window). From the Edit menu, choose New Account to open the Create New Account dialog box, as shown in Figure 6.1. (If you prefer, you can open the same dialog box by pressing Ctrl+N or by clicking on the New button in the Account List window.)

2. Click on a button to select the appropriate account type. Normally, that will be Checking. However, Checking, Savings, Credit Card, and Money Market are all valid account types for Online Banking. On the other hand, Online Banking isn't available for Cash, Investment, Asset, or Liability accounts.

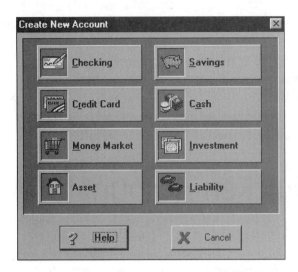

FIGURE 6.1:
Select the account type for your new Online Banking account in the Create New Account dialog box.

TIP — Select the Checking (not Credit Card or Liability) account type to create an account for a line of credit with Online Banking access.

Assuming that you chose the Checking account type, Quicken will open the Checking Account Setup dialog box, as shown in Figure 6.2. (The corresponding dialog boxes for other account types are similar and offer essentially the same online options.)

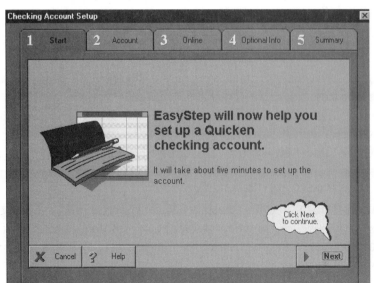

FIGURE 6.2:
The Checking Account Setup dialog box steps you through creating an account.

3. Click on the Next button to step past the Start tab. This will bring up the Account tab, as shown in Figure 6.3. Enter the Account Name and Description, and then click on the Next button.

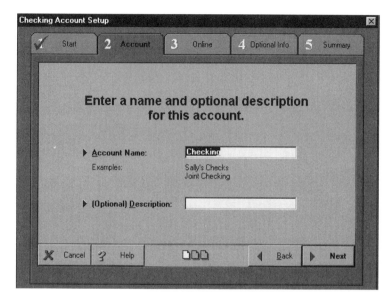

FIGURE 6.3: Begin entering account information in step 2.

4. When the second page of the Account tab appears (see Figure 6.4), click on No and then click on the Next button. Quicken displays a message confirming that it will create your new account with a $0 balance. Click on the Next button again to continue.

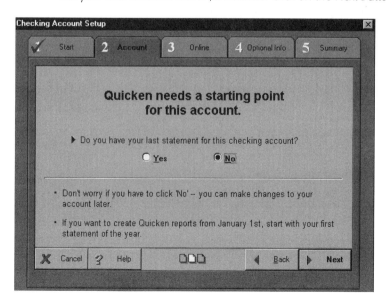

FIGURE 6.4: Since you're creating a new account, you can just say No to entering a starting balance.

5. Now Quicken displays the Online tab, as shown in Figure 6.5. To enable Online Banking for this account, click on the Yes button beside the Online Banking option. (If you'll also be using Online BillPay with this account, you can click on Yes to enable that option at the same time.)

Notice that when you enable one of the online options, Quicken expands the Online tab of the Checking Account Setup dialog box to four pages, as indicated by the four small page icons near the bottom of the dialog box.

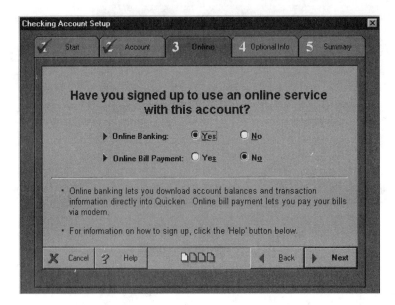

FIGURE 6.5:
Click on Yes to tell Quicken you want to use Online Banking.

6. Click on the Next button to display the next page of online information, as shown in Figure 6.6. This is where you identify the financial institution where you opened your Online Banking account. You must select the correct bank from the Financial Institution drop-down list box. Then, carefully type the bank's routing number into the Routing Number text box. You'll find the routing number in the Online Banking welcome kit you received from your bank.

TIP   Don't be too surprised if the routing number appears, as if by magic, when you select the financial institution. If you've previously set up other accounts at the same financial institution, Quicken will fill in the routing number for you.

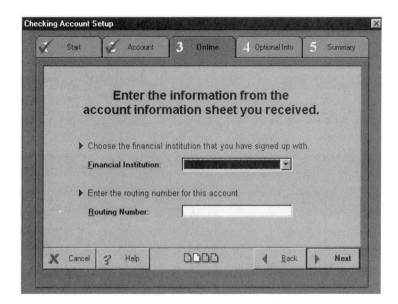

FIGURE 6.6:
This screen lets you identify the bank where you opened your Online Banking account.

7. Click on the Next button once again to bring up the account information page shown in Figure 6.7. In the Account Number box, type the exact account number as supplied by the bank in your Online Banking welcome kit. If necessary, you can modify the account type at this time by selecting Checking, Savings, Money Market, or Line of Credit in the Account Type drop-down list box.

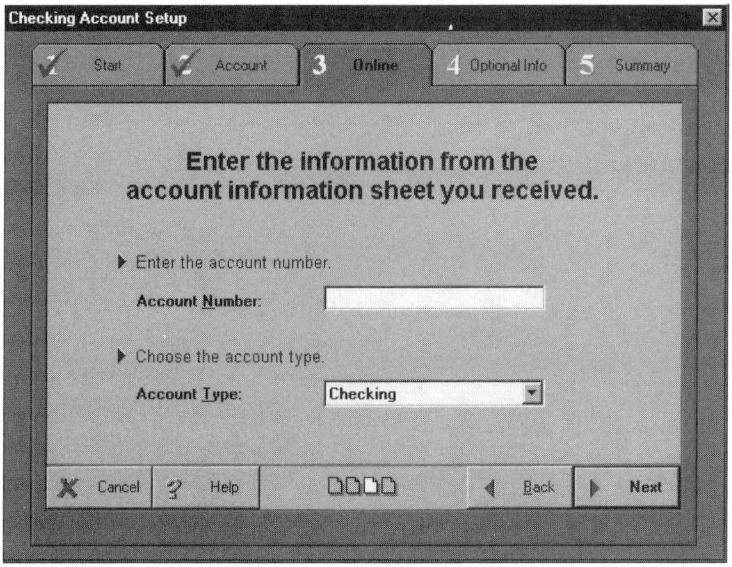

FIGURE 6.7:
Now we're getting specific—identifying the bank account number.

WARNING If you're setting up more than one account at the same bank, you'll need to be especially careful to identify and enter the correct account number for each account.

8. Click on the Next button to display the final page of the Online tab, as shown in Figure 6.8. If you've already signed up for your Intuit membership or created other online accounts, Quicken will fill in the Social Security Number box with the information it has on file. Confirm that the number is correct, changing it if necessary. (For instance, you might need to enter your spouse's Social Security number instead of your own if your spouse is listed as the primary owner of the account at the bank.)

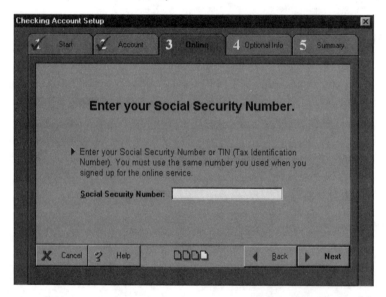

FIGURE 6.8: Make sure the Social Security number is correct.

9. Click on the Next button to move to the Optional Info tab. The first page offers a simple Yes/No choice. Choose Yes, and then click on the Next button to open the second Optional Info page shown in Figure 6.9. As the name implies, this information is optional—it isn't required to create your Quicken account—but it's handy to have for quick reference. You can always add this information later, but I recommend that you do it now, while you're thinking about it and have the welcome kit and other materials on hand.

Type the appropriate information into the Financial Institution, Account

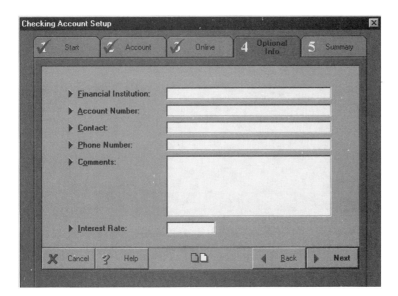

FIGURE 6.9:
Entering this
information is
optional–but
recommended.

Number, Contact, Phone Number, Comments, and Interest Rate boxes. Then click on the Next button to continue.

10. When the first page of the Summary tab appears (see Figure 6.10), check that all the information is correct. You can enter or change any of the information on this screen the same way you entered it earlier. Click on the Next button to move to the next page (shown in Figure 6.11) and do the same. In particular, make sure a check mark appears in the checkbox for the Enable Online Banking

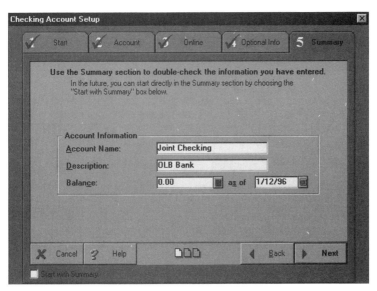

FIGURE 6.10:
The Summary
tab lets you
review and revise
the information
you entered.

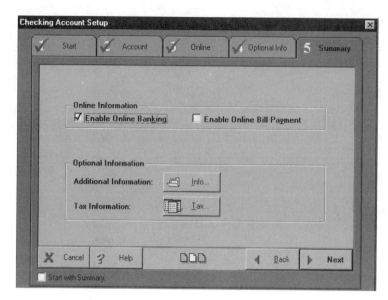

FIGURE 6.11:
Make sure the
Enable Online
Banking option is
checked.

option. When you're confident that the information is correct, click on the Next
button to continue.

11. Check the information in the final page of the Summary tab, as shown in Figure 6.12. Pay particular attention to the routing number and account number.
Once you're sure everything is correct, click on the Done button. Quicken will
close the Checking Account Setup dialog box and create the new account using
the information you've provided.

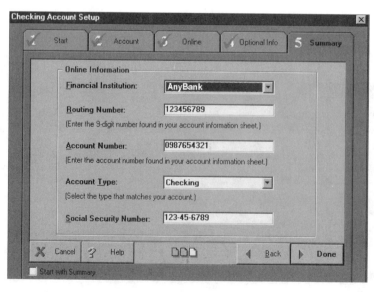

FIGURE 6.12:
One last double
check and you're
done.

When the Account List window reappears, you'll see your new account added to the list (see Figure 6.13). The lightning bolt in the Type column indicates that online access (Online Banking or Online BillPay) is enabled for the account.

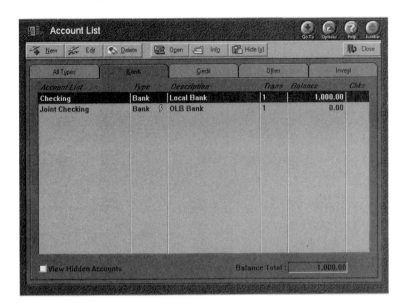

FIGURE 6.13: Lightning bolts designate accounts with Online Banking or Online BillPay enabled.

Enabling Online Banking for an Existing Account

You can enable Online Banking for an existing Quicken account by following these steps:

1. Open your Quicken data file and go to the Account List (click on the Account List icon in the Home Base window or choose Account from the Lists menu).

2. Select the account to which you want to add Online Banking access, and then click on the Edit button. Quicken opens the Edit Bank Account dialog box with the Summary tab displayed, as shown in Figure 6.14.

3. In the Online Information area in the middle of the dialog box, click on the Enable Online Banking option. When the check mark appears in the checkbox beside the option, Quicken adds another page to the Summary tab of the dialog box. Click on the Next button to open the next page, as shown in Figure 6.15.

4. Go to the Financial Institution box and select your bank from the drop-down list.

5. Refer to the welcome kit you received from your bank and enter the routing number and account number in their respective boxes. Be sure to enter the numbers carefully.

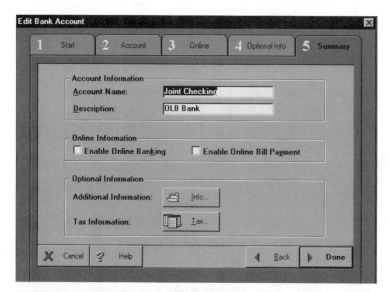

FIGURE 6.14:
Checking the Enable Online Banking option gets things started.

FIGURE 6.15:
This information must be correct for Online Banking to work.

TIP	You can also find the bank routing number and your account number printed on your checks.

6. Check to make sure the account type and Social Security number are correct, changing them if necessary. Then click on the Done button to close the dialog box; Online Banking has now been added to your account.

Deciphering the Numbers on a Check

All the numbers you need to enter into Quicken in order to enable an account for Online Banking are printed on the bottom of your checks. Although the long string of machine-readable numbers appears intimidating, it's not so difficult to decipher once you break it into its component parts. The components are separated by symbols, and include the following:

- Bank routing number
- Account number
- Check number

The bank routing number is the nine-digit number in the lower left corner of the check. It's surrounded by heavy colons.

The other numbers along the bottom of the check are your account number and the check number. The check number often includes a leading zero and might come last or might appear between the routing number and the account number. Regardless of the position, it's pretty easy to identify because it matches the regular check number printed in the upper right corner and changes on each check.

Once you identify the routing number and check number, what's left is your account number. At most U.S. banks, a checking account number has ten digits.

When you return to the Account List window, a lightning bolt should appear in the Type column to indicate that the account has one of the online features (Online Banking or Online BillPay) enabled. (Refer back to Figure 6.13.)

Making the First Online Contact

If you've been following along with this book so far, you have an Intuit membership, an account at a participating financial institution with Online Banking activated, and a corresponding Quicken account with the Online Banking option enabled.

WARNING You must have the PIN supplied by your bank in order to access your account for Online Banking the first time.

Now you're ready to access your Online Banking account. For your initial online session, just follow these steps:

1. Open your Quicken data file and click on the Online Banking icon in the Home Base window, or choose Online Banking from the Online menu. This will open the Online Banking window shown in Figure 6.16.

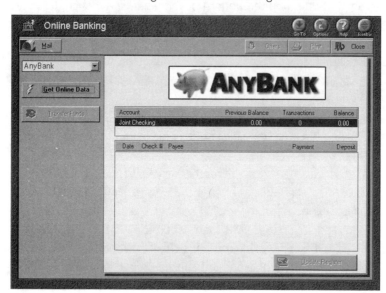

FIGURE 6.16: The Online Banking window is the starting point for all your Online Banking activities.

2. Select the bank you want to contact from the drop-down list box in the upper left corner (under the Mail button). If you have accounts configured for Online Banking at only one financial institution, that's the only one that appears on the list. However, if you have Online Banking–enabled accounts at more than one financial institution—a bank and a credit card company, for instance—you'll need to choose which one you want to contact with this call.

3. Click on the Get Online Data button to begin the online session.

4. Since this is the first time you're accessing an account at this financial institution, Quicken will display the dialog box shown below warning you that you must change your PIN. Click on the OK button to continue.

NOTE
Requiring you to change your PIN is a security measure. You must use the PIN supplied by the bank to access your account for the first time, but it's only good for initial access to the account. After that, you'll use the PIN that you create, and only you know.

WARNING
Don't throw away that PIN you received from the bank. You may need it again. If you forget your PIN, the bank can reset your account to allow you to sign on again with your original PIN.

5.   Quicken opens the Change PIN… dialog box, shown below. Type in the PIN supplied by the bank in the Existing banking PIN box. To keep anyone from reading your private PIN, the number doesn't appear on-screen. You'll see asterisks instead.

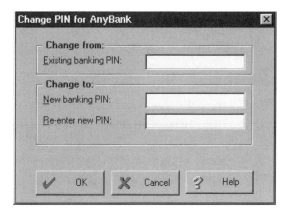

6.   Make up a PIN of your own and enter it in the New banking PIN box. Again, asterisks appear on-screen. Next, retype your new PIN in the Re-enter new PIN box. Although you can't visually confirm that you entered the new PIN as you intended, typing the new PIN twice reduces the possibility of an inadvertent typing error. After entering the PINs, click on the OK button to close the dialog box.

TIP

Make a note of your new PIN and store it someplace safe (but not around your computer). You'll need to use the PIN every time you access your account for Online Banking.

7. Next, Quicken displays the Enter Password dialog box shown below. Type your Intuit membership password in the box, and click on the OK button. This launches your Online Banking session.

If you stored your Intuit password for Online Banking/Online BillPay, the program will skip this step and enter your stored password automatically. See the previous chapter for more information on storing your Intuit membership password.

After you enter the PINs and password, Quicken handles the rest of the online session automatically. The Online Status dialog box (shown below) will keep you informed as Quicken initializes your modem, logs on to the ISC network, and sends your message—your Intuit membership ID, password, and PIN, followed by a request for the current statement for your accounts at the selected financial institution. Quicken retrieves the information from the ISC network and logs off automatically.

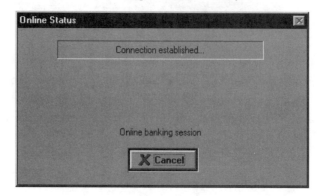

WARNING If you have trouble accessing your new Online Banking account, don't just keep trying repeatedly. Call Technical Support for assistance. After five unsuccessful attempts to log on with your initial PIN, the system will lock you out. You'll have to request another PIN from your financial institution and wait for it to arrive in the mail before attempting to access your account again.

When Quicken completes the Online Banking session, it returns you to the Online Banking window. The online statement area probably won't have changed much from before your online session. Since this was your first access to your account, it's likely that there were no transactions or other account activity to download. Perhaps the balance changed, and that's all. Later, when there's more activity, you can review the transaction details in this window and update your account register with the downloaded information. I'll cover that in the next chapter.

Opting Out – How to Discontinue the Service

Online Banking is so convenient, it's hard to imagine that at some point, you may want to discontinue the service. However, it might happen someday, so you should understand the process. Just as enabling an account for Online Banking involves more than changing a few settings in Quicken, disabling the option requires changes at your bank as well as changes to your Quicken account. To disable Online Banking for an account, you must do the following:

- Request the bank to deactivate Online Banking access to your account
- Disable the Online Banking option for the corresponding Quicken account

Canceling the Online Banking service is like making any other change in your bank account. You must contact the bank and request the change in your account status. Bank policies regarding account changes vary. You might be able to make the request with a simple phone call to the bank's customer service line; you may be able to make your request via e-mail; or you might need to send the bank a written request or visit a bank branch in person.

The bank will contact Intuit Services Corporation and take the necessary steps to deactivate Online Banking access to your account. After the bank disables the Online Banking feature on your account, you can change your Quicken account to reflect the change in status by following these steps:

1. Open your Quicken data file and go to the Account List window by clicking on the Account List icon in the Home Base window.

2. Select the account for which you want to disable Online Banking. Click on the Edit button to open the Edit Bank Account dialog box, as shown in Figure 6.17.

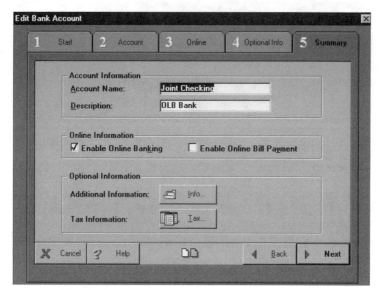

FIGURE 6.17: Removing one check mark disables the Online Banking option for this account.

3. To disable the Online Banking option, simply click on Enable Online Banking to clear the check mark from the checkbox. The Next button changes to Done. Click on the Done button to close the Edit Bank Account dialog box.

4. Quicken displays the warning shown below. Click on the OK button to confirm your change to the Online Banking option.

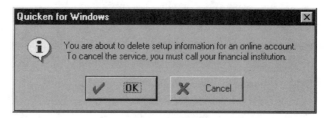

Back in the Account List window, the lightning bolt symbol disappears from the Type column for that account. That's all there is to it. Online Banking for that account is history.

Chapter 7

USING ONLINE BANKING

- **Anatomy of an Online Banking session**
- **Getting an online statement of your account**
- **Reading your online statement**
- **Updating your register**
- **Editing downloaded entries**

Previous chapters covered the general concepts of online personal finance, the players involved in providing the service, and the steps needed to get everything set up for Online Banking. Now let's look at what happens during an Online Banking session, learn how to get an online account statement, and use the downloaded transaction details to update your Quicken account register.

Anatomy of an Online Banking Session

Before you begin step-by-step instructions for an Online Banking session, it helps to have a little background. Remember that true Online Banking requires two-way communication between you and your bank. You send a request (ask for a statement update, send e-mail, or initiate a transfer of funds between accounts), and the bank responds; the information you requested is transferred into Quicken.

Intuit Services Corporation (ISC) is the intermediary between you and the member bank. But all of your interaction takes place with the Quicken software—and it all occurs before and after the Online Banking session itself. The rest of the process is fully automated.

You begin the process in Quicken. Quicken calls ISC automatically. ISC authenticates the validity of *your* request, gets the requested information from your bank, and then transmits that information back to Quicken. After Quicken downloads the data from your bank, you can use it to update your Quicken account register. Figure 7.1 diagrams the flow of requests and information.

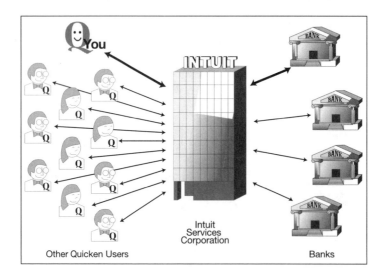

FIGURE 7.1:
Your Online Banking connection goes through Intuit Services Corporation.

Intuit takes the security of Online Banking sessions very seriously. Before you can gain access to account information at any bank, you must supply both a PIN for your bank and your Intuit membership password. Quicken requests your PIN and password (unless you stored your Intuit password) when you start an Online Banking session. Quicken uses the password to log onto the ISC network. After access to the network is established, Quicken uses the PIN to gain access to your bank account information. You must supply both the correct password and the correct PIN to do Online Banking. If either one is incorrect, the system won't allow access to the information in your account.

The Online Banking activity that you'll probably use most is getting an online bank statement. In fact, it may be your main reason for upgrading or purchasing the latest version of Quicken and signing up for the Online Banking service. Let's look at the process of getting an online bank statement and using it to update your account register.

Getting an Online Statement of Your Account

An online statement is much like a paper account statement. It has two main parts:
- Current balance
- List of transactions that have been posted to the account since your last statement

You don't have to go through two separate procedures to get both your account balance and transaction details. Quicken updates all the relevant account data in the same online session. In fact, if you have multiple accounts set up for Online Banking at the same bank, Quicken will download updated account statements for all of them.

TIP An online statement, like its paper counterpart, is easier to work with if it doesn't contain too many transactions. You can adjust how often you get online statements from your financial institution in order to keep the statements an easily manageable size.

Downloading Online Data

To update your Online Banking account statement, follow these steps:
1. Open your Quicken data file and then open the Online Banking window, as shown in Figure 7.2. You can get to the Online Banking window either by clicking on the Online Banking icon in the Home Base window or by choosing Online Banking from the Online menu.

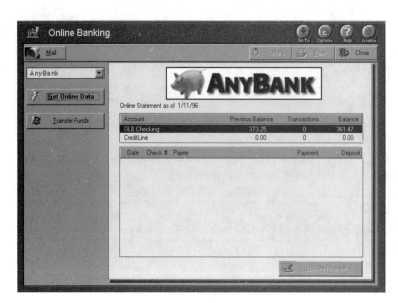

FIGURE 7.2:
The Online Banking window is your starting point for an online session with your financial institution.

2. Start by selecting the financial institution you want to contact from the drop-down list box in the upper left corner of the Online Banking window (just below the Mail button).

> **TIP**
>
> **Remember, you don't have to select which account you want to update. Quicken automatically gets statements for all accounts at the selected financial institution for which you've enabled Online Banking.**

3. Click on the Get Online Data button.
4. Quicken displays the Access to… dialog box shown below. Enter your PIN for this financial institution, and then click on the OK button.

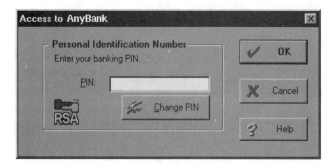

WARNING If you have Online Banking enabled for more than one financial institution, you must make sure you use the correct PIN for the financial institution you are contacting.

5. If you've stored your Intuit membership password for Online Banking (see Chapter 5), Quicken will enter it automatically. Otherwise, the program opens the Enter Password dialog box shown below. Type in your password and then click on the OK button.

6. The Online Banking session proceeds automatically from this point. The Online Status dialog box (shown below) keeps you informed of what's happening.

Quicken initializes your modem and makes the call to the Intuit Services Corporation network. The program logs on to the network, goes through security checks, and then requests the latest data from your accounts at your chosen financial institution. After downloading the requested information, Quicken logs off the network and disconnects your modem.

If there was no new account information available for downloading, Quicken will display the message shown below. Otherwise, the transaction details will appear in the Online Banking window, ready for your review.

Reading Your Online Statement

After you download account data, the Online Banking window starts to look more like a real account statement (see Figure 7.3). It shows not only the account balance, but also details of the transactions that have cleared your bank since your last online statement.

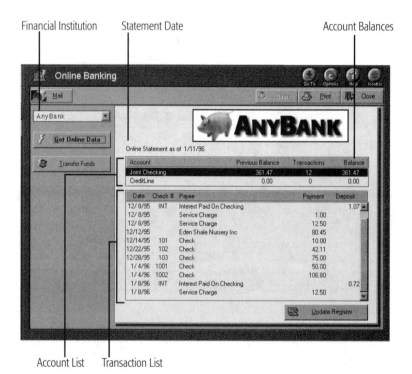

FIGURE 7.3:
The Online Banking window looks similar to an account statement.

The Online Banking window looks enough like a typical paper account statement that you'll probably be able to figure out most of its elements:

Financial institution	If you have Online Banking accounts at multiple financial institutions, you choose which financial institution's accounts to view by selecting it from this drop-down list box.
Statement date	The effective date of this online statement—usually the close of the previous business day.
Account list	Shows the accounts for which you've enabled Online Banking at the selected financial institution. When you click on an account name to select it, Quicken shows the transaction details for that account in the lower part of the window.
Previous balance	Your balance as recorded in the previous online statement.
Number of transactions	The number of transactions included in the current online statement.
Balance	Your current account balance.
Transaction list	Details of the transactions that have cleared the bank since your previous online statement.
Date	The official transaction date. The transactions are sorted by date.
Check #	The check number.
Payee	The payee for the transaction (if it's known by the computer system). Credit card payments and electronic transactions may include descriptive information in the Payee column, but checks will often appear simply as "Check."
Payment/Deposit	The amount of the transaction, listed in the appropriate column.

NOTE

Just how current is the current balance shown on your statement? Financial institutions generally update account information once a day with all the transactions processed before a designated cutoff time. If the cutoff time is 4:00 p.m., then a statement you download today will show the balance and the transactions that have cleared as of 4:00 p.m. yesterday. Normally, there are no updates posted on Sundays or bank holidays.

Updating Your Register

Getting an online account statement is just the beginning. The real advantage of Online Banking is being able to use the information you get from your bank to update and manage your personal finances. In the case of an online account statement, that means using the information from the statement to ensure that your Quicken account register is accurate and up-to-date. You need to make sure the transactions in your account register jibe with the bank's records.

The basic process of checking your account register against the online statement is the same as checking it against the monthly paper statement. First you compare the transactions in your register with those on the statement. Then, if you find transactions on the statement that aren't in your register (such as service charges, interest, forgotten ATM transactions, and so on), you add them to the register.

Quicken's Online Banking features make this process easy. The program automatically makes the comparison between transactions in your online statement and transactions in your register. If there are transactions in the statement that aren't already in your register, it lets you add them to your register without the hassle of having to retype the information.

> **NOTE**
> This section deals with getting an Online Banking statement for a typical checking account. Using Online Banking with a credit card account is basically the same, but there are a few differences. I'll discuss those differences in the next chapter.

Identifying Matching Transactions

Going through a paper account statement and comparing transactions with those in your account register is a tedious chore. But Online Banking can eliminate that chore.

Quicken compares the transactions listed in the online statement to the unreconciled transactions in your account register. The program compares such information as check number, date, and transaction amount. When it finds a match, Quicken marks the transaction in your register with a C in the Clr (cleared) column to indicate that it has cleared the bank. When you reconcile your account, those transactions will already be checked off as cleared.

NOTE At this point, the transaction is marked as cleared (*C*) but not yet reconciled (*R*). Previous versions of Quicken used an asterisk (*) and an *X* instead of the *C* and the *R*.

After downloading your online statement, you can tell Quicken to compare the list of cleared transactions to those in your account register by clicking on the Update Register button at the bottom of the Online Banking window. If Quicken finds matches for all the transactions in the transaction list, it displays a message similar to the one below. If there are cleared transactions listed in the online statement for which Quicken can find no matching transaction in your account register, the program gives you the opportunity to review and edit those transactions before adding them to your register. (This process is covered in the next section.)

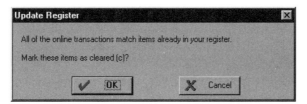

If Quicken finds a discrepancy (usually an incorrect amount) between a transaction from your statement and a transaction in your register, it displays the Duplicate Check Number Found dialog box shown below. When you click on the Continue button, Quicken adds the online transaction to your register and appends the letter *A* to the check number. Later, you can edit the transaction in your register to resolve the conflict.

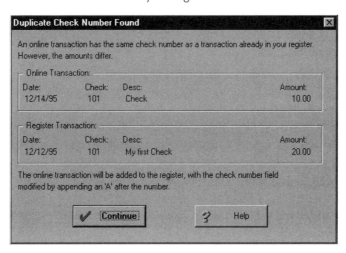

Editing Downloaded Entries

If there are cleared transactions listed in your online statement that aren't in your account register, Quicken can update the register by adding the missing transactions for you. However, you'll need to review and edit the transactions first. You'll want to assign the transactions to the appropriate categories, and you may need to edit the payee as well—especially for those transactions that are listed as "Check."

To review and edit statement transactions in preparation for adding them to your register, follow these steps:

1.	In the Online Banking window, select the financial institution and account to display the online statement. Then click on the Update Register button.

	Quicken compares the transaction list to your account register; if there are any transactions not already listed in your register, the program displays the Update Register dialog box, as shown in Figure 7.4.

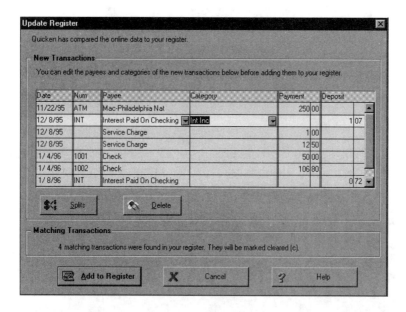

FIGURE 7.4:
The Update Register dialog box lets you edit new transactions before adding them to your account register.

The dialog box is divided into two sections. The New Transactions section displays transactions listed in the online statement for which Quicken couldn't find a matching transaction in your register. Below this list is the Matching Transactions section, where Quicken reports its success at finding matching transactions.

NOTE The Matching Transactions section of the Update Register dialog box will not appear if the program didn't find any matching transactions in your register.

Some, or all, of the transactions in the New Transactions list will need editing before you add them to your register. You can edit the payee and category for each transaction in the New Transactions list. However, you can't alter the other information—at least not while working in this dialog box.

2. To edit a transaction, select a transaction from the list by clicking on it.

3. Click on the Payee field. You can retype or edit the payee using normal text-editing techniques. If your register contains previous entries for this payee, you can save yourself some typing. Just click on the arrow button at the right side of the Payee field, and select the payee from the drop-down list.

4. Next, click on the arrow button in the transaction's Category field. If you want to assign the transaction to a single category, you can simply scroll down the drop-down list and select the appropriate category or transfer account from the list. It's just like specifying the category for a check or register transaction.

If necessary, you can split the transaction among multiple categories. Choose Split Transaction from the Category drop-down list, or click on the Splits button (below the transaction list) to open the Splits dialog box. Splitting a transaction among multiple categories here works just like it does in your register.

5. You may find a transaction in the New Transaction list that you don't want to transfer to your register. Perhaps it's a transaction that Quicken didn't recognize as matching anything in your register, but you're sure it's there.

To remove a transaction from the New Transaction list, select the transaction and click on the Delete button (located below the list). Quicken displays the message box shown below, requesting confirmation of the action. Click on the OK button to remove the transaction from the list. It won't be added to your account register.

6. After editing the transactions in the New Transactions list, you're ready to add them to your account register. Simply click on the Add to Register button at the bottom of the dialog box. Quicken enters the transactions in your register.

Adding Downloaded Transactions to Your Register

When you click on the Add to Register button in the Update Register dialog box as described in step 6 above, Quicken adds all the transactions in the New Transactions list to your Quicken account register for the corresponding account. The program marks each transaction as cleared by placing a C in the Clr column of the register. When you reconcile the account, these transactions will be checked, indicating that they've been identified as transactions that have cleared the bank.

WARNING Just downloading transaction data from your financial institution doesn't add transactions to your account register. You must first review the transactions and verify that they are correct by using the procedure described in the preceding section.

After adding downloaded transactions to your account register, be sure you review the register. Check for duplicate transactions not found by Quicken. (The program is pretty good at matching transactions, but some duplicates can slip through.) This is also your opportunity to add memos to the downloaded transactions.

Chapter 8

EXPLORING OTHER ONLINE BANKING FEATURES

- **Using Online Banking with a credit card account**
- **Reconciling your account register**
- **Transferring funds between online accounts**
- **Using e-mail to communicate with your bank**
- **Dealing with common questions and problems**

The preceding chapter described the most common Online Banking activity—getting an online statement and updating your account register with the downloaded transaction details. But there's more to Quicken's Online Banking feature. At some financial institutions, you can use Online Banking with credit card accounts; Online Banking has a major impact on reconciling your account register; and then there are transfers between accounts and the ability to communicate with the bank using e-mail. Read on to find out more about these other Online Banking operations.

Using Online Banking with a Credit Card Account

It's natural to think of Online Banking as a way to keep tabs on your checking and savings accounts. But Online Banking can work equally well with credit card accounts. If you have an American Express (or Optima) card or a Quicken credit card (IntelliCharge), you can access those accounts with Online Banking. In addition, if you have a credit card issued by a participating financial institution, you *might* be allowed to access that account as well.

Getting an online statement for a credit card works just like Online Banking with a checking account. The procedure is the same, and you can download the same kind of balance and transaction information. There are just a few minor differences when you use Online Banking with a credit card account.

When you select a credit card account in the Online Banking window, you'll notice some changes in the column headings in the transaction list (see Figure 8.1):

- Ref (reference number) instead of Check # (check number)
- Charge/Payment instead of Payment/Deposit

In addition, you'll usually see a bit more information on Payees when you download credit card transactions. Since the credit card processing company has records on each vendor who accepts its card, you're more likely to see a descriptive name in the Payee column instead of the vague "Check" that appears so frequently in checking account statements.

When you download transaction details for a credit card account and add them to your account register, Quicken tries to categorize the new transactions for you. There is a merchant code included with each transaction that helps identify the kind of business a vendor is in. Quicken uses that information to automatically assign a preliminary category to downloaded transactions.

For example, if the merchant code identifies the payee as a restaurant, Quicken assigns the transaction to the Dining category. To refine the process of assigning categories, Quicken searches your account register for other transactions with the same payee. If Quicken finds a matching payee, it will use the same category for the new transaction. If the previous transaction with that payee was split among multiple categories, Quicken will use the first category listed in the split.

This system of assigning categories to new transactions isn't perfect, but it's a start. You'll still have to review and edit the categories for your new transactions in the Update

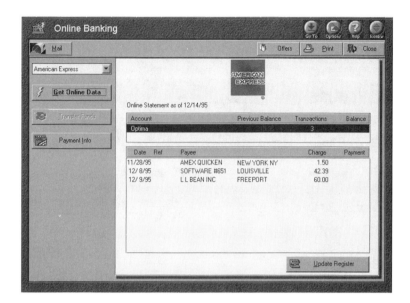

FIGURE 8.1:
The transaction list gets some different headings when you view an online statement for a credit card account.

Register dialog box. The automatic category assignments based on merchant codes are only occasionally the same as the category you want to assign to the transaction. However, the ability to repeat the category assignment of the last transaction with the same payee means that Quicken "learns" how you want to categorize transactions. If you repeatedly deal with the same vendors, the process can work very well.

Paying Your Credit Card Bill

Your monthly paper credit card statement is more than an account summary; it's also a bill. Quicken's Online Banking feature provides a similar capability to let you see not only the account balance, but also the minimum payment due and the due date. Quicken will even generate a check automatically to pay your credit card bill.

To check on your credit card bill, follow these steps:

1. Go to the Online Banking window and select the financial institution where you have your credit card account. From the account list, select the account you want to inquire about. (Obviously, Online Banking must be enabled for this account, and you must have downloaded an online statement.)

2. Click on the Payment Info button. Quicken opens the Credit Card Payment Information dialog box. There's no need to go online to download the information, since it's already in your last online statement. (Of course, that last statement should be reasonably current. You're not going to get accurate payment information if your last online statement update was over a month ago.)

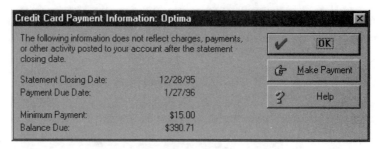

The dialog box presents the following information that you'd normally find in the bill portion of your credit card account statement:

- Statement Closing Date
- Payment Due Date
- Minimum Payment
- Balance Due

3. After examining the contents of the dialog box, you can do one of the following:

    - Click on the OK button to close the dialog box.
    - Click on the Make Payment button to initiate a payment on your credit card bill. This will open the Make Credit Card Payment dialog box shown below.

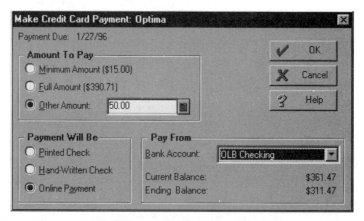

4. Make selections and fill in options in the Make Credit Card Payment dialog box to specify your credit card payment:

    - Amount To Pay—choose Minimum Amount or Full Amount, or, if you want to specify another payment amount, choose Other Amount and enter the planned payment in the text box.
    - Payment Will Be—choose Printed Check, Hand-Written Check, or Online Payment.
    - Pay From—choose which Bank Account you want to pay the credit card bill from.

5. Click on the OK button; Quicken goes to the account register for the selected account and enters a transaction for the payment you specified. All that remains is for you to write or print the check, or send the online payment.

Reconciling Your Account Register

Strictly speaking, reconciling your Quicken account register to your bank statement isn't an Online Banking feature—at least not in the sense that you do the reconciliation online. However, having frequent online access to information about the status of your account has a significant impact on how you reconcile your account. For one thing, you already know what transactions have cleared the bank before you begin the reconciliation (or even open the statement envelope, for that matter).

If Online Banking is enabled for an account, you have two ways to reconcile that account. You can use either of the following:

- The paper statement from your bank
- The online statement you download into Quicken

You must pick one reconciliation method. You can't combine the two methods on the same account or switch back and forth (at least not easily).

The main reason for sticking with one reconciliation method is that the beginning balance for an account reconciliation is based on the ending balance the last time the account was reconciled. If you reconcile your account to an online statement and then try to reconcile to the paper statement when it comes in, the beginning balance will be incorrect. You could overcome that problem, but there's also the fact that when you complete an account reconciliation, the cleared transactions are marked as reconciled. As a result, they no longer appear in the reconciliation dialog box, and Quicken doesn't include them when searching for matches to the cleared transactions in a statement. You could manually change the cleared and reconciled status of all the transactions listed in your paper account statement, but the process would be so time-consuming and error-prone that it's not practical.

I suggest that you reconcile your Quicken account register to the paper statement you get in the mail instead of reconciling it to the online statement. You can still download online statements and use them to check your balance and cleared transactions. However, in case of an error, the paper statement is a written document that all parties can refer to, so it makes sense to reconcile to that document. It's also a separate cross-check of the information you downloaded into the online statements.

Although I suggest reconciling to the paper statement, let's look at both options.

Reconciling to Your Paper Statement

If you've been getting online statements for your account with Quicken, then the paper statement doesn't contain any surprises or new information when it arrives in the mail. The reconciliation process becomes just a final check that everything is in order, instead of a time for making additions and adjustments to discover just what the status of your account really is (or what it was on the statement date a week ago).

If you're familiar with the procedure for reconciling a Quicken account register to the paper statement from the bank, you may notice a few changes when you enable the Online Banking option for the account. The initial dialog box is a bit different, and most of the transactions are already marked as cleared when you start. To reconcile the account to a paper statement, follow these steps:

1. Open your Quicken data file and display the Account List (click on the Account List icon in the Home Base window or choose Account from the Lists menu).

2. Select the account you want to reconcile—one with Online Banking enabled— and then click on the Reconcile button in the toolbar or choose Reconcile from the Activities menu. Usually, Quicken displays the message shown below.

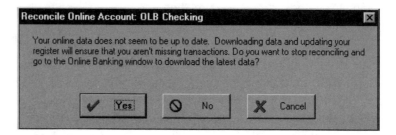

Even if you just downloaded an online statement, it probably carries the previous business day's date, hence this message. If that's the case, you can just click on the No button to close the message box and proceed with the reconciliation. On the other hand, if it's been a while since you downloaded an online statement, you might want to click on the Yes button to discontinue the reconciliation until you've had a chance to update the account.

If you proceed with the reconciliation, Quicken opens the Reconcile Online Account dialog box.

3. Choose the Paper Statement option by clicking on the radio (round) button at the top of the dialog box.

4. In the Ending Statement Date text box, type the closing date listed on your

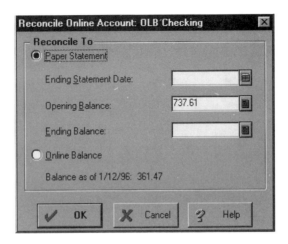

paper statement. To make reconciliation easier, Quicken will not display register transactions posted after this date. This is a change from the way reconciliation works in an account that is not enabled for Online Banking.

5. Enter the Ending Balance information as shown on your statement. Quicken has already supplied the Opening Balance from your last reconciliation for this account, but you can override it here if necessary.

No doubt, those familiar with the reconciliation procedure for non–Online Banking accounts will notice that there is no provision for entering service charges or interest earned. Quicken assumes that you will get these from your online statements, so there's no need to enter them here.

6. After entering the statement information, click on the OK button to open the Reconcile Bank Statement window, as shown in Figure 8.2.

Notice that most (if not all) transactions are already checked off in the Clr column, indicating that they've cleared. Quicken has previously identified the cleared transactions from the online statements.

7. Review the list of transactions and compare it to the paper statement. You may need to check or uncheck a few transactions to match the paper statement. (You can change the cleared status of a transaction by clicking on it.) However, that's the exception rather than the rule when reconciling an Online Banking account. Reconciling becomes a final double check instead of the primary way you determine what transactions have cleared the bank. You can also use the New, Edit, and Delete buttons to create, modify, or remove transactions in your register. These buttons work just as they do when reconciling non–Online Banking accounts, but you'll rarely need them.

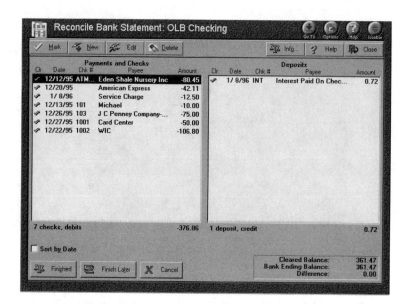

FIGURE 8.2:
Using Online Banking means that most transactions are already marked as cleared when you open the Reconcile Bank Statement window

---

TIP

You might want to note any transactions marked cleared by Online Banking, but unmarked during reconciliation. (There should be just a few.) If you want to record the fact that an online statement indicated that these transactions have cleared the bank, you'll need to manually mark them as cleared in your account register after reconciliation is complete. If that's not important to you, you can just wait until you reconcile the account to the next paper statement. The transactions will appear in the list as uncleared, and you can find them on the paper statement and mark them cleared at that time.

---

8. When you're through checking the list of cleared transactions, your account should balance, as indicated by a 0.00 value in the Difference display in the lower right corner of the dialog box. Click on the Finished button.

9. If your account balanced with the statement, you will see the Reconciliation Complete dialog box with its Congratulations message. If you want to print a reconciliation report, click on the Yes button. Otherwise, click on the No button to close the dialog box.

    If your account is out of balance with the statement, Quicken will offer to enter an adjustment transaction. This is part of normal operations for Quicken—it's no different because of Online Banking.

When you finally return to the account register window, you'll notice that the *Cs* in the Clr column (designating cleared transactions) have been changed to *Rs* to indicate that those transactions have been reconciled. Quicken will no longer consider those transactions when searching for matches to cleared transactions in future online statements.

Reconciling to Your Online Statement

To reconcile your account to the latest online statement, you use essentially the same steps as reconciling to a paper statement. The difference is that you don't do any comparison of the list of cleared transactions to another document. Quicken simply displays the results of its own reconciliation comparison for your acceptance.

If the account balance is off, you can mark and unmark transactions in an attempt to balance it, but without a printed statement for comparison, you're working blind. Fortunately, if you start with a new account (or an existing account that was recently reconciled to the latest paper statement), it's not too difficult to get your first online statement to balance. At most, you'll need to mark only one or two transactions as cleared. After that, the account should reconcile automatically—unless something goes wrong.

To reconcile an account register to the latest online statement, follow these steps:

1. Follow steps 1 and 2 in the preceding section, "Reconciling to Your Paper Statement"; this will start the reconciliation process and open the Reconcile Online Account dialog box.

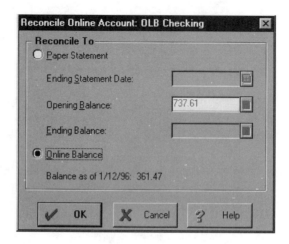

2. Choose Online Balance and then click on the OK button. This will open the Reconcile Bank Statement window, as shown in Figure 8.3.

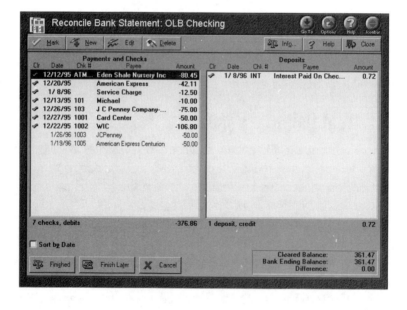

FIGURE 8.3:
When reconciling to an online statement, there's not much to do in the Reconcile Bank Statement window.

3. Many of the transactions that appear in the Reconcile Bank Statement window are already marked as cleared. These are the transactions that were matched to downloaded transactions in the online statements. Other transactions that are listed in your account register are listed here, but they are not checked off as cleared.

Review the transactions in the Reconcile Bank Statement window, and mark or unmark items in the Clr column as needed. When you're through, click on the Finished button.

4. After you complete the reconciliation, you'll have the same options described in step 9 in the preceding section. You can choose to print a reconciliation report, and you can have Quicken insert an adjustment transaction if your account is out of balance.

As with reconciling to a paper statement, when you return to the account register window, the cleared transactions will be marked with an *R* in the Clr column to indicate that they have been reconciled. Quicken will no longer consider these transactions when searching for matches to cleared transactions in future online statements. This is the whole purpose of going through the process of reconciliation to an online statement.

Transferring Funds between Accounts

If you have multiple accounts with the Online Banking option enabled at the same financial institution, Quicken lets you transfer funds between those accounts. You can initiate the transfer from Quicken and send your request to your financial institution through the Online Banking network. It's quick and easy—there are no checks or other paperwork to deal with. It's a great way to move surplus funds from a checking account into an account that earns more interest, or to move funds from a savings account into a checking account to cover the checks you write.

WARNING	Not all banks allow online funds transfers between accounts. Check with your financial institution to see if this feature is supported.

To transfer funds from one Online Banking account to another, follow these steps:

1. Open your Quicken data file and display the Online Banking window (choose Online Banking from the Online menu), shown in Figure 8.4.
2. Select the financial institution where you have the accounts that will be involved in the transfer. Remember, both the source and the destination accounts must be at the same financial institution, and both accounts must be enabled for Online Banking.

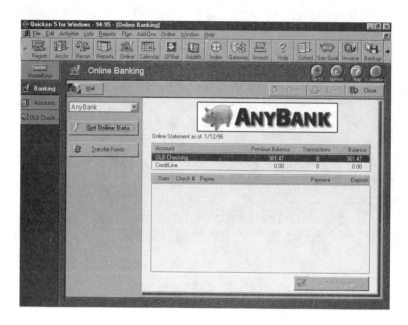

FIGURE 8.4:
The Online Banking window is your starting point for transfers between accounts.

3. Click on the Transfer Funds button to open the Transfer Funds Between Accounts dialog box, shown in Figure 8.5.

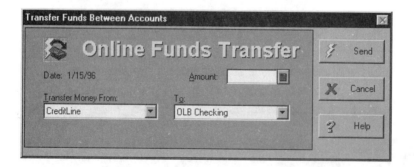

FIGURE 8.5:
The Transfer Funds Between Accounts dialog box

4. Fill in the details for the transfer:
   - Enter the amount you want to transfer in the Amount box.
   - Select the source account for the transfer from the Transfer Money From drop-down list box.
   - Choose the destination for the transferred funds from the To drop-down list box.

WARNING Make sure you specify the correct accounts in the Transfer Money From and To boxes. You don't want to get confused and move funds into the wrong account or request a transfer in the opposite direction from what you intended.

5. When you complete the selections in the dialog box, click on the Send button. Quicken begins the Online Banking session immediately.

6. Quicken displays the Access to... dialog box shown below. Enter your PIN for this financial institution, and then click on the OK button.

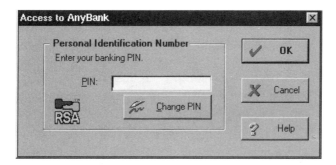

7. If you've stored your Intuit membership password for Online Banking, Quicken will enter it automatically. Otherwise, the program opens the Enter Password dialog box shown below. Type in your password and click on the OK button.

8. The Online Banking session proceeds automatically from this point. The Online Status dialog box keeps you informed of what's happening.

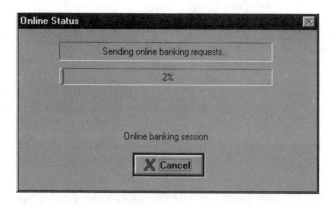

Quicken initializes your modem and makes the call to the Intuit Services Corporation network. The program logs on to the network and goes through security checks. Then the software sends the bank your request for the transfer of funds between accounts. After the bank acknowledges receipt of the request, Quicken logs off the network and disconnects your modem.

Quicken adds the transfer transactions to the affected account registers automatically.

The bank usually processes the transfer on the next business day. Normally, everything will go through without a hitch. However, if you don't have enough funds in the account from which you wanted to transfer the funds, the bank won't make the transfer. If that happens, you'll get a message from the bank informing you of the discrepancy. Then you must manually remove the transfer transactions from the Quicken account registers.

WARNING   **You can't do online funds transfers between accounts at separate financial institutions. It just doesn't work.**

Using E-Mail

E-mail communication with your financial institution isn't exactly an earth-shaking development. It isn't even a major reason to consider using Online Banking in Quicken. E-mail is more of a serendipitous side effect of establishing a two-way online connection with your bank. Despite its peripheral nature, e-mail can be a useful feature at times.

Basically, e-mail provides one more way to communicate with your bank's customer service staff. Although e-mail isn't as fast as a phone call, it works on your schedule. Office hours don't matter, and there's no waiting on hold to reach a customer service representative. You can send an e-mail message at your convenience. Then you log on later—also at your convenience—and get the bank's reply. Financial institutions usually respond to e-mail messages within 48 hours—much faster than a reply via regular mail.

Creating an E-Mail Message

When you want to send an e-mail message to a financial institution where you have established an Online Banking relationship, follow these steps:

1. Display the Online Banking window (choose Online Banking from the Online menu) and select the financial institution with which you want to communicate from the drop-down list box in the upper left corner of the window.

2. Click on the Mail button to open the Online Banking Messages dialog box, as shown below.

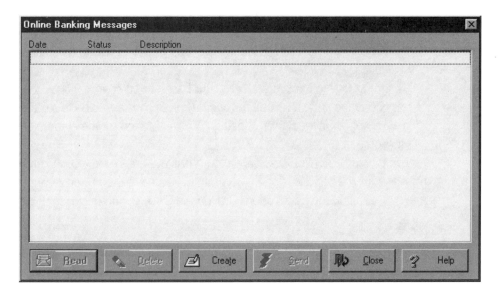

3. Click on the Create button at the bottom of the Online Banking Messages dialog box. This opens the Message to… dialog box, as shown in Figure 8.6.

4. Fill in the header information for your message. Quicken fills in the To and From boxes for you, but you can change those items if you want. Type the appropriate text in the Subject box to help identify the topic of your message. Select the account you're referring to from the Regarding account drop-down list box.

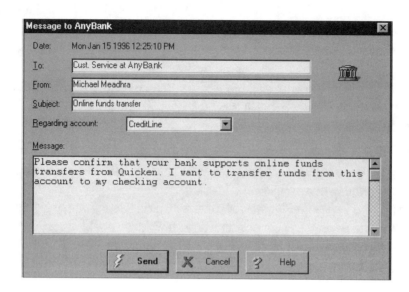

FIGURE 8.6:
Create e-mail to your financial institution in the Message to... dialog box.

5. Type your message in the large text box in the middle of the dialog box.
6. When you finish composing your message, click on the Send button. Quicken starts the Online Banking session and sends your message to the financial institution.

     Like all Online Banking sessions, you'll need to enter your PIN for the financial institution and your Intuit password (unless you've elected to store your password for Online Banking) before Quicken logs on for the automated online session.

After completing the online session, Quicken displays the dialog box shown below to confirm that your message was sent successfully. You have the option of printing your message by clicking on the Print button. Click on the Close button to close the dialog box.

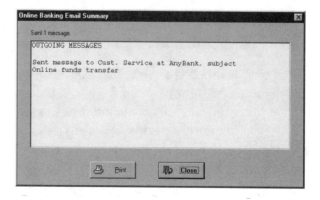

Reading Your E-Mail

Quicken checks for e-mail addressed to you (actually, to your Intuit membership number) when you log on for an Online Banking session with a particular financial institution. It happens automatically; you don't have to do anything special to get your e-mail. If Quicken finds any e-mail waiting, the program downloads it automatically and alerts you by displaying a notice in the Online Session Summary dialog box at the conclusion of the online session.

TIP   If you're expecting an e-mail reply, try to log on for an Online Banking session once each day or so. That way, you'll be sure to get your e-mail in a timely fashion.

Once you receive e-mail messages from your financial institution, you can read them by following these steps:

1. Open your Quicken data file and display the Online Banking window (click on the Online Banking icon in the Home Base window). Then click on the Mail button to open the Online Banking Messages dialog box, as shown below.

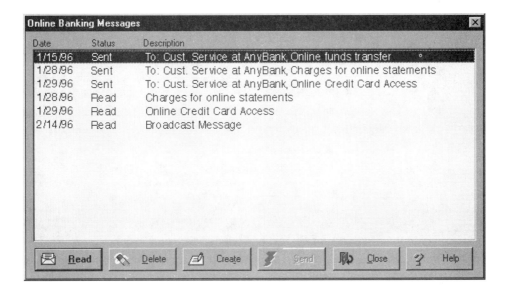

2. Select an e-mail message to read by clicking on it in the list. The Date and Description columns will help you identify each message, and the Status column will indicate which messages you haven't read yet.

3. Click on the Read button to open the Message dialog box, where you can view the contents of the selected message as shown below.

   You can read the message on-screen, and you can also print it by clicking on the Print button at the bottom of the Message dialog box.

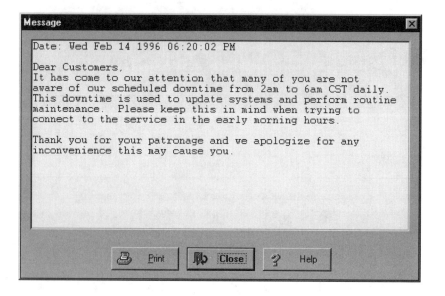

```
Message                                                          X

Date: Wed Feb 14 1996 06:20:02 PM

Dear Customers,
It has come to our attention that many of you are not
aware of our scheduled downtime from 2am to 6am CST daily.
This downtime is used to update systems and perform routine
maintenance.  Please keep this in mind when trying to
connect to the service in the early morning hours.

Thank you for your patronage and we apologize for any
inconvenience this may cause you.



              Print        Close        Help
```

4. When you're through reading the message, click on the Close button to close the Message dialog box. When you return to the Online Banking Messages dialog box, you can select another message to read or you can perform message maintenance, such as deleting messages that you no longer need.

5. Click on the Close button to close the Online Banking Messages dialog box.

NOTE Quicken's Online BillPay feature also includes e-mail capabilities, but it's completely separate from the Online Banking e-mail. As a result, if you need to send or receive messages related to both Online Banking and Online BillPay, you'll need to conduct two separate online sessions, one for Online Banking messages and one for Online BillPay messages.

Dealing with Common Questions and Problems

With a system as complex as the Online Banking features of Quicken, some problems are inevitable. Sooner or later, you'll run into a problem with your Quicken software, your modem, or your connection with Intuit Services Corporation. There's a good chance that it will be caused by something that happens at Intuit Services Corporation or the financial institutions you're trying to contact.

The most important thing to remember when you encounter a problem with Online Banking is not to panic. Quicken can usually recover gracefully, and there is very little chance that your financial data will be corrupted. At worst, most Online Banking problems are a nuisance, forcing you to conclude your Online Banking session at a later time.

When dealing with problems, it helps to know what to expect. So let's look at a few of the more common problems and how to deal with them.

Cannot Connect

When you try to log onto Intuit Services Corporation's network for an Online Banking session, you may get a message similar to the following:

- Cannot Connect. Please try later.

This might be caused by a problem with your modem or phone line, but it's more likely to be the result of a general system overload—too many people trying to call into the Intuit Services Corporation network at the same time. In some cases, you could get this message because the Intuit Services Corporation system is temporarily shut down for maintenance.

If you've connected to Intuit Services Corporation successfully before and haven't changed your modem, the problem isn't likely to be in your system. The best thing to do is to just wait a while and then try your Online Banking session again.

Status Bar Never Reaches 100%

Some Quicken users get concerned because the status bar in the Online Status dialog box doesn't reach 100% during an Online Banking session. They're afraid the transmission was discontinued before all the data got transferred.

Don't worry, this is normal.

The status bar in the Online Status dialog box indicates the time remaining before Quicken will be forced to disconnect. It's not an indication of how much of your data has been transmitted. As long as you didn't get an error message, everything is fine.

Errors in Your Online Statement

If you notice an error in your online statement or transactions, you should contact your financial institution. Dealing with an error in your bank statement is the same whether the error appears in your online statement or your paper account statement.

WARNING   Don't forget to follow the bank's rules regarding time limits for disputing mistakes and requirements for written notice of errors.

Comm Port in Use

If you try to log on to the Intuit Services Corporation network for an Online Banking session, you might get the error message shown below, indicating that Quicken couldn't go online because the Comm Port is in use. Usually, that message is caused by fax software or some other communications program running when you tried to begin the Online Banking session with Quicken. A common culprit is fax software set to automatically answer the phone and receive fax transmissions. It's easy to forget that the fax software is running in the background.

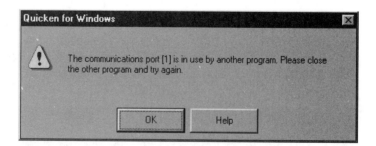

Quicken can't share a comm port and modem with other software. You'll have to exit your other communications programs before attempting to use any online features from Quicken. Once you finish your online chores in Quicken, you can restart your other communications programs.

Quicken Insists on Retrying an Aborted Online Banking Session Before Starting Another

If an Online Banking session is interrupted before it was completed, Quicken will remember what you were trying to do. The next time you attempt to go online, Quicken tries to finish (or redo) the incomplete session before allowing you to access another financial institution. This is Quicken's normal operation, and it usually presents no problem.

However, it *can* be a problem if you're trying to complete online sessions at more than one financial institution when one institution's computer system is temporarily out of service. For instance, suppose you attempt to get an account update from American Express, and your online session is aborted due to a problem connecting to American Express's server. You try a few more times and realize the problem is persistent. You need to wait an hour or two. In the meantime, you'd like to update your account statements at another financial institution, but when you try to do so, Quicken insists on calling American Express again. The failed connection to American Express is preventing you from connecting to the other financial institution. Bummer!

Fortunately, there's a way to work around this problem. Just follow these steps:

1. After experiencing a failed Online Banking session, go ahead and start a second online session with another financial institution. When you do, Quicken will display a message saying that Quicken will complete the first session instead of your current request.

2. When this message appears, hold down the Ctrl+Shift keys as you click on the OK button.

3. Quicken displays another message, asking you to confirm your action discarding the original online session. Click on the OK button.

4. Quicken abandons the aborted online session and proceeds with your new online session. Later, you can start over with the original online session.

Part 3

Online BillPay

Chapter 9

WRITING ELECTRONIC CHECKS

- **How does Online bill payment work?**
- **Anatomy of an online bill payment**
- **Forms of payment**
- **Allowing time for online payments to reach your payees**

The online personal finance feature that many Quicken users will employ most frequently is online bill payment. After all, for most people, paying bills is their most common (and often their most dreaded) financial transaction. Online bill payment may not transform the task of paying bills into a pleasant experience, but the convenience of being able to write and send checks electronically can make the job of paying bills a little less onerous.

Let's start our examination of Quicken's online bill payment feature with an overview of how the process works—how an electronic payment gets from your computer to your payee and the banks.

How Does Online Bill Payment Work?

First of all, you should realize that making online bill payments is separate from Online Banking. Online Banking is the ability to get an online statement from your bank, while online bill payment is the ability to use Quicken's online connections to send payments to others. The two processes are as different as their paper counterparts—getting your monthly bank statement and writing checks to pay your bills. One is a direct communication with your bank, and the other is a communication with the person or company you're paying. (Of course, when you write a check, you know your bank will be involved eventually when it honors the check and pays the funds out of your account.)

Online Banking requires a two-way connection with your bank so that you can request the status of your accounts and the bank can respond. As a result, the service is available only from those financial institutions participating in the Intuit network. Online bill payment, on the other hand, requires no such link to your bank and is available from nearly any account in the United States with checking privileges. Not only that, but you can sign up for ISC's Online BillPay service from up to ten separate accounts.

When you use online bill payment, you send payment instructions to a processing facility—either Intuit Services Corporation or CheckFree—which then issues the payment on your behalf. The payment might be in the form of a paper check, or, less often, an electronic funds transfer (EFT), but either way, the payment travels through normal business channels. Neither your payee nor your bank needs to be a member of the Intuit Services Corporation network in order for online bill payment to work.

Let Someone Else Do the Dirty Work

Quicken's online bill payment feature lets you pay someone else to take care of the tedious part of paying bills. You issue the instructions, and the payment service prints and mails the checks, timed to arrive on the date you specify. You don't have to mess with printing and signing checks, stuffing envelopes, licking stamps, and mailing the bills. If the payee is set up to receive electronic funds transfers, you have the added advantage of even faster processing; payments can be made as soon as the next business day after you issue payment instructions.

Once you get everything set up, using online bill payment is easy. You simply enter a transaction in Quicken, just as if you were recording a handwritten check or preparing a check for printing. Then a few mouse clicks will start an online session and transmit the information to the payment service. It's simpler and faster than printing checks from Quicken. You get instant confirmation that your payment instructions were received by the bill processing center. Later, you can check the status of a payment or issue a stop-payment order, all from within Quicken.

Payment processing for Online BillPay from Quicken is handled by Intuit Services Corporation; a similar service is offered by CheckFree Corporation. Both are specialized companies set up to process online bill payments. As you recall from Chapter 2, Intuit Services Corporation is a subsidiary of Intuit, Inc., the makers of the Quicken software. CheckFree is a separate company that provides bill payment services to corporations and to individual PC users.

Online bill payment is *not* a service provided by your bank (at least not from within Quicken). The advantage of going through a separate service for online bill payment is that there is no need for a connection between Quicken and your bank. As a result, you can arrange to pay bills from almost any bank account. Although the member banks usually offer Online BillPay with ISC as one of the services available with their checking accounts, you're not restricted to using Online BillPay with only the participating financial institutions in the Intuit online banking network.

If you use Quicken 5.0 for Windows, the default service provider is Intuit Services Corporation. If you have used CheckFree's bill payment service with a previous version of Quicken, you'll have the option of continuing to use CheckFree or switching to Intuit Services Corporation's Online BillPay. Users of Quicken for Macintosh will get their online bill payment service from CheckFree.

NOTE See Appendix B for more information on using CheckFree instead of Intuit Services Corporation.

Anatomy of an Online Bill Payment

Before you can use the Online BillPay feature, you must:

- Sign up for the Online BillPay service
- Set up your Quicken account (or accounts) to enable the Online Bill Payment option

Setting aside these preliminaries for the time being, let's look at just what happens when you make an online bill payment using ISC's Online BillPay service.

NOTE See Chapter 10 for instructions on setting up to use Online BillPay.

Creating a Transaction in Quicken

When you pay a bill electronically, you start by creating a payment transaction in Quicken. You can create the transaction using any of Quicken's standard techniques:

- Write a check
- Enter the item into your account register
- Use a payment that Quicken generates automatically, such as payment on your credit card bill

Of course, the payment must be made from an account you've set up for Online BillPay, and you must designate it as an online payment. Also, the bill payment service is going to need to know more than your payee's name as shown on the "Pay to the order of" line. You can choose an established online payee or supply the necessary information (name, address, phone number, and your account number) to define a new online payee.

NOTE See Chapter 11 for detailed instructions on creating Online BillPay transactions and sending them to Intuit Services Corporation for processing.

Starting the Online BillPay Session

Once you create the transaction, you need to send the information to Intuit Services Corporation (ISC) for processing. You don't have to send each payment separately. Quicken lets you create several payments and then send them to the payment center in one online session. The process is highly automated. All you need to do is click on a couple of buttons, enter your PIN and password for security, and let Quicken do the rest.

Processing Your Payment

Once ISC receives your instructions, it will process your payment. For most bills, the service will print a regular paper check and mail it for you. In an effort to have the payment arrive at its destination on the date you specified, ISC mails checks out a few days before the scheduled payment date.

If your payee has made arrangements to accept EFTs from the payment service, the service will contact Automated Clearing House—the facility banks use for transferring funds—and initiate an EFT from your bank account to your payee's account. The transfer will be effective on the payment date you specified.

Figure 9.1 diagrams both these payment processes.

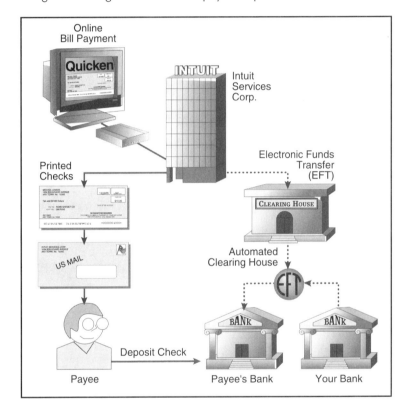

FIGURE 9.1: Intuit Services Corporation pays your bills according to your instructions.

Paying the Bill

The payment arrives at your payee, where it will be posted to your account. Although it arrives without the payment stub that was probably attached to your original bill (the part that is labeled "return this portion with your remittance"), the payment carries with it your name, address, and account number—which should be adequate to allow the merchant to identify and properly credit your account.

If the payment arrived as a check, the payee will deposit it just like any other check. At this point, all that remains is for your bank and your payee's bank to settle accounts by clearing the check (the payee's bank presents the check to your bank for payment). If the payment arrived as an EFT, the funds and the notice of payment reached your payee's bank at the same time.

How Much Does It Cost?

The cost of the Online BillPay service varies, depending on what bank you use. You can get Online BillPay from one of Intuit's participating financial institutions, or you can order the service directly from Intuit Services Corporation. If you work with a member bank, you pay the bank for Online BillPay (probably as part of a package with Online Banking); the bank contracts with ISC, which actually provides the service. If you sign up for Online BillPay from an account at a non-member bank, you deal directly with ISC.

The base price for the Online BillPay service from a given account is $5.95 per month for up to 20 transactions. If you make additional online payments, you'll pay extra for those that exceed your monthly allotment. The extra transactions may be charged individually or in groups. A typical charge is $2.95 per ten additional transactions.

For example, under this pricing scheme, 18 Online BillPay transactions in one month would cost $5.95. If you made 25 online payments, the cost would be $8.90. That's $5.95 for the first 20 transactions plus $2.95 for the next group of ten (even though you used only five of them).

Online BillPay charges are calculated separately for each bank, and they are normally separate from any charges for Online Banking services. However, some financial institutions offer special package deals that combine Online Banking and Online BillPay for one price or incorporate them into the monthly service charge for your account. In some cases, Online BillPay is effectively free if you stay under the monthly allotment of online payment transactions. If you order the bill payment service directly from ISC, you can get Online BillPay for multiple accounts at one bank for the same monthly fee.

No matter what bank you use, your Intuit membership plays a part by providing the initial access to Intuit's online services, including Online BillPay. However, there's no cost to you for this access. ISC gets paid (directly by you, or indirectly by the bank) for providing the Online BillPay service. Your Intuit membership is just part of Intuit's overhead costs of providing that service.

Forms of Payment

When you make an online bill payment, Intuit Services Corporation will send your payment to your payee in one of two forms:

- Paper check
- Electronic funds transfer (EFT)

Regardless of which form the payment takes, you can send Online BillPay payments to anyone in the continental United States. All you need is the payee's name, address, and phone number. You'll also need to supply your account number with the merchant or some other identifying information to enable the payee to properly credit your payment to your account.

Paper Checks

Even in the world of online bill payments, the standard payment method is still a paper check. If your payee isn't among the select few companies that have made arrangements with Intuit Services Corporation to be paid by EFT, then ISC prints a check and mails it to your payee.

When you use Online BillPay, the payee gets a simple paper check drawn on your account, just like your regular handwritten checks or the checks you print from Quicken. The check looks a little unusual (see Figure 9.2), but it is nonetheless a functional check bearing the following easily recognized features:

- Your checking account number and your bank's routing number
- Your name and address
- Your payee's name
- Your account number with the payee
- In place of your signature, an imprint indicating that the check is authorized by a signature on file

FIGURE 9.2: An Intuit Online BillPay check looks a little strange without your signature.

Normally, ISC mails checks three days before the scheduled payment date to allow for time in transit through the U.S. Postal Service. The check *should* arrive on the date you specified for the payment, but it may arrive a day or so on either side of that date.

WARNING Intuit Services Corporation can't control or predict how long it will take for your payment check to arrive at its destination. It may be posted early or late, depending on the speed of the mail. Checks that arrive early might be presented to your bank for payment a day or so sooner than you planned. To avoid overdrafts, you'll need to make sure there are funds available in your account to cover the payment. On the other hand, some payments may take a week or more in transit, arriving at your payee several days later than scheduled.

Once your payee receives the check, it should post the payment to your account the way it always does. Your name, address, and account number on the check should be enough to ensure proper credit. However, because the payment stub is not attached, this may delay handling of the payment by some payees. The lack of a real signature on the check also confuses a few payees. You're not likely to have trouble with a corporate accounting department, but a bookkeeper for the Mom & Pop Shop might wonder if the Online BillPay check is a "real" check.

WARNING The lack of a payment stub enclosed with your check may require "special handling" of your payment by some payees. As a result, there may be a day or two's delay between the time the payee receives your payment and the time it's actually credited to your account.

After posting your payment, your payee deposits the paper check in its bank account, just like any other check. The payee's bank presents the check to your bank for payment, and your bank transfers funds from your account to the payee's bank. You'll get the canceled check in your next paper account statement (assuming your bank returns canceled checks to you).

NOTE CheckFree uses a combination of EFT and paper check for some payments. CheckFree will use an EFT to transfer funds from your account to a CheckFree bank account, and then pay your payee with a check drawn on the CheckFree account. CheckFree uses this technique to reduce paperwork by consolidating payments from multiple clients to the same payee.

Electronic Funds Transfers

Electronic funds transfers, or EFTs, may sound like something strange and new. But you're probably already familiar with them. If you have ever had insurance premiums or utility bill payments automatically deducted from your bank account, you've used electronic funds transfers. ATM withdrawals are a form of EFT. Perhaps you get your paycheck or tax refund by direct deposit—this is also a form of EFT.

When you pay a bill with an EFT, the funds for the payment go from your account directly to your payee's account. The transfer goes through the federal banking system along with other bank-to-bank transactions. Since it's all handled electronically, the payments usually go through the next business day. This makes EFTs faster and more predictable than traditional methods of payment; there's no delay while a piece of paper travels through the mail system.

Increasingly, electronic funds transfers are becoming common business practice. The online bill payment services use EFTs whenever possible to make your online payments. Still, surprisingly few payments are made this way. For now, the weak link in the EFT payment chain is getting reports from the payee's bank to the payee confirming that the EFT payment was made, and then relaying the necessary information to credit the payment to the proper customer (you).

For this reason, payees must be set up and confirmed for EFT transactions with Intuit Services Corporation. The company maintains a list of standard merchants that have made those arrangements. You must select your payee from this list when you make a payment by EFT. Otherwise, the payee will be paid by check.

WARNING Not all ISC standard merchants are paid by EFT. In fact, only a few merchants get EFT payments. The rest get checks.

NOTE CheckFree has slightly different rules for determining which payees get paid by EFT. CheckFree automatically sends payments by EFT if it detects a match between your payee's name and address and a payee on CheckFree's list of EFT-capable merchants.

Lead Times

Online BillPay is convenient, but it doesn't take place instantly. After you send your payment instructions to Intuit Services Corporation, the payment must be processed and handled. In order to allow time for this processing, you must submit your payment instructions a few days before the date you want the payment to take place. This is called the lead time for a payment.

Electronic funds transfers have the shortest lead time. ISC can usually complete EFTs on the next business day after you submit the payments. As a result, EFTs require a lead time of just one or two days, meaning the payment date can be scheduled just one or two days after the date you submit the Online BillPay instructions.

Paper checks are a different story. They usually require a lead time of four or five business days. Actually, ISC claims to be able to process and print paper checks in about one business day. The difference between EFTs and paper checks is that ISC must mail checks three business days before the scheduled payment date. Add the mailing time to the day of processing time, and you get a lead time of four days. For some payees, ISC collects their payments from various customers and sends the batch of checks to the payee by overnight courier. These payees have lead times of two or three days.

> **WARNING**
>
> The lead time of four to five business days allows a rather arbitrary three days for delivery via the U.S. Postal Service. Sometimes that's not enough! If you schedule payments for the minimum lead time, they may not arrive on time. You may want to schedule critical payments a few days early to allow extra time for variations in mail delivery.

Quicken maintains a list of Online BillPay payees, complete with standard lead times, as shown in Figure 9.3. Currently, most payees require paper checks, and consequently most lead times are four days. Those payees accepting EFTs have shorter lead times. As you prepare online bill payments, you need to refer to the payee list for the appropriate lead times for specific payees. If you try to schedule a payment sooner than the date allowed by the lead time, Quicken will display an error message and adjust the payment's effective date.

Theoretically, when a payee agrees to start accepting EFTs, Intuit Services Corporation will update its master list by shortening that payee's lead time to two days. Then, during your next Online BillPay session, Quicken will retrieve the updated information. (As this book goes to press, I haven't seen this happen yet.)

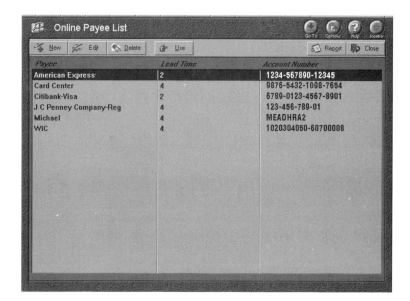

FIGURE 9.3:
The shorter lead times indicate merchants that are paid via EFT.

When Will Online BillPay Payments Be Deducted from My Account?

With Online BillPay, the funds are not deducted from your account when you transmit the payment to ISC. Generally, the funds are not deducted until the scheduled payment date—and sometimes later.

EFTs do take place on the scheduled payment date, and the funds are deducted from your account on that date. Paper checks, on the other hand, are printed and mailed to *arrive* on the scheduled payment date. Once the check arrives at its destination, it must be handled by your payee, deposited into the payee's bank, and then presented to your bank for payment. The funds will be deducted from your account when the check finally clears your bank. That might be as early as the scheduled payment date (or even a day or so earlier), but it's likely to be a few days later.

Chapter 10

GETTING READY FOR ONLINE BILLPAY

- **Setting up your bank account for Online BillPay**
- **Setting up a Quicken account for Online BillPay**
- **Making the first online contact**
- **How to discontinue the service**

Quicken's online bill payment feature lets you pay bills right from your computer. However, writing electronic checks requires more than just your Quicken software. You'll need all of the following in order to use the Online BillPay service from ISC:

- An Intuit membership
- A suitable bank account—which can be just about any account with check-writing privileges
- Arrangements with the bill payment service—Intuit Services Corporation—to draw funds from your account and pay merchants
- A corresponding Quicken account with the Online BillPay feature enabled

Setting up your Intuit membership was covered in Chapter 5. This chapter describes the other steps you'll need to take: activating electronic bill payment from your bank account, contacting the bill payment service, and setting up a Quicken account for Online BillPay services.

Setting Up Your Bank Account for Online Bill Payment

Quicken's online bill payment feature will work with almost any bank account. That includes accounts at financial institutions that are part of Intuit's online banking network, as well as accounts at other U.S. banks. Of course, your Quicken software can't provide this kind of service on its own. There are other parties involved and some setup required before you can use online bill payment.

If you've read the preceding chapter, you have some idea how the online bill payment process works. The bill payment service—most likely Intuit Services Corporation—handles bill payment processing for you (and thousands of other Quicken users). You simply send payment information to Intuit Services Corporation, and they process your payment and send a check or electronic funds transfer (EFT) to your payee. For your bank, it's business as usual as it clears your check or transfers funds according to the EFT instructions.

The basic capability to send online payment requests is built into Quicken. The key to making the feature work is getting signed up with the bill payment service. In order to process payments for you, the bill payment service must have your checking account number and other details about the account from which you want to pay your bills; it also needs your authorization to print checks and initiate EFTs from that account. You will be issued a personal identification number to ensure that only you can send payments drawn from that account.

How you go about signing up for online bill payment will depend on which payment service you use (Intuit Services Corporation or CheckFree) and whether the account you want to use for online bill payment is at one of the financial institutions in the Intuit banking network. The instructions in this chapter assume that you're dealing with Intuit Services Corporation for your bill payment services. For more information on working with CheckFree instead, see Appendix B.

What Accounts Are Eligible for Online BillPay?

The short answer to that question is, any account at a U.S. bank or financial institution that offers checking privileges will work with the Online BillPay feature in Quicken. In other words, if you can pay bills from an account by writing regular checks, you can use the same account to pay bills with Online BillPay.

If you do all your banking with one of the participating financial institutions in the Intuit banking network, you're in good shape. You can have Online Banking and Online BillPay active for multiple accounts at the same member bank, providing the bank supports those features on your accounts.

If you want to use Online BillPay with an account at a bank that's not part of Intuit's online banking network, you can do that too. Instead of contacting the bank to set up the service, you contact Intuit Services Corporation (ISC) directly. ISC can process payments drawn on nearly any account in the United States that has checking privileges. You can even use ISC's bill payment service to write electronic checks from multiple accounts at different financial institutions.

Setting Up an Account at a Member Bank

If you have (or plan to open) an account at one of the more than 35 financial institutions participating in the Intuit online banking network, you'll probably want to use the Online BillPay feature with that account. In fact, if you're beginning a new online banking relationship, it's likely that the availability and cost of the Online BillPay service figured prominently in your selection of a financial institution. On the other hand, since Online BillPay is available from almost any bank account, it's unlikely that you will change banks in order to take advantage of the feature.

NOTE Refer back to Chapter 3 for guidelines on selecting a banking partner for online banking. Also see Appendix C for a comparison of the services offered by participating financial institutions.

You will probably want to activate both Online Banking and Online BillPay for the same account at a member bank. But it doesn't have to be that way; Online Banking and Online BillPay are completely independent features. If your bank supports both features for an account, you can usually activate either one or both—the choice is yours. However, while there are numerous situations in which you might want only Online Banking active on an account, the reverse is seldom true. Online Banking complements Online BillPay by giving you timely, online confirmation when your bill payments clear your bank. Therefore, it makes sense to use the features together if they are both available. For this reason, some banks offer Online Banking and Online BillPay as a package; when you order one, you get both.

Requesting Online BillPay

Ordinarily, Online BillPay isn't activated for a given account until you request it—even if Online BillPay was one of the advertised features of the account. Fortunately, if you want to activate Online BillPay, all you have to do is ask.

To activate Online BillPay from an account at one of the financial institutions participating in the Intuit banking network, contact the bank's customer service department. Nearly all the participating financial institutions have toll-free phone numbers. You can order Online BillPay at the same time you order Online Banking. Usually, you can do both when you open a new account.

> **NOTE** See Chapter 6 for more detailed information about opening a new account at a member bank.

Tell the customer service representative that you want to use Quicken's Online BillPay feature with the account. If the bank needs your request in writing, you may be asked to sign and return a simple form. The bank will take care of notifying Intuit Services Corporation (which will provide the payment processing service) and getting everything set up. Your account should be ready to use for Online BillPay in a few days or so.

> **WARNING** If your account is at one of the member banks, you must have your bank (or Intuit Services Corporation) activate your account for Online BillPay. This is separate from your Intuit membership and anything you set up in your Quicken software.

If Online BillPay is the first online service you've signed up for with your financial institution, you'll get an Online Banking welcome kit containing the following:

- A supplemental Quicken manual covering the Online BillPay and Online Banking features
- A letter with the information (the bank's routing number and your account number) that you'll need to enable your Quicken account for Online BillPay

- A personal identification number (PIN) that you'll need to access your account
- A disk that will update your Quicken software to include your bank in the Financial Institution drop-down list (you won't receive this if your bank is already in the list)

For security reasons, the PIN is mailed separately, timed to arrive a couple of days before or after the rest of the welcome kit. You need both the account information and the PIN in order to use Online BillPay with your account in Quicken.

If you have other online services active for this account or other accounts at the same financial institution, you should already have all the information you need to enable your Quicken account for Online BillPay. You can use your existing banking PIN for online access to the account as soon as the bank and Intuit Services Corporation process the change in account status. That should take only a couple of days.

> **TIP** Your PIN from a member bank is good for all online accounts and all online services at that bank. You'll use the same PIN for Online Banking and Online BillPay.

Setting Up an Account at a Non-member Bank

If you have an existing account with a local bank that is not one of the financial institutions participating in Intuit's banking network, you can still use Quicken's Online BillPay feature. All you need to do is make arrangements with Intuit Services Corporation (ISC) to make online payments from your existing account. ISC must activate the Online BillPay feature for each account you wish to use for making online payments.

Note that you must contact ISC—not your bank—to make the arrangements. If your bank is not a member of the Intuit banking network, it can't give you a valid PIN and arrange for access to the bill payment service from Quicken. In fact, your bank may not even know what you're talking about when you request Online BillPay from your account. Fortunately, Online BillPay can work without your bank being involved except to cover the checks ISC will write on your behalf.

> **WARNING** To use Online BillPay with an account at a non-member bank, contact Intuit Services Corporation directly. Do *not* go through the bank to activate the service.

Signing up for Online BillPay with ISC is easy. You'll find the Quicken Online Enrollment Form packaged in the box with your Quicken software. Just do the following:

- Fill out the form, making sure you check the option to activate Online BillPay.
- Sign the form. (If you're setting up Online BillPay from a joint account, both parties must sign.)
- Enclose a voided check from the account you want to activate.

> **TIP**
>
> If the Quicken Online Enrollment Form is missing from your package, call Intuit Services Corporation at 708-585-8500. A customer service representative can help you get signed up for Online BillPay service.

Intuit Services Corporation will obtain your bank's name and routing number as well as your account number from your voided check. That information, along with your authorizing signature, will allow ISC to provide you with bill payment service from the account. ISC will then send you an Online Services welcome kit containing the following:

- A supplemental Quicken manual covering the Online BillPay and Online Banking features
- A letter with the information (your bank's routing number and your account number) that you'll need to enable your Quicken account for Online BillPay
- A personal identification number (PIN) that you'll need to unlock access to the online bill payment service
- A disk that will update your Quicken software to include your bank in the Financial Institution drop-down list (you won't receive this if your bank is already in the list)

For security reasons, the PIN is mailed separately, just like the PIN for an ATM card. You need both the account information and the PIN in order to access your account from Quicken.

> **TIP**
>
> If your Online BillPay PIN arrives before the rest of the welcome kit, you can probably go ahead and get started with Online BillPay right away. The account information you need to set up your Quicken account is usually available on your checks and bank statement.

Setting Up a Quicken Account for Online BillPay

After you make arrangements with your bank or Intuit Services Corporation for online bill payments from your chosen bank account, the next step is to enable the corresponding Quicken account for Online BillPay. You can either

- Enable Online BillPay when you set up a new account
- Add the Online BillPay feature to an existing account

To set up the Online BillPay option, you'll need your account number and the bank's routing number. You'll find this information in the welcome kit you received from the bank. If you're adding Online BillPay to an existing account, you can get the same information from one of your checks. You'll also need a PIN supplied by the bank (or Intuit Services Corporation) in order to log on for the first time. If you already have online access to other services at the same financial institution, you can use your existing PIN for Online BillPay as well.

NOTE The procedure for setting up a new account with Online BillPay enabled is the same as setting up a new account with Online Banking. If you're already familiar with the process, you'll probably want to skip the next few pages.

Setting Up a New Account

You can create a new Quicken account and enable the Online BillPay feature for that account by following these steps:

1. Open your Quicken data file and display the Account List (click on the Account List icon in the Home Base window). Then click on the New button in the Account List window to open the Create New Account dialog box, as shown in Figure 10.1.
2. Click on a button to select the appropriate account type. Usually, that will be Checking. However, Savings and Money Market are also valid account type choices. In contrast, Online Banking isn't available for Credit Card, Cash, Investment, Asset, or Liability accounts.

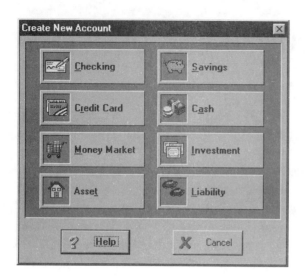

FIGURE 10.1:
Select the account type for your new Online BillPay account in the Create New Account dialog box.

Assuming that you chose the Checking account type, Quicken will open the Checking Account Setup dialog box, as shown in Figure 10.2.

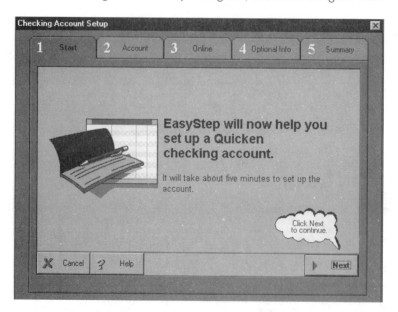

FIGURE 10.2:
The Checking Account Setup dialog box steps you through creating an account.

3. Click on the Next button to step past the Start tab. This will bring up the Account tab shown in Figure 10.3. Enter the Account Name and Description and then click on the Next button.

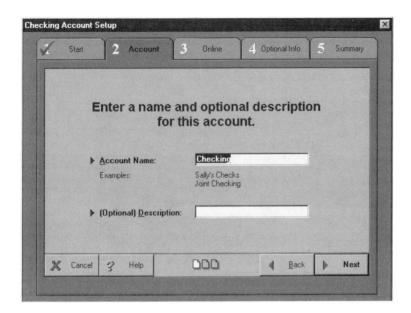

FIGURE 10.3:
Begin entering your account information here.

4. When the second page of the Account tab appears (see Figure 10.4), click on No and then click on the Next button. Quicken displays a message confirming that it will create your new account with a $0 balance. Click on the Next button again to continue.

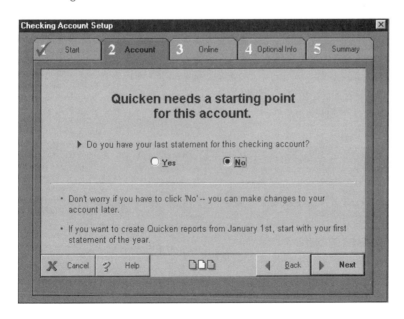

FIGURE 10.4:
Since you're creating a new account, you can just say No to entering a starting balance.

5. Now Quicken displays the Online tab, as shown in Figure 10.5. To enable Online BillPay for this account, click on the Yes button beside the Online Bill Payment option. (If you'll be using Online Banking with this account, you can click on Yes to enable that option at the same time.)

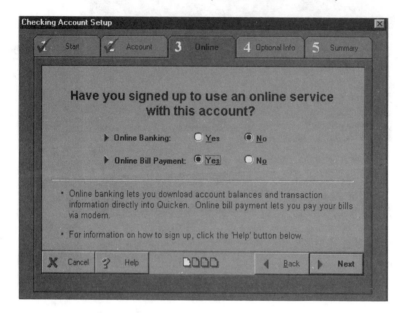

FIGURE 10.5: Click on Yes to tell Quicken you want to use Online Bill Payment.

6. Click on the Next button to display the next page of online information, as shown in Figure 10.6. This is where you identify the financial institution where your Online BillPay account resides.
   - If your bank is a member of Intuit's banking network, select the correct bank from the Financial Institution drop-down list.
   - If your Online BillPay account is at a non-member bank, select Other from the Financial Institution drop-down list.

   You must also type the bank's routing number into the Routing Number box. You'll find the routing number in the Online Banking welcome kit you received from your bank.

7. Click on the Next button once again to bring up the account information page, as shown in Figure 10.7. In the Account Number box, type the exact account number as supplied by the bank in your Online Banking welcome kit. If necessary, you can modify the account type at this time by making the appropriate selection from the Account Type drop-down list.

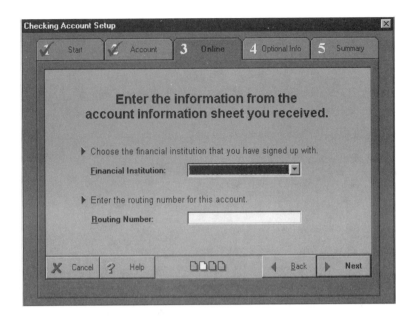

FIGURE 10.6:
This screen lets you identify the bank where you opened your Online BillPay account.

WARNING

If you're setting up more than one account at the same bank, you'll need to be especially careful to identify and enter the correct account number for each account.

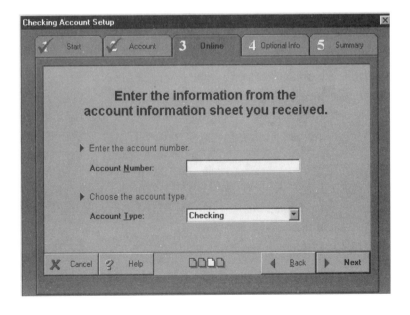

FIGURE 10.7:
Now we're getting specific—identifying the account number.

8. Click on the Next button to display the final page of the Online tab, as shown in Figure 10.8. If you've already signed up for your Intuit membership or created other online accounts, Quicken will fill in the Social Security Number box with the information it has on file. Confirm that the number is correct or change it if necessary. (For instance, you might need to enter your spouse's Social Security number instead of your own if your spouse is listed as the primary owner of the account at the bank.)

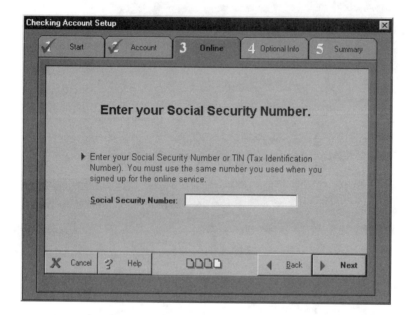

FIGURE 10.8: Check to make sure the Social Security number is correct.

9. Click on the Next button to move to the Optional Info tab. The first page offers a simple Yes/No choice. Choose Yes and then click on the Next button to open the Optional Information page (see Figure 10.9). As the name implies, this information is optional—it isn't required to create your Quicken account—but it's handy to have for quick reference. You can always add this information later, but I recommend that you do it now, while you're thinking about it and have the welcome kit and other materials on hand.

   Type the appropriate information into the Financial Institution, Account Number, Contact, Phone Number, Comments, and Interest Rate boxes. Then click on the Next button to continue.

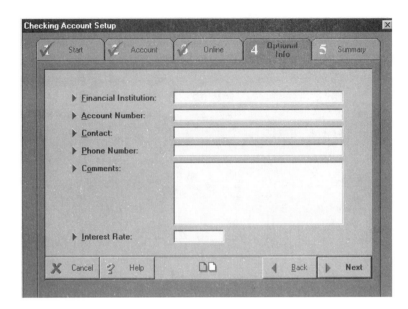

FIGURE 10.9:
Entering this information is optional–but recommended.

10. When the first page of the Summary tab appears (see Figure 10.10), check that all the information is correct. You can enter or change any of the information on this screen, the same way you entered it in the first place. Click on the Next button to move to the next page (shown in Figure 10.11) and again look over

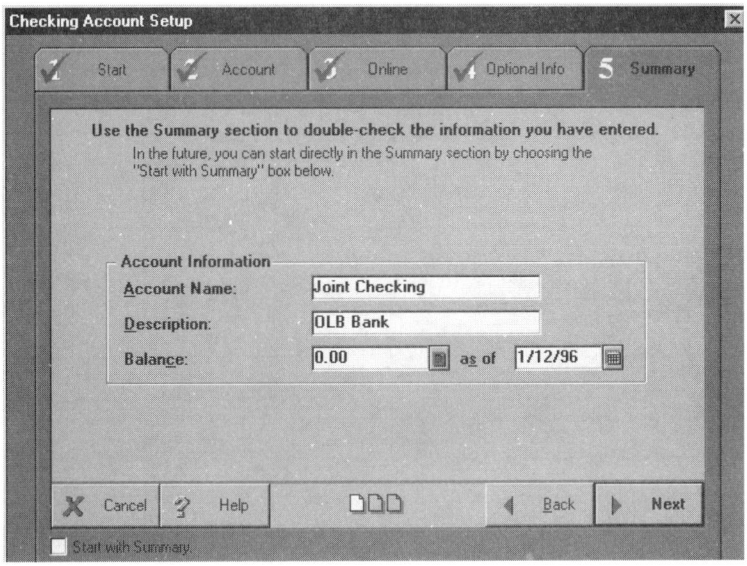

FIGURE 10.10:
The Summary tab lets you review and revise the information you entered.

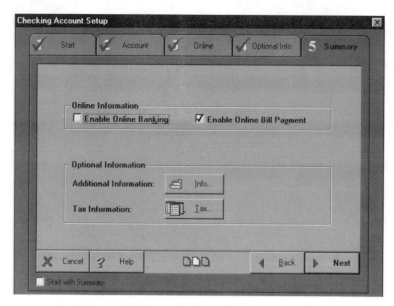

FIGURE 10.11: Make sure the Enable Online Bill Payment option is checked.

the information. In particular, make sure a check mark appears in the Enable Online Bill Payment checkbox. When you're confident that the information is correct, click on the Next button to continue.

11. Review the information in the final page of the Summary tab, shown in Figure 10.12. Pay particular attention to the routing number and account number. Once you're sure everything is correct, click on the Done button. Quicken will

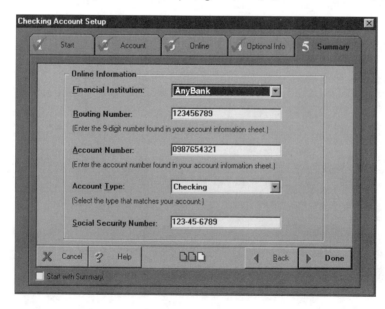

FIGURE 10.12: One last double check and you're finished.

close the Checking Account Setup dialog box and create the new account using the information you've provided.

When the Account List window reappears, you'll see your new account added to the list (see Figure 10.13). The lightning bolt in the Type column indicates that online access (either Online Banking or Online BillPay) is enabled for the account.

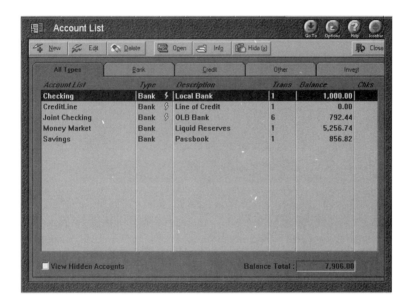

FIGURE 10.13:
Lightning bolts designate accounts with Online Banking or Online BillPay enabled.

Enabling Online BillPay for an Existing Account

More than likely, you'll be adding the Online BillPay option to an existing account, either a long-standing account at your usual bank or a more recently opened account at a member bank to which you're adding features one at a time. Either way, you probably have an existing Quicken account and simply want to add the Online BillPay option.

You can enable Online BillPay for an existing Quicken account by following these steps:

1. Open your Quicken data file and go to the Account List (click on the Account List icon in the Home Base window or choose Account from the Lists menu).

2. Select the account you want to enable for Online BillPay, and then click on the Edit button. Quicken opens the Edit Bank Account dialog box with the Summary tab displayed, as shown in Figure 10.14.

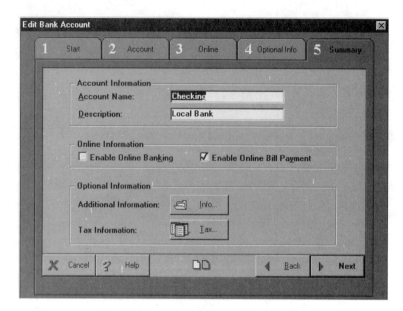

FIGURE 10.14: Checking the Enable Online Bill Payment option gets things started.

3. In the Online Information area in the middle of the dialog box, click on the Enable Online Bill Payment option. Click on the Next button to open the next page of the Summary tab, as shown in Figure 10.15.

4. Go to the Financial Institution box and select your bank from the drop-down list. If the account isn't at one of the banks that are participating in Intuit's banking network, select Other (at the bottom of the list).

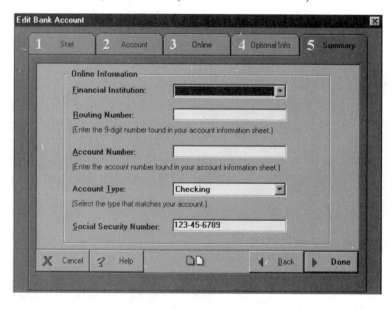

FIGURE 10.15: This information must be correct for Online BillPay to work.

5. Refer to the welcome kit you got from your bank and enter the routing number and account number in their respective boxes. Be sure to enter the numbers carefully.

> **TIP**
>
> You can also find the bank routing number and your account number printed on your checks. See the section "Deciphering the Numbers on a Check" in Chapter 6 if you need help identifying the significant numbers in the code at the bottom of your check.

6. Make sure the account type and Social Security number are correct, changing them if necessary. Then click on the Done button to close the dialog box and add the Online BillPay feature to your account.

When you return to the Account List window, a lightning bolt should appear in the Type column, indicating that the account has one of the online features (Online Banking or Online BillPay) enabled (refer back to Figure 10.13). Notice that the lightning bolt appears beside all online-enabled accounts. You can't tell from the Account list which accounts have Online Banking, which ones have Online BillPay, and which ones have both.

Making the First Online Contact

Once you get everything set up for online bill payments from Quicken, you'll probably be anxious to try the system out. The next chapter will show you how to make an online payment. In the meantime, you can log on to test your connection to Intuit Services Corporation. This will also give Quicken the opportunity to download a list of standard merchants. You'll need that information later when you begin paying bills online.

> **WARNING**
>
> You'll must have the PIN supplied by your bank in order to access your account for Online BillPay for the first time.

Now you're ready to access your Online BillPay account. Just follow these steps for your initial online session:

1. Open your Quicken data file and choose Online Bill Payment from the Online menu. This will open the Online Bill Payment window, as shown in Figure 10.16.

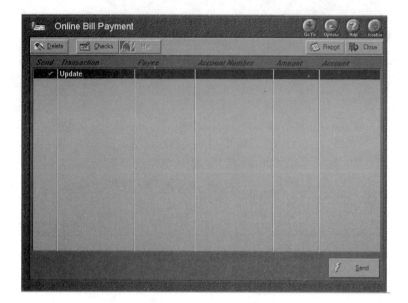

FIGURE 10.16:
The Online Bill Payment window is the starting point for all your Online BillPay activities.

2. Since you haven't created any online payments yet, the transaction list is empty except for the Update item, which is highlighted. Click on the Send button in the lower right corner of the window to begin the online session.

3. If this is the first time you're accessing either Online BillPay or Online Banking at this financial institution, Quicken will display the dialog box shown below, warning you that you must change your PIN. However, if you've already accessed this account for Online Banking, you won't see the warning, and you can skip steps 4 and 5 below. If you see the warning, click on the OK button to continue.

NOTE **Requiring you to change your PIN is a security measure. You must use the PIN supplied by the bank or Intuit Services Corporation to access your account for the first time, but it's only good for one use. After that, you'll use the PIN that you create, and only you know.**

4. Quicken opens the Change Banking PIN dialog box shown below. Type in the PIN supplied by the bank (or ISC) in the Existing banking PIN text box. To prevent anyone else from reading your private PIN, the number doesn't appear on-screen. You'll see asterisks instead.

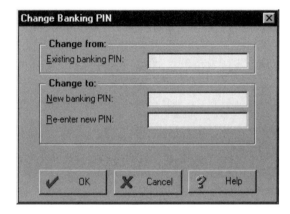

5. Make up a PIN of your own and enter it in the New banking PIN text box. Again, asterisks appear on-screen. Next, retype your new PIN in the Re-enter New PIN text box. Although you can't visually confirm that you entered the new PIN as you intended, typing the new PIN twice reduces the possibility of an inadvertent typing error. After entering the PINs, click on the OK button to close the dialog box.

TIP **Make a note of your new PIN and store it someplace safe (but not around your computer). You'll need to use the PIN every time you access your account for Online BillPay.**

6. Next, Quicken displays the Enter Password dialog box shown below. Type your Intuit membership password in the box, and click on the OK button. This launches your Online BillPay session.

If you stored your Intuit password for Online Banking/Online BillPay, the program will skip this step and enter your stored password automatically. See Chapter 5 for more information on storing your Intuit membership password.

After you enter the PINs and password, Quicken handles the rest of the online session automatically. The Online Status dialog box (shown below) will keep you informed of Quicken's progress as it initializes your modem, logs on to the Intuit Services Corporation network, and sends your online banking message—your Intuit membership ID, password, and PIN, followed by a request for any updates for your Online BillPay account. Quicken retrieves the information from the Intuit Services Corporation network and logs off automatically.

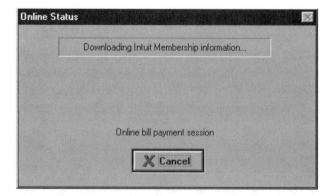

WARNING If you have trouble accessing your new Online BillPay account, don't just keep trying repeatedly. Call Technical Support for assistance. After five unsuccessful attempts to log on with your initial PIN, the system will lock you out. You'll have to request another PIN from the financial institution (or ISC) and wait for it to arrive in the mail before attempting to access your account again.

When Quicken completes the online session, it returns you to the Online Bill Payment window. If Quicken found any messages or other information, the program displays a report in the Online Bill Payment Transmission Summary dialog box. Otherwise, you'll see a message similar to the one shown below.

How to Discontinue the Service

Online BillPay is a terrific service, but there may come a time when you want to discontinue it. Perhaps your needs will change, or you'll want to switch your bill-paying activity to another account. Whatever the reason, if you want to disable Online BillPay for a given account, you must do the following:

- Tell your bank (or Intuit Services Corporation) to deactivate Online BillPay for the account
- Disable the Online BillPay option for the corresponding Quicken account

If the Online BillPay account is with a member bank, you need to contact the bank's customer service department. If the account is with a non-member bank, you must contact Intuit Services Corporation directly.

Bank policies regarding account changes vary. A simple phone call might be all that's needed to make the change. You may be able to make your request via e-mail; or you might need to send the bank a written request. Once you make the request to discontinue Online BillPay service, the bank will contact Intuit Services Corporation and take the necessary steps to deactivate Online BillPay for your account.

Once you drop the service, there's no point having the option enabled in your Quicken account. You can change your Quicken account to reflect the change in status by following these steps:

1. Open your Quicken data file and go to the Account List window by clicking on the Account List icon in the Home Base window.

2. Select the account for which you want to disable Online BillPay. Click on the Edit button to open the Edit Bank Account dialog box, as shown in Figure 10.17.

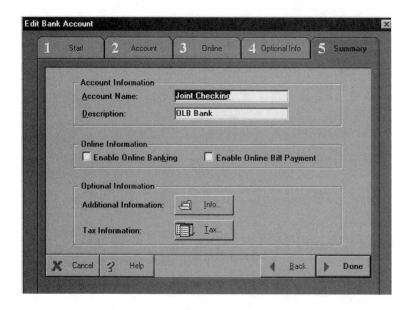

FIGURE 10.17: Removing one check mark disables the Online Bill Payment option for this account.

3. To disable the Online Bill Payment option, simply click on Enable Online Bill Payment to clear the check mark from the checkbox. Click on the Done button to close the Edit Bank Account dialog box.

NOTE Disabling Online BillPay for an account has no effect on Online Banking access to the same account.

4.   Quicken displays the warning shown below. Click on the OK button to confirm your change in the Online Bill Payment option.

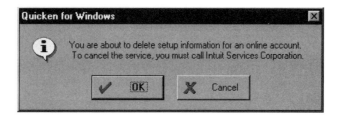

Back in the Account List window, the lightning bolt symbol disappears from the Type column for that account (unless the Online Banking option is still active). That's all there is to it. Online BillPay is no longer operational for that account.

Chapter 11

MAKING ONLINE BILL PAYMENTS

- **Writing an electronic check**
- **Making online payments from your account register**
- **Sending online payments**
- **Maintaining your list of online payees**
- **Adding standard merchants to your online payee list**

Quicken's Online BillPay feature is really just one more way to access the funds in your bank account and disburse them to someone you need to pay. Along with handwritten checks, ATM cards, debit cards, and automatic withdrawals, online bill payment gives you another method for moving your money from your account.

As I pointed out in Chapter 9, what starts out as an online bill payment in Quicken may end up as either a printed check or an electronic funds transfer. But as far as you're concerned, you just write a check in Quicken and send it out electronically instead of printing and mailing it yourself. The online bill payment service will take care of the rest.

Writing an Electronic Check

Quicken's Online BillPay feature lets you use familiar tools to create your online payments. Once you enable an account for Online BillPay, you'll have the option of designating checks and register transactions as online payments. The biggest difference between writing a regular check and making an online payment is that you'll need to supply more information about the payee.

When you generate a regular check, it can include just the payee's name; there's space for the payee's address in case you want to print it on the check, but that information is optional. Not so with online payees! Intuit Services Corporation needs the payee's full address, plus an account number and phone number, in order to get your payment to the correct payee.

To create an online payment in the Write Checks window, follow these steps:

1. Start by clicking on the Online Bill Pay icon in the Home Base window. Quicken will open the Write Checks window, as shown in Figure 11.1.

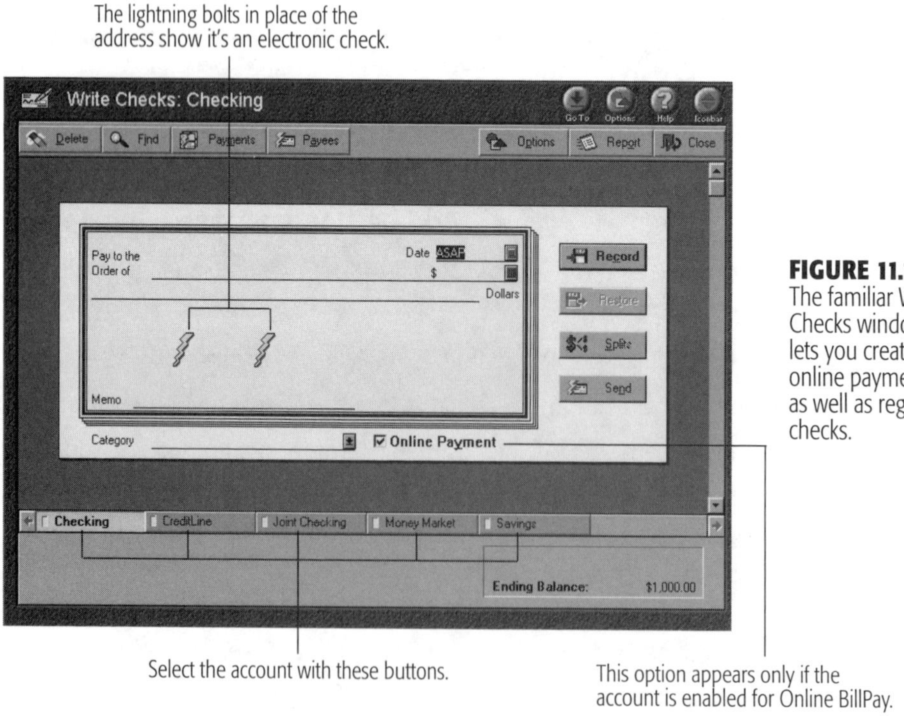

The lightning bolts in place of the address show it's an electronic check.

FIGURE 11.1: The familiar Write Checks window lets you create online payments as well as regular checks.

Select the account with these buttons.

This option appears only if the account is enabled for Online BillPay.

This window probably looks familiar, but there are a few differences to accommodate online payments. For instance, notice those big lightning bolts in place of the address. Unlike a regular check, for an online payment you don't enter the payee's address in this window. You'll use a separate dialog box to supply information about the payee.

Then there's the Online Payment option that appears below the check when you're writing checks on an account that's enabled for Online BillPay. It lets you switch back and forth between online payments and regular checks. Just clear the check mark to enter conventional checks from an online-enabled account.

Also, the date looks strange—ASAP instead of today's date. That's because online payments are not available for the current date. Quicken will fill in the date based on the minimum lead time required for the payee. You can always specify a later date if you prefer.

2. Select the account from which you want to make this payment. When you enter the Write Checks window to create online payments, Quicken defaults to the first online-enabled account. You can select a different account by clicking on one of the account buttons along the bottom of the window. Of course, it must be an Online BillPay–enabled account.

TIP Make your first online bill payment to yourself. There's no better way to see how the system really works and confirm that your first payment reached its destination. You'll also get to see what the online bill payment check looks like when it arrives in the mail.

3. Click on the Pay to the Order of line and type the payee's name. For this first online payment, I suggest using your own name. Then press Tab to move to the next field; Quicken will check the payee entry, and when it can't find information on the payee in its files, will display a message similar to the one below.

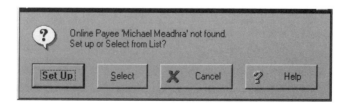

When you enter an unrecognized payee name while creating an online payment, Quicken gives you the option to set up or select the payee. If you chose Select, Quicken would open the Online Payee List window. To select a payee from the list, you would click on the payee you wanted to use and then click on the Use button, or just double-click on the payee. Quicken would then return to the transaction you were creating and insert the selected payee.

4. Since you haven't built your Online Payee List yet, there's nothing to select from. Click on the Set Up button to open the Set Up Online Payee dialog box shown below.

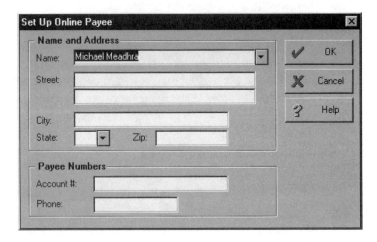

5. Quicken transfers the payee's name from the check; you need to fill in the other fields in the dialog box:

- Type the payee's street address and city; select the state from the drop-down list, and then enter the zip code.

- Move down to the Payee Numbers section of the dialog box and enter the account number or other information that identifies you to the payee. This (along with your name and address on the check) is how the payee will know how to credit your payment. Use your account number—such as a credit card number or loan number—if you have one. Otherwise, enter anything that will help the payee identify what the payment is for. If you can't think of anything else, enter your last name.

- Next, type the payee's phone number in the Phone text box. Intuit Services Corporation will use this number to contact the payee should there be any question or problem with your payment.

WARNING Quicken requires you to enter *something* in the Account # and Phone text boxes.

- Click on the OK button to close the Set Up Online Payee dialog box and return to the Write Checks window.

6. Now you've not only defined the payee for this check, you've also made the first entry in your Online Payee List. The next time you want to make an online payment to the same payee, you can just select the payee from the list. To see your Online Payee List, click on the Payees button at the top of the Write Checks window. This will open Online Payee List window, as shown in Figure 11.2. To return to the Write Checks window, click on the Checks quick tab.

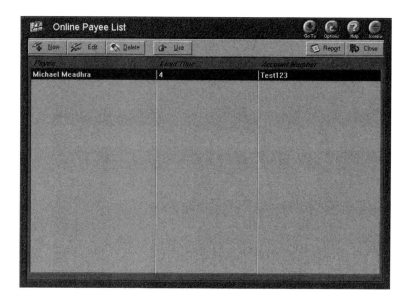

FIGURE 11.2:
Quicken keeps a list of the online payees you set up.

7. Back in the Write Checks window, you can finish filling out the check normally:
- Notice that Quicken has changed the date from ASAP to a new date reflecting the four-day lead time required to get online payments to most payees. This is the soonest you can schedule the payment, but if you prefer, you can change the date to instruct Intuit Services Corporation to make the payment on a later date. You can schedule a payment up to 60 days in advance.

WARNING Don't schedule payments too close to the due date. Remember that Intuit Services Corporation can't guarantee that the payment will arrive on the scheduled date. If the payment is delayed in the mail and arrives late, your payee may assess late fees or other penalties.

- Enter the payment amount as a number. As usual, Quicken spells it out for you on the line below.
- If you want, you can type a brief note on the Memo line. The memo is for your records only; it appears here and in the account register, but the memo is not printed on the online payment check or transmitted to the payee with an EFT payment.

WARNING The Memo line does *not* appear on the payment sent to your payee. You can't use the Memo line to communicate information to the payee, such as the purpose of the payment.

- Select a category for your transaction from the Category drop-down list, just as you would with any regular check. The finished online check should look similar to Figure 11.3.

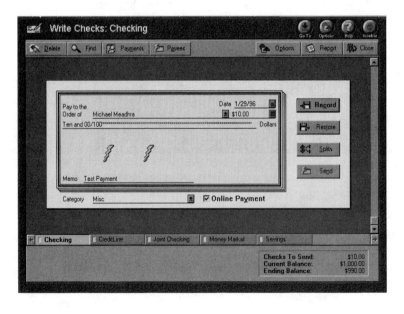

FIGURE 11.3:
A completed online check is very similar to a regular check.

8. Click on the Record button to record the finished online payment. Quicken adds the transaction to your account register and also lists it in the Online Bill Payment window, ready to be sent to Intuit Services Corporation for processing.

At this point, you could click on the Send button to go to the Online Bill Payment window and begin an online session immediately. But first, check out the account register to see what an online payment looks like there.

Making Online Payments from Your Account Register

In addition to creating online payments from the Write Checks window, you can create online payments from your account register. An online payment is like other register transactions, with just a few key differences. Those differences include:

- Designating the transaction as an online payment
- Selecting a payee from the Online Payee List or setting up a new payee
- Post-dating the transaction to allow for online processing lead time

To create an online payment in your account register, follow these steps:

1. Click on the Account List icon in the Home Base window to open the Account List window.
2. Select the account from which you want to make the online payment, and click on the Open button to open the account register.
3. Start a new transaction by pressing Ctrl+N or by choosing New Transaction from the Edit menu.
4. Press Tab to skip past the Date column; we'll come back to that later.
5. In the Num column, click on the arrow button and choose Send from the drop-down list. This designates the item as an online payment—one you'll "send" to the bill payment service for processing. Press Tab to move on to the Payee field.

1/29/96	Send	Michael Meadhra		10	00					990	00
		Misc	Test Payment								
1/23/96	Send ±	*Payee*		15	00		*Deposit*				
		\<Edit\>		ord		Edit	Splits				
		\<New\>									
		ATM									
		Deposit									
		EFT									
		Next Chk#									
		Print									
		Send									
		Transfer									

6. Click on the arrow button in the Payee field to open a drop-down list of payees. Since you've already defined this as an online payment, only online payees appear in this list. So far, you have set up only one online payee—yourself. Select an online payee by clicking on the item in the list.

1/29/96	Send	Michael Meadhra		10	00					990	00
		Misc	Test Payment								
1/23/96	Send		±	*Payment*			*Deposit*				
		Michael Meadhra		-10.00 Misc			Test Pay...				

> **TIP**
>
> You can define a new online payee in the account register just as you can in the Write Checks window. Both techniques work anywhere Quicken asks you to supply a payee for an online payment transaction.

7. When you select the payee, Quicken checks the transaction date against the lead time required for that payee. If the date is too early, the program displays a message similar to the one shown. When you click on the OK button, Quicken adjusts the transaction date and enters the amount, category, and memo from your previous transaction with the selected payee (unless you've disabled Quicken's automatic transaction-memorizing or auto-complete features).

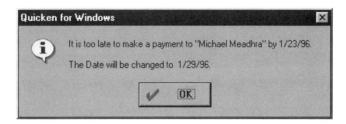

8. Edit the transaction if necessary by changing the date, amount, category, and/or memo. When the transaction is complete, click on the Record button to record the transaction. Figure 11.4 shows the account register with two online payments ready for you to send to the bill payment service.

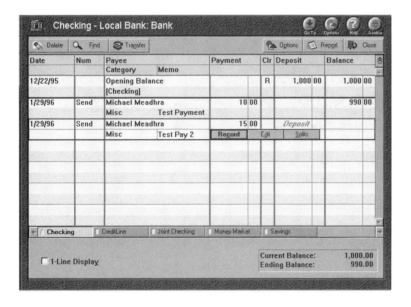

FIGURE 11.4: These two online payments are ready to go.

Sending Online Payments

You've created an online payment in the Write Checks window and another in the account register. The next step is to send them to the bill payment service—Intuit Services Corporation—for processing. It's roughly equivalent to printing regular checks; you're just instructing ISC to do the printing and mailinginstead of doing it yourself.

To send your online payments to Intuit Services Corporation, follow these steps:

1. Choose Online Bill Payment from the Online menu to open the Online Bill Payment window, as shown in Figure 11.5.

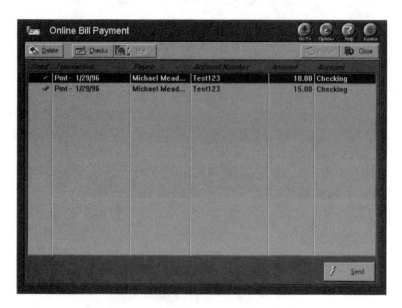

FIGURE 11.5: Send payments to Intuit Services Corporation from the Online Bill Payment window.

The Online Bill Payment window is your command center for online sessions with Intuit Services Corporation's bill payment service. It shows a list of pending online payments with enough detail to identify each one. You can see the kind of transaction, the date, the payee, your account number, the amount, and which Quicken account the payment is made from. If you have more than one account enabled for Online BillPay, this window will consolidate transactions from all your online accounts.

2. Select which payments to send to the bill payment service.

A check mark in the Send column indicates that the payment will be sent to Intuit Services Corporation during the next online session. By default, all the pending payments are checked. However, you can pick and choose which payments to send by clicking on a transaction to toggle the check mark on and off.

TIP If you need to edit one of the online payments before sending it, just double-click on the payment in the Online Bill Payment window. Quicken will jump to that transaction in the account register. Make your changes, and click on the Record button. Then click on the Bill Pay quick tab to return to the Online Bill Payment window.

3. Now that you have selected which payments to send, click on the Send button to start the online session.

4. If you have payments designated for accounts at more than one financial institution, Quicken displays the Multiple Financial Institutions dialog box (shown below) asking you to choose which financial institution you want to send payments from. Select a financial institution from the list and click on the OK button.

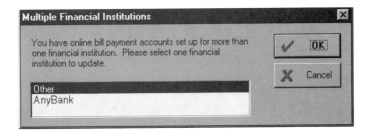

You can send payments from only one financial institution at a time. Payments drawn on multiple accounts at the same financial institution are fine, but payments from an account at another financial institution will need to be sent in another online session.

5. Next, the Online Authorization dialog box appears, as shown below. Enter your PIN for the chosen financial institution and click on the OK button.

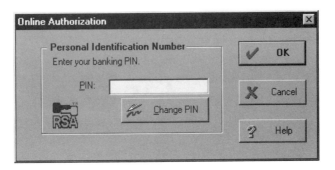

6. Now the Enter Password dialog box appears. Type in your Intuit membership password and click on the OK button. (If you choose to store your password for Online Banking/Online BillPay, Quicken skips this step and enters your password automatically.)

NOTE   **See Chapter 5 for instructions on storing your Intuit membership password.**

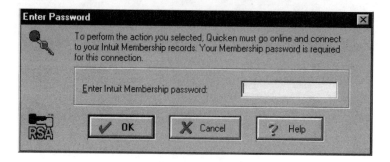

7. Once you enter your PIN and password, Quicken goes online and makes contact with Intuit Services Corporation's bill payment service. The Online Status dialog box keeps you informed of Quicken's progress as it goes through the process:

- Setting up the modem
- Dialing the phone number
- Logging onto the Intuit Services Corporation network
- Sending your online payments
- Getting confirmation that the payments were received
- Logging off the network

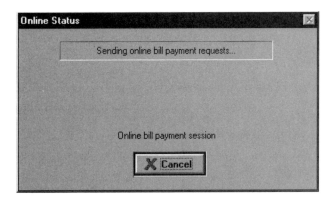

8. After Quicken logs off the Intuit network, the program reports its success in the Online Bill Payment Transmission Summary box, shown below. Here you can view a summary of what Quicken accomplished in the online session. If you want a permanent record, click on the Print button to print a report. When you're through viewing the summary, click on the Close button to close the dialog box and return to the Online Bill Payment window.

WARNING Once you close the Online Bill Payment Transmission Summary box, you can't open it again to review the information or make a printed record.

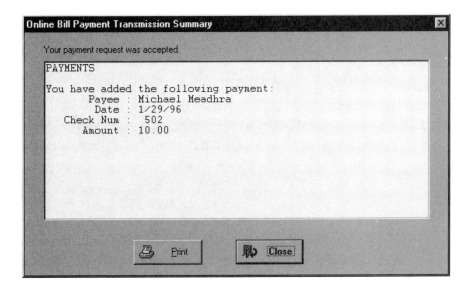

9. After your online session, click on the account quick tab to see your online account register. Notice the changes in the online payment transactions (see Figure 11.6). The Send label in the Num field has been replaced by the check number that was assigned by Intuit Services Corporation. A lightning bolt beside the check number designates the transaction as an online payment.

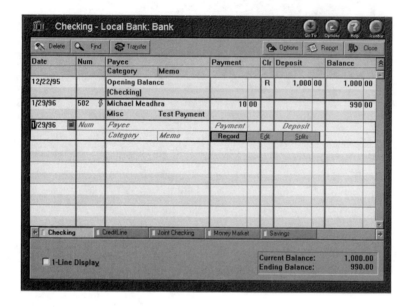

FIGURE 11.6:
A lightning bolt in the Num column is the mark of a completed online payment.

Deleting Payments

Sometimes you not only don't want to send a particular payment to the bill payment service in the next online session, you want to get rid of the transaction completely. Perhaps it's a duplicate transaction or some other kind of error. You can delete the transaction from the Online Bill Payment window by following these steps:

1. Select the payment you want to delete by clicking on it.
2. Click on the Delete button at the top of the Online Bill Payment window. Quicken jumps to the account register, deletes the transaction, and returns to the Online Bill Payment window automatically.

Maintaining Your Online Payee List

Quicken maintains a list of your online payees so that, for future online payments, you can select payees from the list instead of entering all that information each time. As you saw when you created your first online payment, Quicken adds payees to the list automatically when you define a new payee. You can also add new payees directly to the Online Payee List and delete or edit out-of-date payees.

When you want to work with your list of online payees, choose Online Payees from the Lists menu to open the Online Payee List window, as shown in Figure 11.7.

NOTE If you double-click on a payee while working in the Online Payee List window, Quicken opens the Write Checks window with the selected payee already entered in a new check.

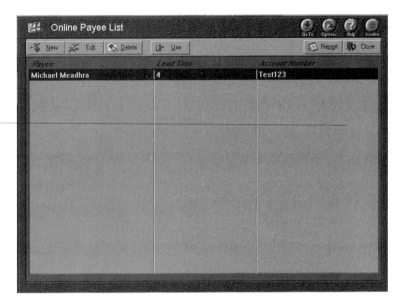

FIGURE 11.7: Quicken maintains a list of your payees for online payments.

Defining a New Payee

Follow these steps to add a new payee to the Online Payee List:

1. Click on the New button at the top of the Online Payee List window to open the Set Up Online Payee dialog box.

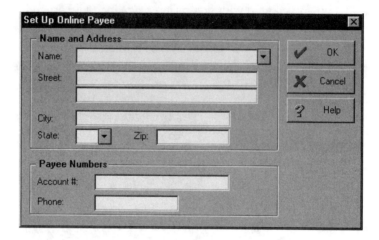

2. Fill in the name, address, account number, and phone number just as you did to define a new payee in the Write Checks window. (Refer back to the section "Writing an Electronic Check" earlier in this chapter for more detailed instructions.)
3. When you're through entering the payee information, click on the OK button. Quicken adds the payee to the list in the Online Payee List window.

Editing an Existing Payee

To make changes in the information on file for an existing online payee, follow these steps:

1. In the Online Payee List, select the payee you want to update.
2. Click on the Edit button at the top of the Online Payee List window to open the Edit Online Payee dialog box.

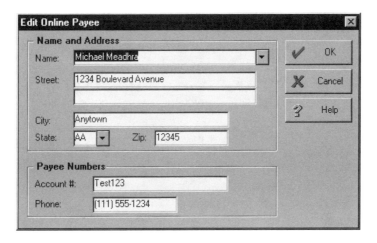

3. The Edit Online Payee dialog box is essentially same as the dialog box you used to define the payee in the first place. You can edit any of the fields as needed.

4. When you finish making changes to the payee information, click on the OK button to close the dialog box.

If you attempt to edit a payee for which you have any sort of pending transactions, Quicken will display the message shown below.

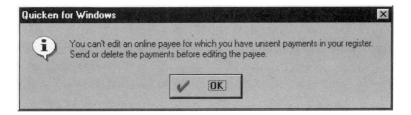

The program won't allow you to edit a payee if you have unsent transactions or scheduled transactions to that payee. You must first send or delete any pending payments and cancel any scheduled transactions; only then can you edit the payee to update a changed address or other information. After you edit the payee, you can redo the deleted payments and reschedule the recurring transactions. It's a hassle, but that's the way it works (at least for now).

WARNING You can't edit a payee if there are any pending payments to that payee.

Adding Standard Merchants to Your Online Payee List

It's probably no surprise that some of the same payees are used by hundreds, perhaps thousands, of Quicken users. Intuit Services Corporation has developed relationships with a number of these merchants to facilitate handling online payments from Quicken users. In some cases, these "standard merchants" are set up to accept payment by electronic funds transfers.

Quicken downloaded the list of standard merchants during your first Online BillPay session. The system automatically downloads updates to the list during subsequent online sessions.

At the very least, using a standard merchant entry can save you some time setting up a payee. If the payee accepts payment by EFT, you'll also gain the advantage of a much shorter lead time for payments to that payee.

To add a standard merchant to your online payee list, follow these steps:

1. In the Online Payee List window, click on the New button to open the Set Up Online Payee dialog box.

2. Click on the arrow button in the Name field. This opens a drop-down list of potential payees, as shown below. You'll notice that some of the items on the list are labeled Standard Merchant.

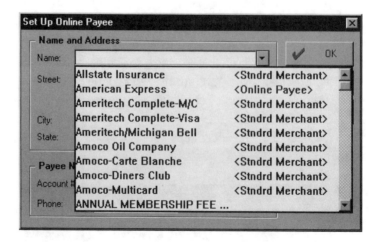

3. Scroll through the list to locate the standard merchant entry you want to use, and click on it. Quicken automatically enters the name and address in the Set Up Online Payee dialog box, as shown below.

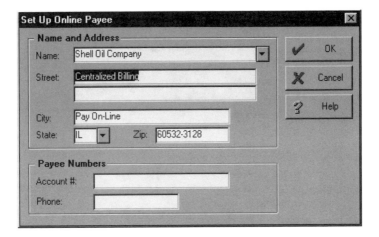

 **Don't change the name or address information for a standard merchant.**

4. Add your own information in the Account # and Phone text boxes.
5. Click on the OK button to close the dialog box and return to the Online Payee List window. If the new standard merchant accepts EFT payments, the lead time shown in the payee list will be two days instead of the typical four days.

Removing Payees from the List

Eventually, your list of online payees will accumulate some outdated entries: loans that you've paid off, credit cards that you've canceled, merchants that you no longer patronize. If you don't expect to need some payees again, you can clean up the list by deleting the obsolete items. To delete a payee, follow these steps:

1. Select the unwanted item from the Online Payee List.

2. Click on the Delete button at the top of the window.
3. When Quicken displays a message similar to the one shown below, click on the OK button. Quicken removes the payee from the list.

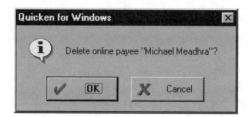

Chapter 12

MORE ONLINE BILLPAY TECHNIQUES

- **Stopping online payments**
- **Checking the status of payments**
- **Making e-mail inquiries**
- **Automating recurring payments**
- **Dealing with common problems**

Most online payments are simple, straightforward transactions. You enter the payment and send it off for processing; the bill payment service makes the payment according to your instructions, and that's it. You're happy; your payee is happy.

But sometimes things aren't so simple. Perhaps you need to make a change in a payment you've already sent to the processing center, or you want to check the status of a particular payment. Maybe you're looking for a way to automate some of those recurring payments you make every month. This chapter shows you how.

Stopping Online Payments

One of the nice things about Online BillPay is that you can create payments up to 60 days ahead of the scheduled payment date. As soon as you receive a bill, you can enter the payment into Quicken and send it while you're thinking about it. Intuit Services Corporation will hold your payment instructions and process the payment just in time for delivery on the date you indicate. Payment processing normally occurs three days before the payment date for paper checks, one day before the payment date for EFTs.

If you discover that you need to make a change in a payment after you've sent it to the bill payment center, you can recall the payment and prevent Intuit Services Corporation from processing it. You can stop a payment in this manner up until the time it is processed. Then, if necessary, you can create a replacement payment.

To stop an online payment you've already sent, follow these steps:

1. Open the account register containing the payment you want to stop.
2. Right-click on the transaction to open the pop-up menu shown at left, and then choose Stop Payment. (You can also choose the Stop Payment command from the Edit menu.)
3. Quicken displays a message similar to the one below, asking for confirmation. Click on the OK button to issue the stop-payment order.

4. Quicken places a stop sign in the Num column, as shown below, to indicate that you've requested a stop-payment order.
5. Next, choose Online Bill Payment from the Online menu. You'll find the stop-payment order in the list of pending online transactions.

1/29/96		502		Michael Meadhra			10	00					990	00
				Misc	Test Payment	Record			Edit		Splits			

6. The stop-payment request won't take effect until you transmit the instructions to Intuit Services Corporation. You can click on the Send button to begin an online

session immediately, or you can send the stop-payment request with other transactions in a later online session. When you complete the online session, Quicken will display the Online Bill Payment Transmission Summary dialog box, containing a message similar to the one shown below. This confirms that Intuit Services Corporation received your request and canceled processing of the payment.

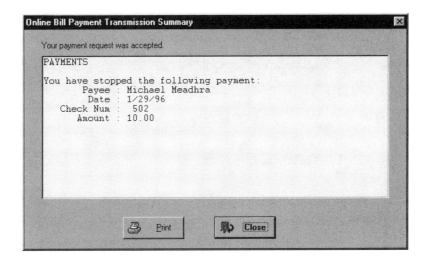

7. Click on the Close button to close the dialog box, and then open the account register containing the stopped payment. Once the stop-payment order is completed, Quicken marks the transaction void, as shown below.

1/29/96	502	**VOID**Michael Meadhra		R		1,000	00
		Misc Test Payment					

Checking the Status of Payments

You get immediate confirmation when you send online payments to Intuit Services Corporation. But you don't have to rely on your memory or on printouts from the Online Bill Payment Transmission Summary dialog box. The same information is available in your account register as well. In addition, you can get updated information once the payment is processed, and you can even send e-mail messages to the bill processing center to inquire about payments.

Making Payment Inquiries from Your Account Register

To check the status of an online payment from your account register, follow these steps:

1. Open the account register containing the payment you want to investigate.
2. Right-click on the transaction and choose Payment Inquiry from the pop-up menu, or choose Payment Inquiry from the Edit menu. Quicken displays the Payment Inquiry dialog box shown below.

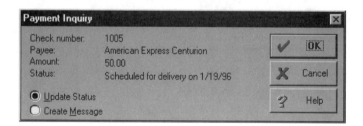

Initially, the Payment Inquiry dialog box shows the status of the payment when it was sent to the processing center. The check number and scheduled delivery date are the same as they appeared in the transmission summary following the online session in which you sent the payment. If that's all the information you need, you can click on the OK button to close the dialog box. Otherwise, proceed to step 3.

> **WARNING** The scheduled delivery date may be different from the transaction date shown in your account register. If you requested a payment date that falls on a bank holiday, the processing center will adjust the scheduled delivery to avoid the holiday. The adjusted delivery date shows up in the Payment Inquiry dialog box, but not in your account register.

3. To get updated information on the status of the payment, click on the Update Status button in the Payment Inquiry dialog box, and then click on the OK button. The update doesn't happen instantly. Quicken must first contact the bill processing center to get the information.

4. Choose Online Bill Payment from the Online menu to open the Online Bill Payment window. You'll notice that Quicken has added a payment inquiry request (see below) to the list of pending online transactions.

5. The payment inquiry will be processed during your next online session, at which time Quicken will download information on the current status of the payment. After the online session, you'll see the results of the payment inquiry in the Online Bill Payment Transmission Summary dialog box. You now have confirmation of the payment processing date.

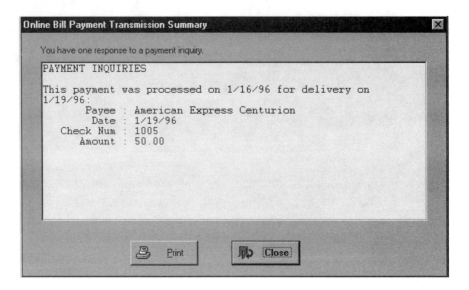

6. Return to the account register and again open the Payment Inquiry dialog box as you did in step 2. If your payment has been processed, the updated status report confirms the payment date.

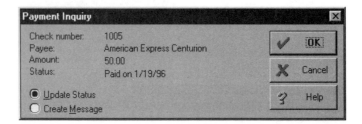

WARNING The "Paid" date is the date your payee was expected to receive the payment—usually three business days after processing by the bill payment service. It doesn't guarantee that your payee actually received the payment on that date. Variations in mail delivery may mean that the payment arrived earlier or later. Internal handling by your payee might add another day or two before your payment is posted to your account.

Making E-Mail Inquiries

If you need more information about a payment than is available from the Payment Inquiry dialog box, you can send an e-mail message to Intuit Services Corporation (ISC). The customer support staff will send a reply, which Quicken downloads automatically during a subsequent online session.

To send an e-mail message to ISC's payment processing center, follow these steps:

1. Open the account register containing the online payment transaction you want to inquire about.

2. Open the Payment Inquiry dialog box by right-clicking on the transaction and choosing Payment Inquiry from the pop-up menu, or by choosing Payment Inquiry from the Edit menu.

3. Click on the Create Message button. When you do, the dialog box expands as shown below.

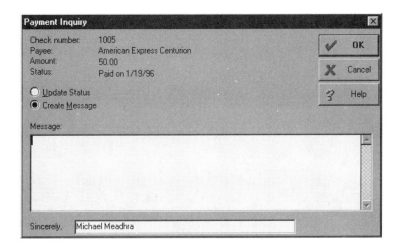

4. Click on the Message box and type your message. Quicken automatically includes references to the specific payment and a closing signature, so you don't have to duplicate that information.

5. When you click on the OK button, Quicken closes the Payment Inquiry dialog box and adds your message to the list of pending online transactions.

6. Open the Online Bill Payment window. You'll see your message listed as a pending transaction, as shown on the next page.

7. If you want to see more detail about the message, click on the Mail button to open the Online Bill Payment Messages dialog box. It lists your unsent message, as shown below. You can review the content of the message by clicking on the Read button. Click on the Close button to close the dialog box.

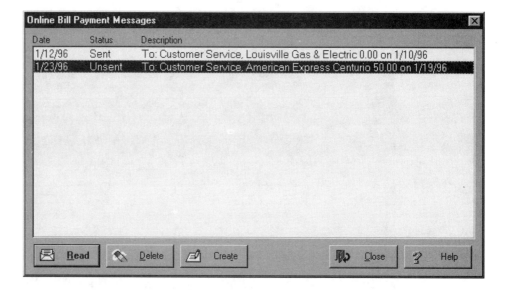

8. Now you can either click on the Send button to start an online session immediately, or wait until later and send the message along with other transactions. After your online session, Quicken will display the Online Bill Payment Transmission Summary dialog box, confirming that your message was sent.

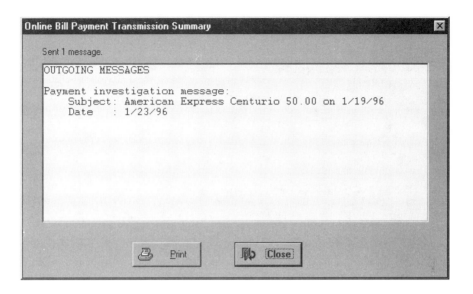

ISC staff will read and respond to your e-mail message. Their stated goal is to respond within two business days. However, the early popularity of Quicken's Online BillPay feature has overwhelmed the staff, and, as this book goes to press, much slower responses to e-mail messages have been the norm. The situation should improve as ISC expands its personnel.

Reading Your E-Mail

The whole purpose of sending an e-mail message is to get a response that answers your questions. In most cases, the ISC staff will respond to your e-mail inquires by e-mail as well. Quicken will pick up the incoming messages automatically during your regular online sessions. You don't need to do anything special to download the messages. After your online session, you should see a notification of incoming mail in the Online Bill Payment Transmission Summary dialog box, as shown on the next page. (You *do* read the summary after each online session, don't you?)

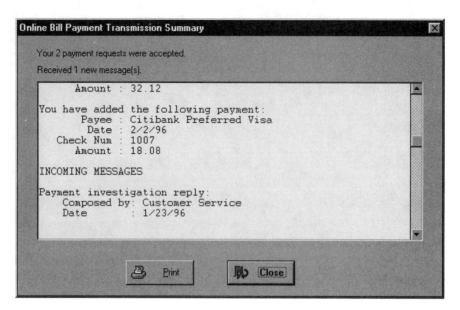

To read the e-mail messages you receive from Intuit Services Corporation, follow these steps:

1. In the Online Bill Payment window, click on the Mail button to open the Online Bill Payment Messages dialog box, as shown below. This box lists the messages available to read.

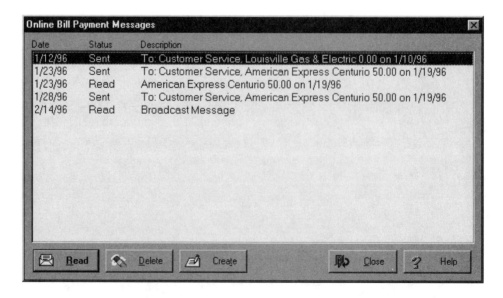

2. Click on the message you want to read, and then click on the Read button to display the message in the Message dialog box, as shown below.

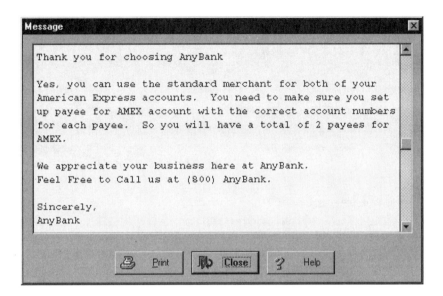

3. Read your message. If you want to make a hard copy for permanent record, click on the Print button. When you're through reading, click on the Close button to close the Message dialog box. Then click on the Close button to close the Online Bill Payment Messages dialog box.

Automating Recurring Payments

Some payments, such as rent, mortgage, or car payments, are the same time after time—the same amount due on the same day each month (or some other recurring schedule). Quicken gives you two ways to handle recurring payments online. You can either

- Schedule transactions in Quicken to automate the process of creating online recurring online payments
- Set up repeating payments to be made automatically by the bill payment service

I prefer scheduling payments in Quicken. Although it's a little more work to generate the payments in Quicken and send them in each month, that involvement in the process gives you more flexibility and control. Giving the bill payment service instructions to repeat payments automatically without your further involvement is more convenient, but it's a bit harder to manage the process and deal with problems if they arise. I'll show you both methods, and you can choose the one that fits your needs.

Scheduled Transactions

If you have Online BillPay enabled for at least one account, your scheduled transactions can include online payments as well as traditional checks and transfers. Setting up an online payment as a scheduled transaction is really no different than setting up any other scheduled transaction in Quicken. You define the transaction and set it up to recur on a regular basis. You can instruct Quicken to either add the transaction to your account register automatically, or prompt you to add it on a certain date. Once the scheduled transaction is entered in your register, you can send it for online processing just like any other online payment.

To create a scheduled transaction for an online payment, follow these steps:

1. From the Lists menu, choose Scheduled Transaction to open the Scheduled Transaction List window, as shown in Figure 12.1.

FIGURE 12.1: The Scheduled Transaction List window is the starting point for both scheduled transactions and online repeating payments.

2. Click on the New button to open the Scheduled Transaction Type dialog box shown below.

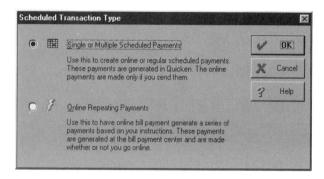

3. Select the Single or Multiple Scheduled Payments option, and click on the OK button. This opens the Create Scheduled Transaction dialog box shown below.

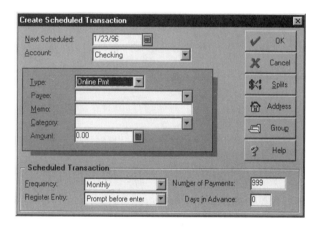

4. Fill in or choose the appropriate information to define the scheduled transaction:
   - Select the next scheduled date for the payment and the account from which to make the payment. Be sure to specify an account that is enabled for Online BillPay.
   - From the Type drop-down list, choose Online Pmt to specify an online payment.
   - Select the payee and fill in the other transaction details.
   - Set the frequency, number of payments, and instructions for entering the transaction into your account register.

5. When you finish defining the scheduled transaction and click on the OK button, Quicken adds the item to the Scheduled Transaction List, as shown below. Notice that the Type column indicates that the new transaction is an online payment.

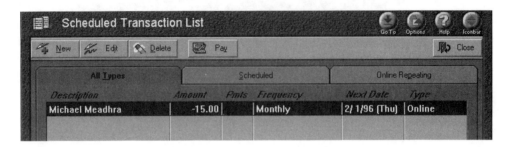

Depending on how you set up the scheduled transaction, Quicken will automatically enter the transaction in your account register or remind you to do so on the appropriate date. Once the transaction is entered, it's just like any other online payment that you send to ISC for processing.

When you use this technique to automate recurring payments, the automation is limited to your local copy of Quicken. The program simply helps you enter transactions, which you can then review and edit before sending them to the bill processing center. However, when the payment arrives at ISC for processing, there's nothing to indicate that it's a recurring payment.

Repeating Payments

Repeating payments differ significantly from scheduled transactions. You send instructions for a repeating payment only once. From then on, Intuit Services Corporation makes payments automatically until the specified number of payments have been made or until you send explicit instructions to stop or alter the repeating payments. The repeating payments continue without your active participation in the process. They continue even if you don't log on for an online session for a month or more.

This degree of automation is both the strength and the weakness of repeating payments. You could take a three-month sabbatical from your computer, and your repeating payments would continue without interruption. On the other hand, automation makes it harder to detect and correct problems, should they occur. ISC's Online BillPay service is relatively new, so it's too soon to say how trouble-free repeating payments will be.

Defining a Repeating Payment

To define a repeating online payment, follow these steps:

1. Choose Scheduled Transaction from the Lists menu to open the Scheduled Transaction List window.

2. Click on the New button to open the Scheduled Transaction Type dialog box, as shown below.

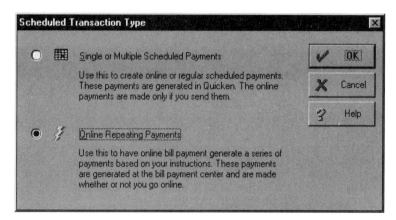

3. Select the Online Repeating Payments option and click on the OK button. When you do, Quicken will open the Create Online Repeating Payment dialog box, as shown below.

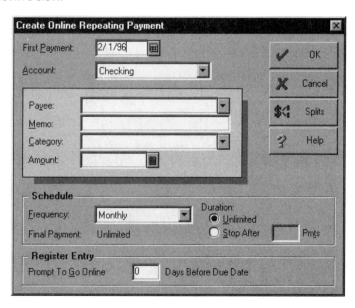

4. Select or fill in the appropriate information in the dialog box to define the repeating online payment:

- Specify the date of the first payment and the account from which you want to make the payment. Of course, the account must have the Online Bill Payment option enabled.
- Select the online payee, and specify the other details of the transaction.
- Schedule the payment frequency and how long the payments should continue.
- Specify when you want Quicken to remind you to go online for updates on the repeating payments.

5. When you're finished defining the repeating payment, click on the OK button to close the dialog box. Quicken adds the repeating payment to the Scheduled Transaction List, as shown below. Notice the listing in the Type column—Rept-Send—which indicates a repeating payment ready to send to Intuit Services Corporation.

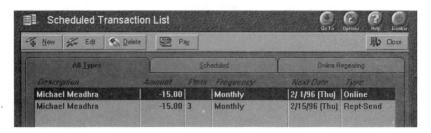

6. Choose Online Bill Payment from the Online menu to open the Online Bill Payment window. You'll see the repeating payment in the pending transaction list, as shown below.

7. You can send the repeating payment instructions during your next online session. Intuit Services Corporation will confirm receipt of your repeating payment instructions and will schedule the first payment in the series. After the online session, the Online Bill Payment Transmission Summary dialog box will show the results (see next page). Click on the Close button to close the dialog box.

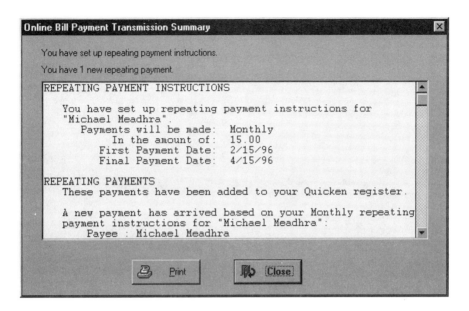

8. During the online session, Quicken downloaded transaction details for the first payment in the repeating series and recorded it in your account register. Open the account register to see the results, as shown below.

2/15/96	503	§ Michael Meadhra		15 00			985 00
		Misc Repeating Payr					

Linking a Repeating Payment to a Loan

Repeating payments are especially useful for loan payments. Once you create a repeating payment, you can link it to a loan and take advantage of Quicken's ability to automatically adjust the split between the principal and interest components of a loan payment.

To link a repeating payment to a loan, follow these steps:

1. Define a repeating payment for the correct amount.
2. Choose Loans from the Activities menu to open the View Loans window.
3. Define a new loan or select an existing loan to which you want to link the repeating online payment.
4. Click on the Edit Payment button to open the Set Up Loan Payment dialog box, as shown on the next page.

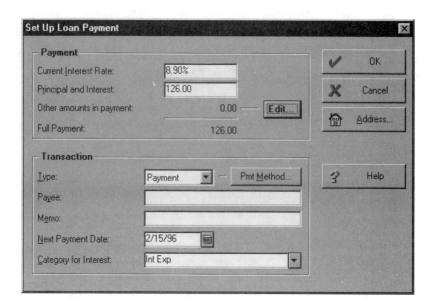

5. Click on the Pmt Method button in the middle of the dialog box. This opens the Select Payment Method dialog box shown below.

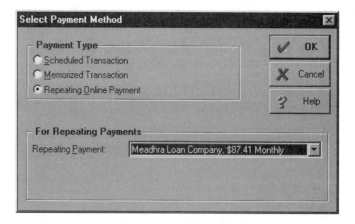

6. Choose the Repeating Online Payment option, and then select the payment you want to link to the loan from the Repeating Payment drop-down list.

7. Click on the OK buttons to close the Select Payment Method and the Set Up Loan Payment dialog boxes.

Changing a Repeating Payment

Once you define a repeating payment and send it to the bill processing center, it's not cast in stone. You can make changes to the repeating payment definition and submit the changes to ISC. The revised instructions will apply to future payments.

These are the steps to follow to revise a repeating payment:

1. Choose Scheduled Transaction from the Lists menu to open the Scheduled Transaction List window. Click on the Online Repeating tab to display just the repeating payments (see below).

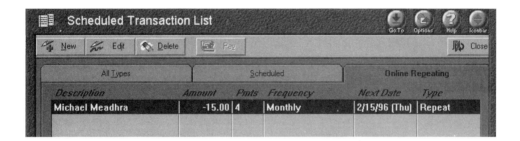

2. Select the repeating payment you want to modify, and click on the Edit button to open the Edit Online Repeating Payment dialog box shown below.

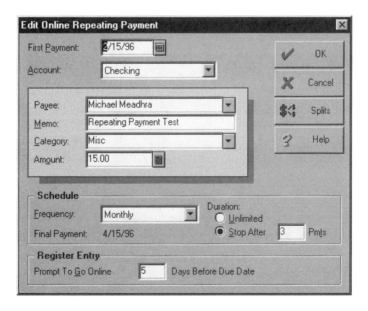

3. Change the specifications for the repeating payment by editing any of the fields, and then click on the OK button. Quicken will close the dialog box and update the Scheduled Transaction List. The program also adds a transaction to the Online Bill Payment list.

4. During your next online session, Quicken will send the updated instructions to the bill processing center. Basically, you're sending instructions for a new repeating payment series that replaces the previous instructions.

Canceling a Repeating Payment

Sooner or later, you'll probably have occasion to stop or cancel a repeating payment. Here are the steps you'll need to take:

1. Choose Scheduled Transaction from the Lists menu to open the Scheduled Transaction List window. Click on the Online Repeating tab.

2. Select the repeating payment you want to cancel, and then click on the Delete button. Quicken displays a message similar to the one below, asking you to confirm the action.

3. When you click on the Delete button, Quicken closes the dialog box and adds your instructions to the list of pending transactions in the Online Bill Payment window, telling ISC to cancel the repeating payment.

4. Choose Online Bill Payment from the Online menu to open the Online Bill Payment window. You'll see the Delete Repeating Payment transaction listed there, as shown below. The next time you go online, Quicken will transmit those instructions to the processing center.

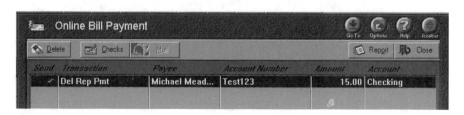

5. When ISC gets the deletion order, it will cease making payments based on the repeating payment instructions. The payment service will cancel all pending payments and stop generating new payments in the repeating payment series. After the online session, the Online Bill Payment Transmission Summary dialog box will display the cancelation results (see below).

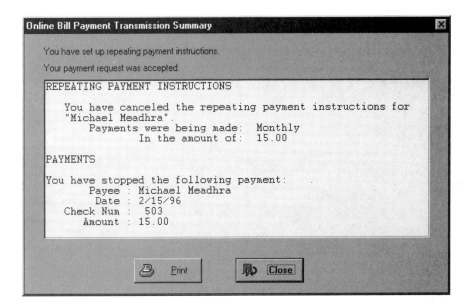

Canceling pending payments has the same effect as issuing a stop-payment order. The transactions in your account register will be marked void, as shown below.

2/15/96	503	**VOID**Michael Meadhra		R			1,000	00
		Misc Repeating Payr						

Dealing with Some Common Problems

The following sections will help you deal with some of the more common error messages you might encounter when using Online BillPay.

Leaving Quicken without Sending Pending Transactions

If you attempt to exit Quicken or close your Quicken data file without first sending all pending online transactions to the processing center, Quicken will display the following message.

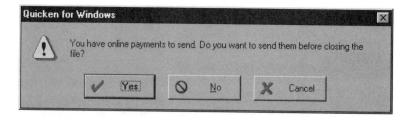

If you click on the Yes button, Quicken opens the Online Bill Payment window, where you can go online and send the transactions. If you click on the No button, Quicken closes the file without sending the pending Online Bill Payment transactions. If you choose this option, be sure to come back later and send the transactions. If you wait too long, the processing center will have to change the dates on your payments. Your third choice is clicking on the Cancel button to tell Quicken you didn't really mean to quit.

Recovering from an Interrupted Online Session

Occasionally, your online session may be interrupted for some reason. The next time you try to go online (whether for Online Banking or Online BillPay), Quicken will display the following message, offering to complete the previous session before starting another online session.

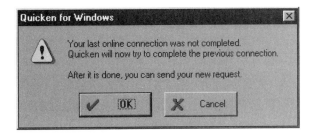

It's possible to override this message and start a new online session, as explained at the end of Chapter 8. However, that's not advisable with an interrupted Online BillPay session. Failing to complete the Online BillPay session may cause Quicken to lose some payments. The best advice is to keep trying until Quicken completes the online session successfully.

Avoiding Check Number Conflicts

By default, Intuit Services Corporation assigns online payments in a given account sequential numbers beginning with 101. If these numbers conflict with the regular paper check numbers in your account, you can have ISC change the numbering scheme for your electronic checks. Call ISC's customer service department (if your online account is with a member bank, you should call the bank directly) and request a new starting number; I suggest a high round number such as 5,000. Future online payments will use the new number sequence.

Misplaced Lightning Bolts in Your Register

Online payments are supposed to be indicated by lightning bolts in the Num column of your account register. However, I've seen some instances where the lightning bolts seem to get misplaced. They disappear from Num field of some online payments and show up beside other transactions.

The problem seems to occur in accounts containing Savings Goal transactions. The lightning bolts get shuffled around when you hide Savings Goal transactions and reappear in the proper places when the Savings Goals are displayed in the register.

If you experience this problem, take a look at the Hide Sav Goal $ option at the bottom of the account register window. Make sure it's not checked.

Payments That Arrive Late

You sent an online payment to pay a bill by the due date, but then you get a call or notice from the payee saying your payment is late and they are assessing a penalty, or even threatening to disconnect your cable TV (or whatever). What happened?

The most common cause of late payments is scheduling payments too close to their due date. If you schedule a payment to be made exactly on the date the payment is due, you're courting disaster. ISC's policy is to process and mail your payment in time to allow three days for mail delivery. Often, the payment *will* arrive in that amount of time, but not always. If the payment is delayed in the mail, it will arrive at your payee late.

> **NOTE**
> The timing of payments made by EFT is much more dependable than that of checks sent through the mail. If payees in the standard merchant's list have a one- or two-day lead time, they probably receive payments from ISC by EFT. You can usually schedule payments to these payees as late as one day before the due date.

It's important to schedule payments a few days before the due date to allow for variations in mail delivery and handling by the payee before the payment gets credited to your account. The more critical the payment, the more time you should allow as a cushion between the scheduled payment date and the due date.

> **TIP**
> To reduce the risk of late payments, schedule payments for three to five days before the due date.

If you do have problems with a merchant over a late payment, you're not stuck without an ally. Intuit Services Corporation will go to bat for you with the payee. If you schedule a payment to be made before the due date but it arrives at the payee after the due date, contact ISC's customer service department and explain the situation. ISC will contact your payee and attempt to get the late charges waived and a notation added to your account explaining the late payment. Many merchants and lenders are understanding if you made a good-faith effort to pay the bill on time (at least the first time it happens). However, some are real hard cases, so there's no guarantee that ISC will be able to get the late fees waived. In some cases, ISC may reimburse you for late fees you must pay, but that doesn't erase the late payment from your record with the vendor.

Part 4

Financial Information & Other Services

Chapter 13

PORTFOLIO PRICE UPDATE

F E A T U R I N G

- **What is Portfolio Price Update?**
- **Signing up for Portfolio Price Update**
- **Using Portfolio Price Update**
- **Going beyond the basics**

Quicken has offered investment tracking capabilities for several years now. However, keeping your investment portfolio up-to-date by manually entering current prices has been a tedious, time-consuming, and error-prone endeavor. Portfolio Price Update solves that problem by allowing you to check security prices online and automatically update your Quicken portfolio with the latest information.

Whether you're using Quicken to track numerous securities or just keeping tabs on a couple of mutual funds in your IRA or 401k, read on to find out how you can use this new online personal finance feature.

What Is Portfolio Price Update?

Portfolio Price Update supplies a better alternative to searching the newspaper for yesterday's prices on the stocks you own and meticulously entering them into Quicken. This built-in Quicken feature lets you avoid the hassle of manual price updates by going online and getting the current prices for the stocks and mutual funds in your Quicken investment accounts. It's fast, easy, and relatively inexpensive.

You can use Portfolio Price Update at your convenience—the service is available around the clock, every day of the week. In one online session, you can check prices on up to 200 securities, which can include stocks and mutual funds traded on the following markets:

- New York Stock Exchange
- American Stock Exchange
- NASDAQ

Portfolio Price Update can also get updates on the popular stock market indexes. This lets you see how your securities compare to the market as a whole and to certain key market segments. Portfolio Price Update does not update the prices of bonds or stock options.

The speed and convenience of Portfolio Price Update makes it practical to keep your investment portfolio up-to-date with current prices. You can even add securities you don't own to a "watch list" and monitor their performance—a good way to track securities you're interested in buying or to keep an eye on your company's (or a competitor's) stock.

How Current Are the Prices?

Although regulations don't permit Portfolio Price Update to retrieve up-to-the-minute stock prices during the business day, the price updates are current enough to meet the needs of most investors. When the market is open, the stock prices are continually updated, but they are delayed by about 20 minutes. After the market closes, you can get the closing prices.

Mutual funds are handled differently. When you check mutual fund prices, you'll get the latest available *closing* prices—updated each business day at about 5:30 p.m. EST. As a result, if you update your mutual fund prices during the business day, you'll get the closing prices from the preceding day. An evening update will retrieve that day's closing prices.

The following table summarizes the type of update you can expect for the various categories:

Stocks	Current prices, delayed by 20 minutes (during the business day)
	Latest closing prices (after hours)
Mutual funds	Latest closing prices
Market indexes	Real-time information or closing prices

How Much Does It Cost?

Intuit lets you try the Portfolio Price Update service at no cost—your first three sessions are free. After that, there is a monthly fee for the service. This fee includes a monthly allotment of six updates, and you are charged the fee whether you use the service or not. If you update your portfolio more often, you'll incur an extra charge for each Portfolio Price Update session in excess of the monthly allotment. Your Portfolio Price Update access fees are billed to your credit card each month. The price for Portfolio Price Update is as follows:

- $2.95 per month for up to six updates
- $.50 for each additional Portfolio Price Update session

Each Portfolio Price Update session can update your entire portfolio up to 200 securities. There's no difference in price whether you update a single stock price or a list of 100 securities.

What Do You Need?

In order to use Portfolio Price Update, you need the following:

- A modem
- An Intuit membership
- At least one defined Quicken investment account
- At least one security in the security list
- Ticker symbols for the securities you want to update

The need for a modem and Intuit membership is obvious. (You may remember from previous chapters that Portfolio Price Update is one of the Quicken features that are supplied through Intuit Services Corporation.) Also, since Portfolio Price Update is specifically designed to update your Quicken portfolio, there's nothing for it to update until you have defined an investment account and a security. But the main point here is that Portfolio Price Update looks up securities based on their ticker symbols, not on their names. You must have the correct ticker symbol to update a security price with Portfolio Price Update.

Signing Up for Portfolio Price Update

Before you go through the sign-up procedure, you can use Portfolio Price Update's three free trial sessions. No sign-up is needed to take advantage of the free trials.

To use one of your free Portfolio Price Update sessions, simply choose Portfolio Price Update from the Online menu. Quicken displays a message (see below) describing the service and showing how many free updates you have left. Click on the OK button to proceed with the Portfolio Price Update session, as described in "Updating Your Portfolio" later in this chapter. The fourth time you use Portfolio Price Update, Quicken will prompt you to sign up.

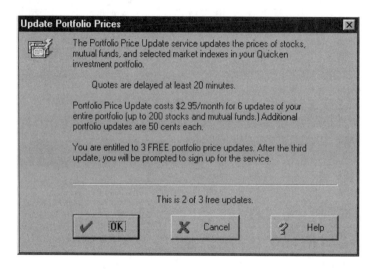

If, after using the three free Portfolio Price Update sessions, you've decided that you want to subscribe to the service, just follow these steps:

WARNING If Portfolio Price Update is grayed-out on your Online menu, it's probably because you don't have an investment account set up. You must define at least one investment account and have at least one security in your Security List before Portfolio Price Update will have anything to update.

1. To start your fourth Portfolio Price Update session, choose Portfolio Price Update from the Online menu. Quicken displays the About Portfolio Price Update dialog box shown below, with its prompt to begin the sign-up procedure.

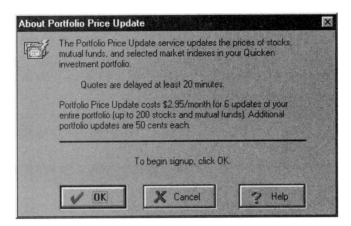

2. Click on the OK button to close that dialog box and open the Portfolio Price Update dialog box, as shown below.

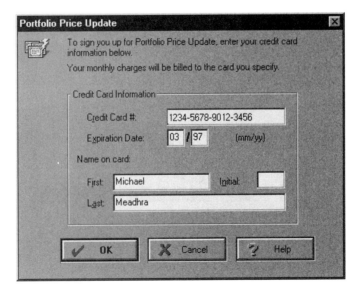

3. You should have already signed up for your Intuit membership, so all that you need to supply here is the information necessary for Intuit Services Corporation

to bill your credit card for the Portfolio Price Update fees. Fill in the following text boxes:

- Credit Card #—enter your credit card number; spaces or hyphens are optional, but may make it easier to read and check the number. Intuit Services Corporation accepts MasterCard, Visa, and American Express.
- Expiration Date—enter the month and year, with two digits in each box.
- Name on card—enter your name exactly as it appears on your credit card.

After you finish entering the billing information, click on the OK button.

4. When the Portfolio Price Update Signup dialog box appears (see below), read the Portfolio Price Update Service Agreement, and then click on the Accept Agreement button.

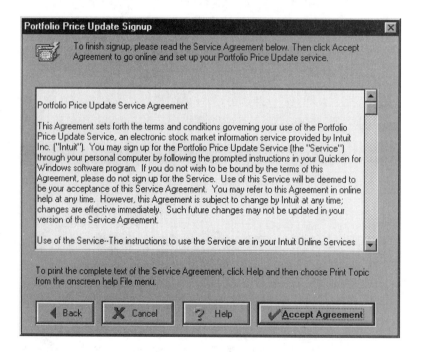

5. Next, the Enter Password dialog box appears. Enter your Intuit membership password, and click on the OK button to continue.

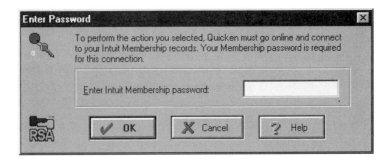

6. Quicken logs onto the Intuit Services Corporation network and signs you up for the Portfolio Price Update service. The Online Status dialog box (see below) keeps you informed of Quicken's progress during the automated online session.

7. After the Portfolio Price Update sign-up is complete, Quicken displays the following message, confirming that the service has been activated. The dialog box also gives you the option of launching a Portfolio Price Update session. Click on the Yes button to update prices, or on the No button to close the dialog box.

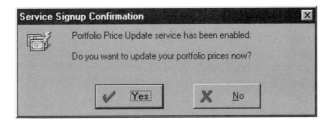

Using Portfolio Price Update

Updating your portfolio with current security prices is easy with Portfolio Price Update. The process is almost totally automatic. All it takes is a few mouse clicks to initiate a Portfolio Price Update online session. However, for Portfolio Price Update to work properly, you'll need to make sure it has the information it needs—namely, ticker symbols for your securities.

Checking Your Security List

Portfolio Price Update searches for securities based on ticker symbols. The program can't update a security's price unless Quicken has the proper ticker symbol on file. Therefore, before you use Portfolio Price Update, your first task is to check the items in your Security List and make sure they have the correct ticker symbols.

Entering Ticker Symbols

To edit (or enter) a security's ticker symbol, follow these steps:

1. Pull down the Lists menu and choose Security to open the Security List window, as shown in Figure 13.1.

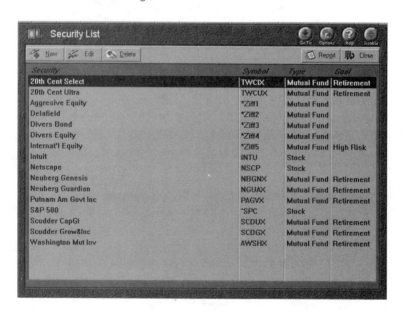

FIGURE 13.1:
Make sure all your securities have ticker symbols before using Portfolio Price Update.

2. Select a security from the list and click on the Edit button. This will open the Edit Security dialog box shown below. (You can set up a new security by clicking on the New button. This will open the Set Up Security dialog box, which is identical to the Edit Security dialog box except for the name in the title bar.)

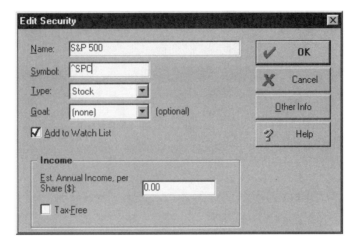

3. Check (or enter) the security name and other information in the dialog box. Pay particular attention to the ticker symbol in the Symbol box. Make sure that it's correct, including capitalization. (Most ticker symbols aren't case-sensitive, but some are.) Check or clear the Add to Watch List checkbox according to your preference for this security.

WARNING Make sure that you use the real ticker symbol, not some non-standard abbreviation for the security that you might find in the local newspaper. Check the *Wall Street Journal*, stock prospectus, your brokerage statement, or other references for the correct ticker symbol for your security.

4. When you're sure the information in the Edit Security dialog box is correct, click on the OK button to close the dialog box.
5. Repeat steps 2, 3, and 4 for the other securities in the Security List.

> **TIP** If you have Quicken 5 Deluxe for Windows, you have another way to find ticker symbols for mutual funds—Mutual Fund Finder. You can run this handy program and search for a mutual fund by name or other classification. Double-click on the name of a mutual fund in one of the Mutual Fund Finder lists to see more detail on the fund—including its ticker symbol.

Skipping a Security

You may have some securities in your Security List that you don't want or need updated by Portfolio Price Update. Fortunately, it's easy to tell Portfolio Price Update to ignore a security. Just follow these steps:

1. Open the Security List window and select the security you want Portfolio Price Update to ignore.
2. Click on the Edit button to open the Edit Security dialog box.
3. In the Symbol box, add an asterisk (*) in front of the ticker symbol as shown below.

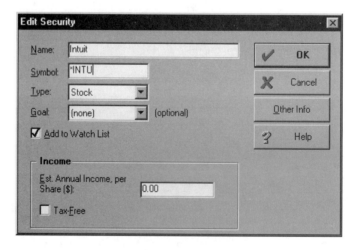

4. Click on the OK button to close the dialog box.

Portfolio Price Update ignores any security that has an asterisk at the beginning of its ticker symbol. You can use this technique if you need to reduce the number of securities in your file to stay within Portfolio Price Update's limit of 200 securities in a price update.

It lets you tell Portfolio Price Update which securities to ignore, instead of simply having the program ignore the extra securities at the bottom of the list. You can also use this technique if you don't know the ticker for a security and don't want Portfolio Price Update to display an error message (such as the one shown below) every time you attempt to get an update.

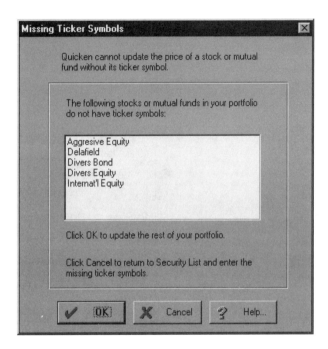

Entering Tickers for Market Indexes

In addition to stocks and mutual funds, Portfolio Price Update updates stock market indexes. To get a current index value along with your stock and mutual fund prices, simply add the indexes you want to see to your Security List, just as you would add any other security. The indexes use special ticker symbols beginning with a caret (^), as shown in the following table:

^DJB	Dow Jones 20 Bonds
^DJBI	Dow Jones 10 Industrial Bonds
^DJBU	Dow Jones 10 Utility Bonds
^DJC	Dow Jones Commodity
^DJS	Dow Jones Commodity Spot

^DJA	Dow Jones Composite (65 stocks)
^DJI	Dow Jones Industrial Average
^DJT	Dow Jones Transportation Average
^DJU	Dow Jones Utilities Average
^IXIC	NASDAQ Composite
^NYA	New York Stock Exchange Composite
^RUI	Russell 1000
^RUT	Russell 2000
^RUA	Russell 3000
^SPO	S&P 100
^SPI	S&P 400 Industrial
^SPM	S&P 400 Midcap
^SPC	S&P 500 Composite Index
^SPF	S&P Financial
^SPT	S&P Transport
^SPU	S&P Utility
^VLIC	Value Line Composite (from KCBOT)
^VLII	Value Line Industrials
^VLIR	Value Line Railways
^VLIU	Value Line Utilities

Updating Your Portfolio

Once you get the preliminaries out of the way by supplying the ticker symbols for your securities, you're ready to use Portfolio Price Update to update your security prices. Getting a price update with Portfolio Price Update is a simple process—it's easy to start the online session, and once it's started, Portfolio Price Update does its thing automatically.

Follow these steps to update your portfolio prices with Portfolio Price Update:

1. You can start a Portfolio Price Update session in one of two ways:
   - Pull down the Online menu and choose Portfolio Price Update.
   - Pull down the Activities menu and choose Portfolio View to open the Portfolio View window, and then click on the Update button.

2. When Quicken displays the Enter Password dialog box (see below), enter your Intuit membership password and click on the OK button.

> **NOTE** Quicken will skip this dialog box and enter your Intuit membership password automatically if you stored your password for Portfolio Price Update. See Chapter 5 for more on storing your password.

3. The Portfolio Price Update session itself is fully automated. Quicken sets up your modem, dials the number, logs onto the Intuit Services Corporation network, downloads the prices for the securities in your Security List, and then logs off. The Online Status dialog box keeps you apprised of Quicken's progress.

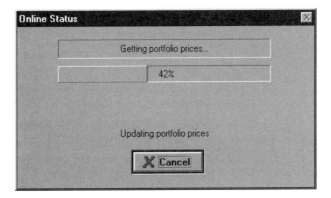

4. After completing the online session, Portfolio Price Update displays the following confirmation message. Click on the OK button to close the dialog box.

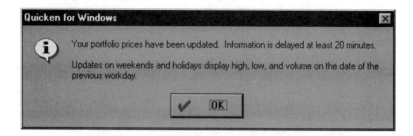

If Portfolio Price Update was unable to update some of the securities in your Security List, you'll see an enlarged version of the confirmation message (shown below) listing which securities the program could not update. The problem is usually caused by incorrect ticker symbols. Make a note of the problem securities, and then click on the OK button to close the dialog box.

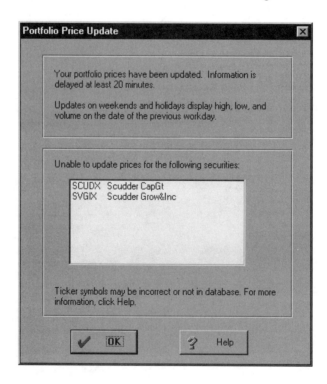

5. After Portfolio Price Update does its job, it automatically opens the Portfolio View window, where you can view the updated security prices, as shown in Figure 13.2.

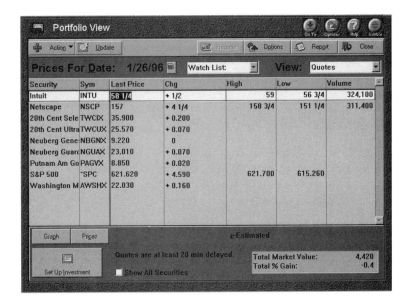

FIGURE 13.2:
See the latest security price updates in the Portfolio View window.

Reading the Results of a Portfolio Price Update Session

Portfolio Price Update doesn't present the newly downloaded security price information in a special window. Instead, you'll see the current prices displayed in Quicken's regular Portfolio View window (see Figure 13.2). You can see the Last Price (the closing price or latest available quote) for all the securities Portfolio Price Update found. For most securities, Portfolio Price Update also shows you the change (Chg) from the previous closing price. In addition, Portfolio Price Update will download High, Low, and Volume information if it's available. (High, Low, and Volume data are usually available for stocks but not for mutual funds.) In order to see the impact of the latest prices on your entire investment portfolio, you can change which investment accounts are shown in the Portfolio View window by selecting different views in the View drop-down list box.

WARNING After running Portfolio Price Update, you may see an *e* appear beside the price, indicating that it's an estimated price, even though you just downloaded the latest closing prices. Quicken compares the date of the last price to the current date. If they don't match, Quicken assumes that the price is an estimate. Reset the Prices For Date to the last trading day to get rid of the erroneous estimate indications.

Beyond the Basics

Using Portfolio Price Update to update security prices in your Quicken investment portfolio is a pretty straightforward process. However, if you maintain multiple Quicken data files or very long lists of securities, you might run into some of the following situations that go beyond the normal use of Portfolio Price Update.

Using Portfolio Price Update with More Than One Quicken File

Most Quicken users keep all their financial data for the current year in one Quicken data file. However, there are some instances when you might need multiple files, such as to separate business and personal finances.

You have two options for using Portfolio Price Update with more than one Quicken data file:

- Establish separate Portfolio Price Update accounts—one for each file
- Link multiple Quicken data files to one Portfolio Price Update account

To choose the first option, you just set up a separate Intuit membership and Portfolio Price Update account in each Quicken data file. The procedure for establishing the second account is the same as for the first. (One extra dialog box will appear when you set up your second Intuit membership, giving you the choice of using an existing membership or setting up a new membership. Choose Set Up New Intuit Membership. Everything else is the same.) You will get two separate billings each month for your Portfolio Price Update sessions.

The second option lets you use one Portfolio Price Update account to update securities in more than one Quicken data file. You can get portfolio updates for security prices in any of the linked Quicken data files, and yet receive only one Portfolio Price Update bill each month. To link a second (or subsequent) Quicken data file to an existing Portfolio Price Update account, follow these steps:

1. Set up your Intuit membership and Portfolio Price Update account in your first Quicken file.

2. Open (or create) a second Quicken data file, but do not set up an Intuit membership in the second file.

3. Create at least one investment account in the second file, and set up securities in the Security List.

4. Choose Portfolio Price Update from the Online menu to begin the Portfolio Price Update setup process.

5. Quicken displays the About Portfolio Price Update dialog box, as shown below. Notice that there are no free updates available—they were used up in the first Quicken file. Click on the OK button.

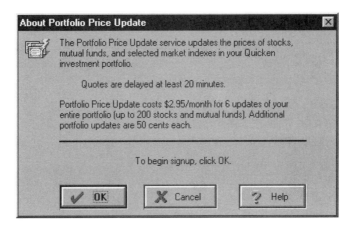

6. Next, Quicken displays the About Intuit Membership dialog box. Click on the Use existing Intuit Membership button.

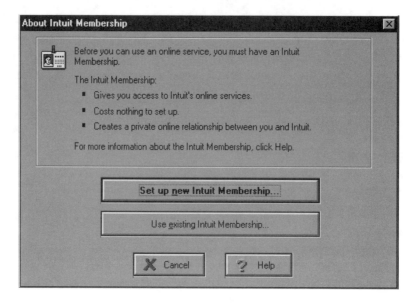

7. In the Existing Intuit Membership dialog box (see below), enter your existing Intuit membership number, or select it from the drop-down list. Then enter your Intuit membership password, and click on the OK button.

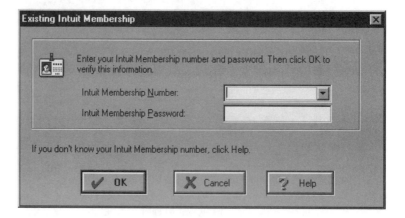

8. Quicken links the current data file to your existing Intuit membership and Portfolio Price Update account and displays the Service Signup Confirmation dialog box. At this point, you have the option of going online using the existing

Portfolio Price Update account. Click on the Yes button to start a Portfolio Price Update session, or click on the No button to close the dialog box without starting an update.

Tracking More Than 200 Securities

Portfolio Price Update is limited to 200 securities in any one update. Although that's enough for most people, an active investor might want to track an even greater number. If Portfolio Price Update encounters more than 200 securities in your Security List, it will update the prices on the first 200 items in the list and ignore the rest.

If you're just a few items over the 200-security limit, you could make Portfolio Price Update ignore some securities by prefacing their ticker symbols with asterisks. After getting one update with Portfolio Price Update, you could edit the ticker symbols in the Security List by removing the asterisks from the previously ignored securities and adding asterisks to others, so that the active list stays below 200; you could then get a second portfolio update. This technique works in a pinch, but it's too cumbersome to use on a regular basis or on large numbers of securities.

If you need to track significantly more than 200 securities, a better solution is to create a second Quicken data file for tracking some of the securities. That way you can keep the Security List in each file below the 200-security limit. Just follow the steps outlined in the previous section to link the second Quicken data file to your existing Portfolio Price Update account. Then follow the steps below to update securities spread across two (or more) Quicken data files:

1. Open your first Quicken data file.
2. Use Portfolio Price Update to update the security prices in the file.
3. Open the second Quicken data file.
4. Use Portfolio Price Update again to update security prices in the second file.
5. Repeat steps 3 and 4 for additional Quicken data files if necessary.

Each time, Portfolio Price Update updates only the securities in the current file. As long as no one file contains more than 200 securities, you can update prices on as many securities as you like (and care to pay for).

Updating Your Credit Card Information

At some point, Quicken may display a dialog box requesting updated credit card information to use for billing your Portfolio Price Update account. This can happen for a number of reasons—your credit card may have expired, or perhaps you made a mistake when you entered your credit card information during sign-up, and the card was invalid or declined. If you see a dialog box requesting updated credit card information, simply supply the updated information in the dialog box and click on the OK button.

Canceling Portfolio Price Update

If you should ever decide that you want to discontinue using Portfolio Price Update, you must explicitly cancel the service. Just ceasing to use Portfolio Price Update isn't enough—you will still be charged the monthly fee until you notify Intuit Services Corporation that you no longer want the Portfolio Price Update service.

To cancel Portfolio Price Update, call Intuit Services Corporation technical support at 708-585-8500, and request cancelation of the service. You'll need to supply your Intuit membership number, as well as your mother's maiden name for identification. The ISC customer service representative can make the change effective immediately. Later, if you want, you can reinstate the Portfolio Price Update feature by repeating the sign-up process.

TIP   To display your Intuit membership number, point to Intuit Membership in the Online menu, and then choose View Details from the fly-out menu. Your Intuit membership number appears in the upper right corner of the Intuit Membership Detail dialog box.

Chapter 14

INVESTOR INSIGHT

- **What is Investor Insight?**
- **Starting up Investor Insight**
- **Setting up your Watch List**
- **Setting up portfolios**
- **Downloading information**
- **Generating charts and reports**

Portfolio Price Update is a nice feature, as far as it goes. However, simply getting security price updates might not be enough for the serious investor. If you're one of those serious investors, you would probably like to track additional securities, review historical data, and follow breaking news that affects the securities you're tracking. That's where Investor Insight comes in.

What Is Investor Insight?

Unlike Portfolio Price Update, Investor Insight isn't a built-in feature of Quicken. It's a separate Windows program designed to complement Quicken. Although Investor Insight comes included with Quicken's Deluxe version, the program operates independently. It doesn't even go through a connection to Intuit Services Corporation.

Like Portfolio Price Update, Investor Insight can download security prices and use that information to update your Quicken investment portfolio. But Investor Insight can do much more, including:

- Get information on more than 16,000 securities
- Get price quotes for stocks and mutual funds traded on the American Stock Exchange, New York Stock Exchange, and NASDAQ
- Download five years of historical data on each security
- Get news reports from Dow Jones News Service (including *The Wall Street Journal*) and *Barons*
- Order detailed company profiles from Standard & Poors that include income statements, balance sheets, earnings estimates, and analysts' ratings
- Set up portfolios to track the performance of specific holdings
- Generate a variety of charts and reports that let you compare securities to each other and to market indexes

In short, you get a wealth of information for making buying and selling decisions from some of the same information sources used by professional stock analysts and brokers.

What Does It Cost?

The Investor Insight software is included in the price of Quicken Deluxe. For the Investor Insight information service, you'll pay a monthly fee. The fee is based on the number of securities you're tracking, not the number of times you access the service. You can get an unlimited number of updates on the securities on your watch list for the same monthly fee.

> **NOTE**
> You can try Investor Insight (the Basic Plan) free for one month. Then, if you continue to use Investor Insight, you will be billed on your credit card.

The Investor Insight pricing plans are as follows:

- Basic Plan (up to 10 securities)—$9.95 per month
- Premium Plan (20 to 50 securities)—$19.95 per month
- More than 50 securities—add $1.00 per month to the Premium Plan for each additional set of 5 securities. For example, tracking 63 securities would cost $22.95 ($19.95 for the first 50 securities plus $3.00 for 13 extra, which count as 15).
- Company Reports—$4.95 each

The Investor Insight service must be billed to a valid credit card. The billing is in monthly cycles starting on the day you sign up for the service, *not* on the first of the month. The monthly fee is based on the number of securities in your largest single update during the billing cycle. You can add securities to your Watch List and delete others during the month, but you won't be charged for the total number of securities on which you've gotten information—only the number in the largest single download.

Starting Up Investor Insight

Investor Insight is installed on your hard drive along with the Quicken software—unless you chose not to include it. If that's the case, you can add Investor Insight to your system by running the Setup program from your Quicken Deluxe program disks or CD and selecting Investor Insight for installation.

Once the program is installed, you can run Investor Insight for the first time and sign up for the service by following these steps:

1. Start Investor Insight by doing one of the following:
   - Run the Quicken Deluxe Gateway and double-click on the Investor Insight icon
   - In Quicken, pull down the Online menu and choose Investor Insight
2. The first time you run Investor Insight, the Investor Insight Overview appears, as shown in Figure 14.1. You can learn more about the program by clicking on the buttons. When you're through, click on the Exit button in the lower right corner to close the overview and go into Investor Insight.

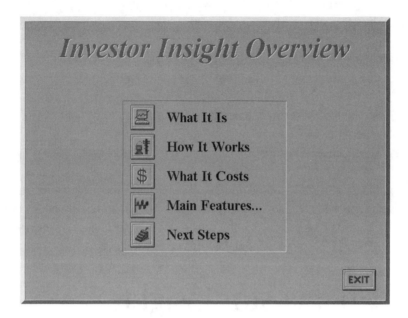

FIGURE 14.1:
This interactive introduction to Investor Insight appears the first time you start the program.

3. Next, the Investor Insight window appears (see Figure 14.2) with still more introductory help in the form of an Easy Steps dialog box. Click on the Next button to step through the instruction screens. Click on the close button to close the dialog box when you're through.

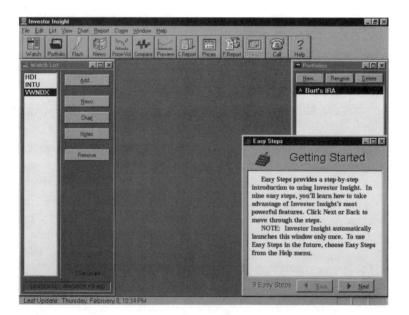

FIGURE 14.2:
The Investor Insight window greets you with Easy Steps instructions.

4. To get things started, click on the Call button in the toolbar. The program displays a status message as it auto-configures your modem, followed by the Modem Autoconfigure Completed message box. Click on the OK button to close the message box.

WARNING If you have any other communications program running, it will interfere with Investor Insight's modem setup. Be sure you disable any fax or voicemail software before attempting to go online from Investor Insight.

5. Next, the Set Up Modem dialog box appears (see below). You shouldn't have to change anything in this dialog box unless you need to add a dialing prefix to get an outside line or disable call waiting. If necessary, you can click on the Advanced button to open another dialog box where you can edit the modem reset and initialization strings. Click on the OK button when you're ready to continue.

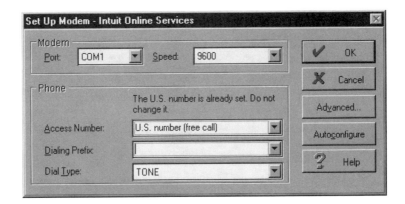

TIP The preprogrammed access number is a toll-free call for most people. However, if you live in a rural area, or are charged for local calls, you can instruct the software to use an 800 number for its calls; just choose Always Use Secondary Number from the Access Number dropdown list in the Set Up Modem dialog box.

6. The program may display a dialog box asking if you have previously registered a user name and password for Investor Insight. Normally, you would just click on the No button. However, you can click on the Yes button if you're reinstalling the software and want to link it to your existing Investor Insight account.

7. When the Subscription Agreement dialog box appears, as shown below, click on the Read Terms of Service button to open a Help window where you can read all the details and disclaimers attached to the Investor Insight service. After you read it, close the Help window and click on the Accept button.

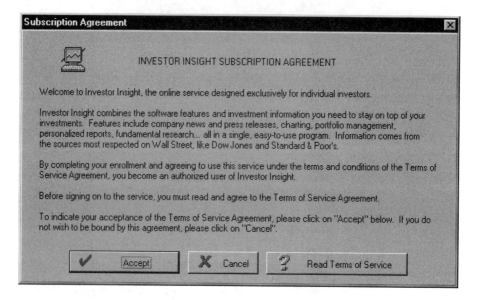

8. The User Registration dialog box (shown on the next page) appears next. Complete the Personal Information section, and then fill in credit card information for the card you want your Investor Insight fees billed to. In the Account Information area, enter a user name and make up a password. When the information is complete, click on the Register Now button.

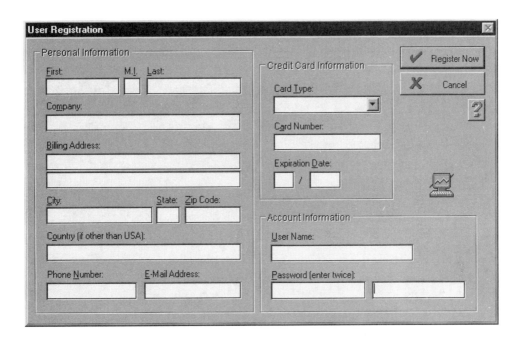

NOTE The system will routinely add a number or symbol to your user name to make it more distinctive. You will receive an e-mail message in Investor Insight informing you of your new user name.

9. Investor Insight initializes your modem, makes a call, and logs onto the network. The Download Status message box shown below gives you a graphic representation of what's happening.

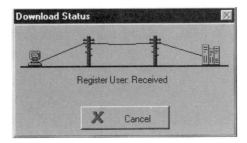

10. Once the program logs off the network, it will display the following message to confirm that you have registered for the Investor Insight service.

Now you're registered to use Investor Insight. You'll need to call again to download information and get your first price updates.

Setting Up Your Watch List

A watch list is simply a list of the securities you want to track. You may have noticed the Watch List window in Figure 14.2 with its short list of sample ticker symbols. These are the securities for which Investor Insight will download prices and information.

Securities in Your Portfolio

Obviously, you'll want your own investments to be included in the Watch List. The easiest way to start is to import the information from your Quicken investment portfolio. To import your Quicken investment records into Investor Insight, follow these steps:

1. From the File menu, choose Get Quicken Investments. Investor Insight searches for your current Quicken file and begins reading the investment information from it. (Be patient, this can take a minute or two.)
2. If Investor Insight finds any ticker symbols in your Quicken file that it doesn't recognize, you'll see the Missing or Invalid Symbols dialog box shown on the next page. Make a note of any securities listed in the box, and click on the OK button.

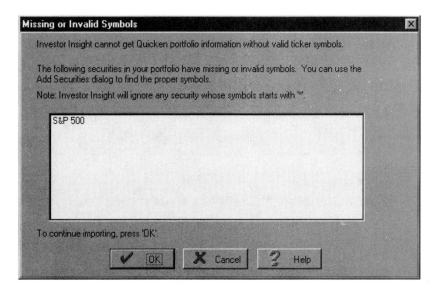

3. Next, the program displays the Get Quicken Accounts dialog box shown below. Select which accounts you want to import, and click on the Get Data button.

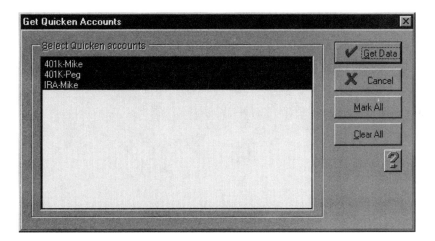

4. Investor Insight will import the Quicken investment accounts and convert them to Investor Insight Portfolios (more about portfolios in the next section). Investor Insight adds ticker symbols to the Watch List for all the securities in your investment accounts. When it's finished, the program displays the following message. Click on the OK button to close the message box.

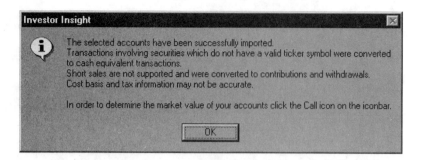

Compare the Watch List and Portfolios List in Figure 14.3 to those in Figure 14.2. You'll see that the information imported from Quicken has been added to the lists.

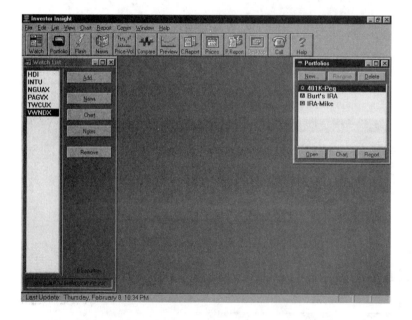

FIGURE 14.3:
Start building your Watch List and Portfolios List by importing investment information from your Quicken file.

Securities You Don't Own

When you want to track securities that aren't in any of your investment portfolios, it's easy to add them to your Watch List. Just follow these steps:

1. Click on the Watch List window. (If the Watch List window isn't already open, open it by choosing Watch List from the Lists menu.) Click on the Add button to open the Add Securities to Watch List dialog box.

2. To find a security, click on either the Name button or the Symbol button, and type the first few letters of the security's name or ticker symbol in the text box. Investor Insight will scan its database and display the closest match in the list box, as shown below.

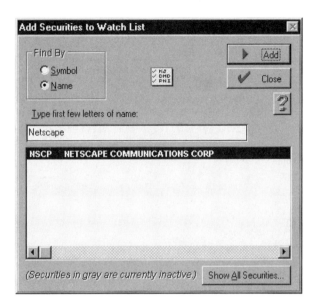

You can speed up the search and give yourself another way to select securities in the future by clicking on the Show All Securities button at the bottom of the dialog box. Investor Insight will ask you to confirm that you want to create an index of the securities in its database. The process takes a few minutes, but you need to do it only once, so click on the OK button. After creating the index, Investor Insight displays securities in a scrollable list, as shown on the next page. You can choose a security by typing the name or by clicking on it in the list.

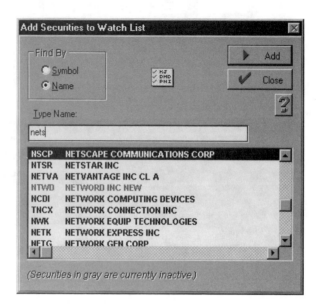

3. When you locate the security you want to add to the Watch List, click on the Add button.

4. Repeat steps 2 and 3 to add more securities to the Watch List as needed. When you're through adding securities, click on the Close button.

5. The program displays the Changed Watch List dialog box, as pictured below. To start an online session immediately for information and price updates on the newly revised list of securities, click on the Call Now button. To defer the online session, click on the Call Later button.

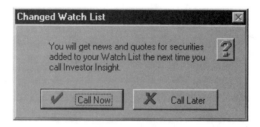

Setting Up Portfolios

Investor Insight Portfolios let you track specific groups of securities. You can use portfolios to keep track of your retirement account, a brokerage account, a group of related stocks, or the recommendations of an analyst or broker.

Investor Insight Portfolios come in three types:

- Simple
- Advanced
- Quicken

The Simple Portfolios are easiest to set up and let you track the current value and gain or loss on a group of securities. Advanced Portfolios contain more detailed information needed to support time-based performance calculations. Quicken Portfolios are similar to Advanced Portfolios, except that you enter all the buy and sell transactions in Quicken and import the details into Investor Insight instead of entering all the transactions directly in Investor Insight.

You'll probably start your Portfolios List with the investment accounts you import from Quicken. The Get Quicken Investments command on the File menu creates portfolios from your Quicken investment accounts at the same time it imports ticker symbols into your Watch List. (The procedure is described in the preceding section, "Setting Up Your Watch List.") The Quicken Portfolios are identified by a *Q* preceding the name in the Portfolios List, as shown below.

Other portfolios you'll want to create and maintain completely within Investor Insight.

Simple Portfolios

To create a Simple Portfolio, follow these steps:

1. Click on the New button in the Portfolios window to open the Create Portfolio dialog box shown below.

2. Type in a name for your portfolio and click on the Simple option, then click on the OK button.

3. Investor Insight creates the portfolio and opens the Add to Portfolio dialog box shown below. Select the security you want to add to the new portfolio, and click on the Add button.

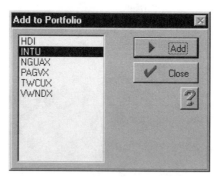

4. When the Enter Holdings dialog box appears, enter the number of shares and price per share in the appropriate text boxes, and then click on the OK button.

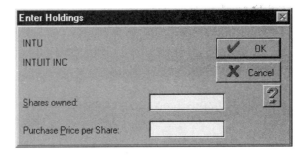

5. Repeat steps 3 and 4 to add other securities to the portfolio. When you are finished adding securities, click on the Close button in the Add to Portfolio dialog box.

6. Investor Insight shows the results of your additions in the Simple Portfolio window shown below. You can use the buttons along the right side to add, edit, or delete the securities listed in the window, or undo the last change. When you're through defining the portfolio, close the Simple Portfolio window.

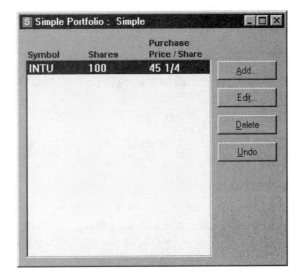

Advanced Portfolios

Creating an Advanced Portfolio is a little more involved, especially if you need to enter a lot of transaction details. But the effort can pay off in the more detailed reports and analysis you can get from an Advanced Portfolio. To create an Advanced Portfolio, follow these steps:

1. In the Portfolios window, click on the New button to open the Create Portfolio dialog box.

2. Type in a name for your portfolio and click on the Advanced option, and then click on the OK button.

3. Investor Insight opens the Advanced Portfolio Start Date dialog box. Use the arrow buttons to adjust the starting date, and then click on the OK button.

4. The next dialog box asks you to enter a beginning cash balance for the portfolio. Type in a value and click on the OK button. When you do, Investor Insight opens the Advanced Portfolio window shown below.

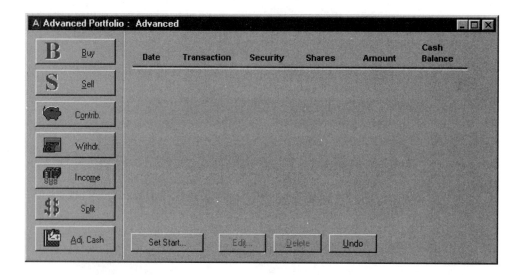

5. The portfolio starts out empty. You'll need to build the portfolio by entering the details of the transactions that have taken place so far. There are separate buttons that will open dialog boxes where you can enter common transactions:

    - Buy
    - Sell
    - Contribute (add cash to the portfolio)
    - Withdraw (cash)
    - Income (interest, dividends, capital gains)
    - Split (stock splits)
    - Adjust cash

To continue the example with a stock purchase, click on the Buy button to open the Buy Shares dialog box, pictured here.

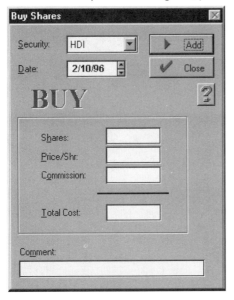

6. Select the security from the drop-down list, and enter the date of the transaction. Type in the number of shares, price per share, and either the commission or the total cost (fill in any three; Investor Insight will calculate the fourth value). Add a comment if you like.

7. When you click on the Add button, Investor Insight adds the transaction to the portfolio. You can add another buy transaction, or click on the Close button to close the dialog box. The Advanced Portfolio window (see below) now shows the stock purchase.

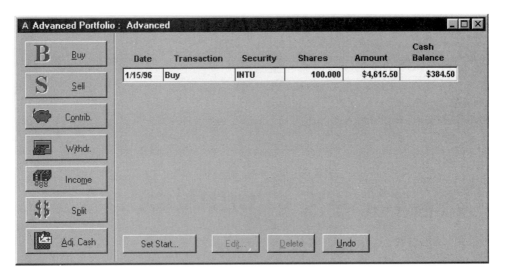

8. Build the portfolio history by adding other transactions. When you're finished, close the Advanced Portfolio window.

Editing Portfolios

You can reopen a portfolio to make any necessary changes by selecting it from the Portfolios List and clicking on the Open button. In the case of Simple and Advanced portfolios, this will open the same window you used to define the portfolio. You can add, delete, and edit transactions in the portfolio freely. In contrast, when you open a Quicken Portfolio such as the one shown below, you see a list of transactions but no way to edit them. That's because any new transactions should be entered in Quicken, not Investor Insight. To update a Quicken Portfolio in the Investor Insight portfolio, click on the Update button; this will import the latest version of the Quicken investment details, overwriting the old information in Investor Insight.

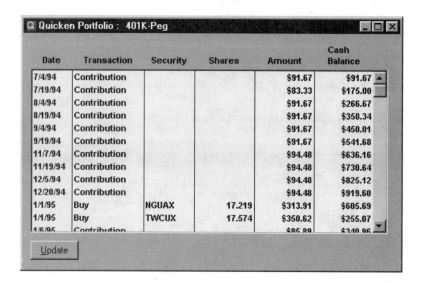

Date	Transaction	Security	Shares	Amount	Cash Balance
7/4/94	Contribution			$91.67	$91.67
7/19/94	Contribution			$83.33	$175.00
8/4/94	Contribution			$91.67	$266.67
8/19/94	Contribution			$91.67	$358.34
9/4/94	Contribution			$91.67	$450.01
9/19/94	Contribution			$91.67	$541.68
11/7/94	Contribution			$94.48	$636.16
11/19/94	Contribution			$94.48	$730.64
12/5/94	Contribution			$94.48	$825.12
12/20/94	Contribution			$94.48	$919.60
1/1/95	Buy	NGUAX	17.219	$313.91	$605.69
1/1/95	Buy	TWCUX	17.574	$350.62	$255.07
1/6/95	Contribution			$85.89	$340.96

Downloading Information

Once you've registered for the Investor Insight service, set up your Watch List, and set up portfolios, you've gotten the preliminaries out of the way. Now you're ready to put Investor Insight to work.

To download information into Investor Insight, follow these steps:

1. From the Investor Insight window, click on the Call button in the toolbar. Investor Insight opens the Download dialog box shown on the next page.

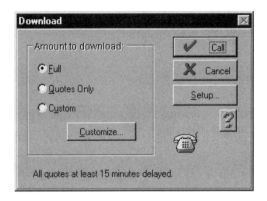

2. Select what to download: Full, Quotes Only, or Custom. For your first download, be sure to choose Full to get historical data and news as well as the latest prices. Later, you may want to select Quotes Only for a quick price update. If you want to download information about some securities on your Watch List but not others, choose the Custom option and click on the Customize button to open the Custom Download dialog box.

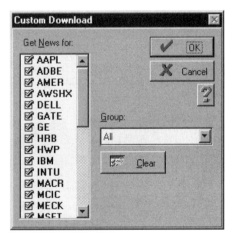

Investor Insight will download information about the checked items only. Click on a symbol to toggle the check mark on or off. When the proper symbols are checked, click on the OK button to close the Custom Download dialog box and return to the Download dialog box.

3. Click on the Call button in the Download dialog box to start the online session.

Investor Insight makes the call to the network, logs on, and begins downloading information. The program displays the Download Status message box (see below) to keep you informed of its progress as it downloads quotes, news, and other information.

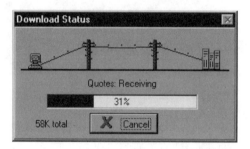

> **NOTE**
>
> **Investor Insight downloads 5 years of historical price information and 90 days of news reports for each new security on the Watch List. As a result, your first download (or the first download after you add several new securities to the Watch List) might take a while. Subsequent downloads only need to update the data and will go much faster.**

4. After Investor Insight completes the download, it displays the following message. Click on the OK button to close the message box. Investor Insight records the newly downloaded information on your hard disk.

5. If you had any e-mail messages from Investor Insight customer service, the program will display the Inbox window at the completion of the online session. To view your messages, click on a message in the list at the top of the window and read it in the lower panel. After reading a message, you can click on the Delete button to remove it from your Investor Insight file, or just leave it in your Inbox for future reference. When you're through reading your messages, close the Inbox window.

Automating Downloads

In addition to initiating an online session manually as described in the preceding section, you can set Investor Insight to automatically call in for an update at a fixed time; you can even configure it to make the automatic call every day. To do this, choose Timer from the Comm menu to open the Timer dialog box, as shown on the next page. Set the frequency and time of the automatic call. You can also instruct Investor Insight to automatically print the latest news or a Personal Report about your securities at the completion of the call. After adjusting the settings to your liking, click on the OK button.

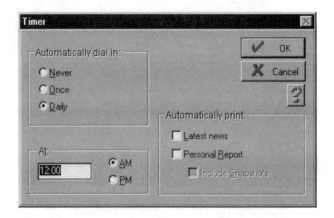

Exchanging Price Data with Quicken

Investor Insight works closely with Quicken to keep your Quicken investment portfolio up-to-date with the latest prices. When you open Quicken, it automatically gets the latest security prices from your Investor Insight files and updates the security prices in Quicken. At least that's the way it works for securities with matching symbols.

Although Quicken automatically updates the current prices of securities, it doesn't automatically import historical price data from Investor Insight—you have to do that yourself. Just follow these steps:

1. Start Quicken, and then choose Portfolio View from the Activities menu to open the Portfolio View window, as shown in Figure 14.4.

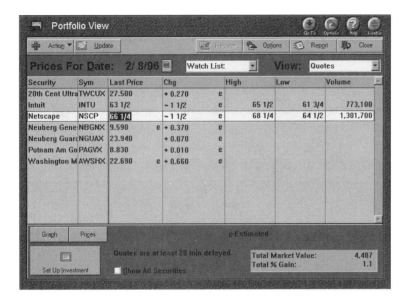

FIGURE 14.4:
You can import historical price data from Investor Insight into Quicken from the Portfolio View window.

2. Select the security for which you want to import prices. Right-click on the security, and choose Import Historical Prices from the pop-up menu that appears. Quicken opens the Import Investor Insight Quotes dialog box.

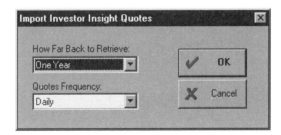

3. Choose the time span and quotes frequency from the drop-down lists, and then click on the OK button. Quicken imports the requested prices from your Investor Insight files.

Generating Charts and Reports

Investor Insight provides several ways for you to view the data it collects. A wealth of charts and reports is available with just a few clicks of your mouse. I can't begin to show you all the charts and reports within the confines of this chapter. The following examples are just a sampling of Investor Insight's offerings. The rest await your exploration.

> **TIP** Be sure to check out the kinds of charts and reports you can create by clicking on the **Chart** and **Report** buttons in the **Portfolios** window.

Charts

From the Chart menu, choose Price-Volume Overview to display the Chart Overview window shown below. This window gives you thumbnail-size previews of the Price-Volume charts for all the securities on your Watch List.

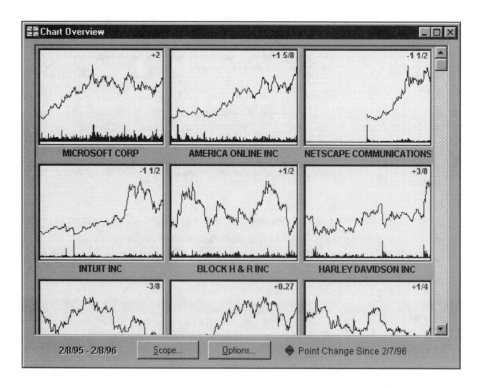

Double-clicking on a thumbnail chart in the Chart Overview window opens a full-size version of that chart in its own window, as shown below.

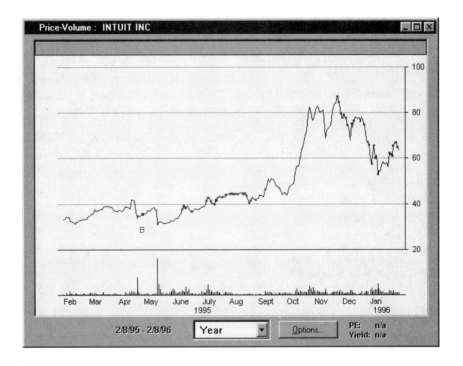

A Price-Volume chart such as this one contains a surprising link to the news reports Investor Insight collects about each security; red dots on the price plot line indicate that Investor Insight has a news story about the security from that date. If you double-click on one of these "hot spots," Investor Insight will open a Browse dialog box like the one shown on the next page where you can read the news report.

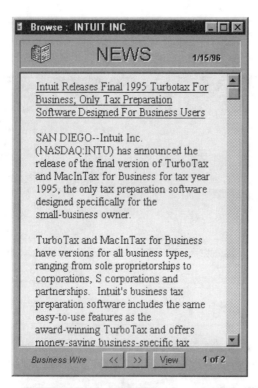

Investor Insight also includes an assortment of comparative charts that let you compare a security to other securities, to market indexes, or to your own portfolios. You can also display charts of the popular market indexes.

The Company Preview feature lets you view Price-Volume charts from a collection of 4,000 securities without adding them to your Watch List. Choose Company Preview from the Chart menu to open the Company Preview dialog box, as shown below. Select a company from the list on the left side of the box, and Investor Insight will display the chart on the right. If the security looks interesting, click on the Add To Watch List button to add it to your Watch List so you can get more information.

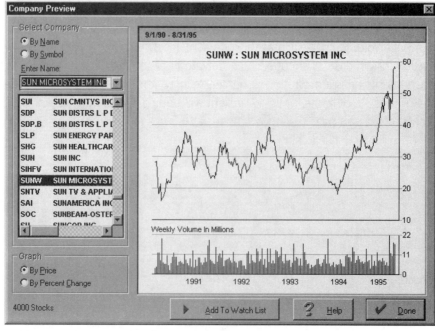

Reports

One of Investor Insight's most useful features is collecting news reports and press releases that mention the securities you're tracking on your Watch List. To view these news reports, choose News from the Report menu to open the News window, as shown below.

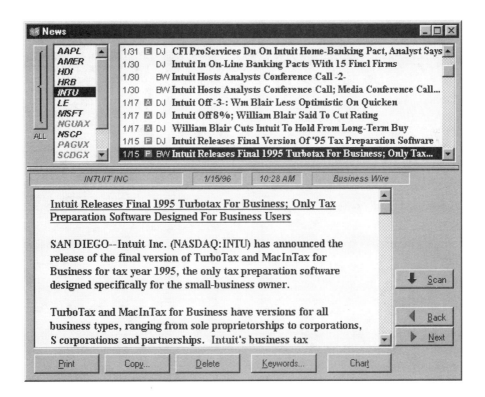

Select a security's symbol from the list in the upper left corner; related headlines appear on the right. When you click on a headline, the story appears in the lower half of the window.

Another type of report, the Flash Report (shown on the next page), presents a condensed summary of significant changes since the previous report. This window appears automatically after each online session; you can also display it manually by choosing Flash Report from the Report menu. Click on the Options button at the bottom of the window to open a dialog box where you can customize the parameters for the report.

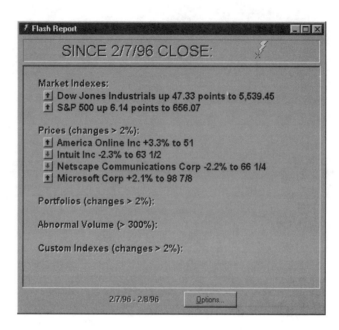

To create a newsletter-style report on the securities in your portfolio or in your Watch List, choose Personal Report from the Report menu. You can customize the report by clicking on the Scope button. Click on the Preview button to view it on-screen (see Figure 14.5), or click on the Print button to print your personalized market newsletter.

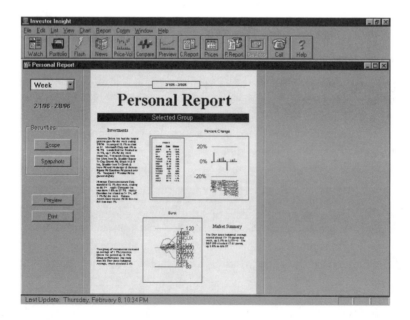

FIGURE 14.5:
The Personal Report lets you create a personalized newsletter about your investments.

Choosing Current Prices from the Report menu opens the Current Prices dialog box, as shown below. This table gives you a concise report on the prices of securities in your Watch List. If you need more details on any security, try the Historical Prices Report to see the numbers behind the Price-Volume charts.

Current Prices

Name	Current Price	Point Change	Percent Change	Volume
AMERICA ONLINE INC	51	+1 5/8	+3.3%	7,946,300
APPLE COMPUTER INC	27 7/8	-3/8	-1.3%	5,569,000
BLOCK H & R INC	38 1/4	+1/2	+1.3%	1,017,600
HARLEY DAVIDSON INC	34 3/4	+3/8	+1.1%	730,800
INTUIT INC	63 1/2	-1 1/2	-2.3%	1,365,300
LANDS END INC	15 3/8	+1/4	+1.7%	32,000
MICROSOFT CORP	98 7/8	+2	+2.1%	10,592,100
NETSCAPE COMMUNICATIONS CO|	66 1/4	-1 1/2	-2.2%	3,286,000
NEUBERGER & BERMAN EQUITY FD	23.94	+0.1	+0.4%	0
PUTNAM AMERN GOVT INCOME FD	8.83	+0.01	+0.1%	0
SCUDDER EQUITY TR CAP GROWTH	21.98	+0.19	+0.9%	0
SCUDDER INVT TR GRWTH & INCM	21.38	+0.17	+0.8%	0
TWENTIETH CENTY INVS INC ULTR|	27.5	+0.27	+1.0%	0
VANGUARD / WINDSOR FD INC	15.1	-0.02	-0.1%	0

2/7/96 - 2/8/96   Since 2/7 ▼   Scope...   Options...

Requesting Company Reports

Investor Insight can download detailed reports from Standard & Poors that give you in-depth information about a company. These Company Reports include earnings forecasts, income statements and balance sheets, analysts' ratings, and much more.

Investor Insight does *not* download Company Reports for each of your securities automatically. These are special-order items. As such, you must explicitly request each Company Report, and you'll be charged $4.95 for each one. To give you a sample of the kind of information these reports contain, Investor Insight includes a Company Report on Intuit, Inc.

Viewing a Company Report

To view a Company Report, follow these steps:

1. From the Report menu, choose Company Reports. Investor Insight opens the Company Reports dialog box shown on the next page.

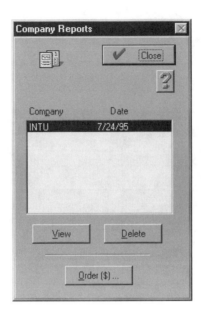

2. Select a company from the list, and then click on the View button to open the Company Report dialog box.

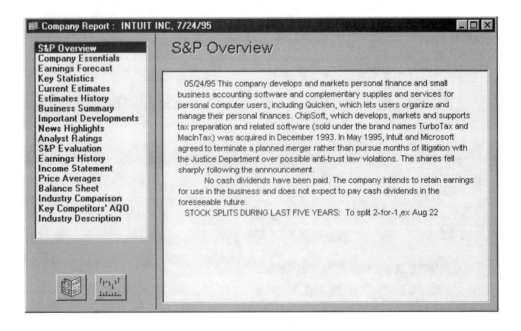

3.   When you select a topic from the list on the left side of the dialog box, that portion of the report (text, table, or chart) is displayed in the panel on the right. The buttons in the lower left corner let you open separate windows to view news stories and the company's Price-Volume chart.

Ordering a Report

If you want to order a Company Report for one of the securities in your Watch List, follow these steps:

1.   Choose Company Reports from the Report menu to open the Company Reports dialog box.
2.   Click on the Order button. Investor Insight opens the Order Company Report dialog box shown below.

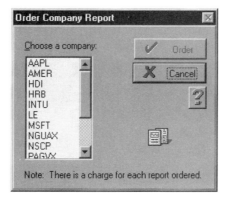

3.   Select a company from the list, and then click on the Order button.
4.   Investor Insight responds with a message box informing you that the order has been placed in your Outbox. Click on the OK button to go back to the Company Reports dialog box.
5.   Repeat steps 2, 3, and 4 to order another Company Report, or click on the Close button.

6. When the Ordered Company Report dialog box appears (see below), you'll have the option of starting an online session to receive the Company Reports immediately, or waiting until later.

If you choose the Call Later button, Investor Insight will request the Company Reports the next time you call for an update. In the meantime, if you decide you don't want the report after all, you can cancel it by removing the request from your outgoing e-mail. To cancel the request, choose Outbox from the Comm menu. In the Outbox window (shown below), select the Company Report order from the list at the top of the window, and then click on the Delete button.

Chapter 15

OTHER ONLINE SERVICES

- **Shopping from the Intuit Marketplace**
- **Exploring the Quicken Financial Network**
- **Using NETworth**
- **Accessing the Internet from Quicken**
- **Entering QFN from the Internet**
- **Finding Quicken information on the commercial online services**
- **Using Quicken Quotes on CompuServe**

Previous chapters have dealt with setting up your Intuit membership and signing up for Online Banking, Online BillPay, Portfolio Price Update, and Investor Insight—all the major online personal finance features available in Quicken.

But the online capabilities of Quicken and Intuit don't end there. You can order supplies and software online from the Intuit Marketplace. You also have access to all the information on the Quicken Financial Network, which is found on the Internet. Then there are the support forums and utilities that Intuit sponsors on the commercial online services. This chapter summarizes these online extras.

> **TIP**
>
> As another online service, when you install Quicken it gives you the option of registering the software online instead of sending in the traditional postcard. However, if you do this, you should *not* send in the registration postcard that came in the software box. You can register by using either method, but it's not necessary to do both.

Shopping from the Intuit Marketplace

The Intuit Marketplace isn't new; it's been around a while. However, you may not have been aware of the feature, tucked away as it was in previous versions of Quicken. Now, you're more likely to notice the Intuit Marketplace command sharing space on the Online menu with the better-known online options.

Basically, the Intuit Marketplace lets you fill out an on-screen order form for checks, envelopes, or other supplies, as well as Intuit software. Once you fill out the form, you can submit your order in one of three ways:

- Print the order and mail it to Intuit
- Print the order and fax it to Intuit
- Send the order directly to Intuit via modem

Using the Intuit Marketplace is simple. Just follow these steps:

1. From the Online menu, choose Intuit Marketplace. The program displays a logo screen that you can dispatch by pressing any key, or simply wait a few seconds; the Intuit Marketplace dialog box will appear, as shown on the next page.

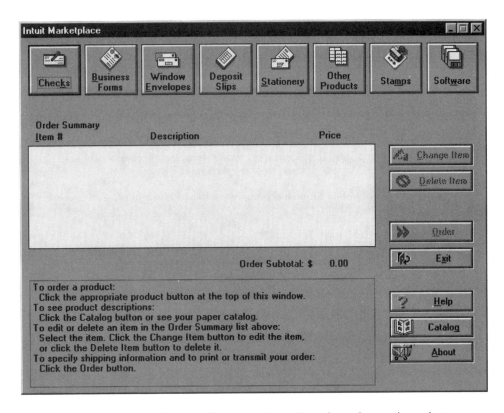

2. Optional: To provide you with more information about the products that are available, the Intuit Marketplace includes an online catalog in Windows Help format. Click on the Catalog button in the lower right corner to open the Intuit Marketplace Help window. Click on an underlined topic to get more details. After viewing the catalog information, click on the Close button or press Escape to close the dialog box.

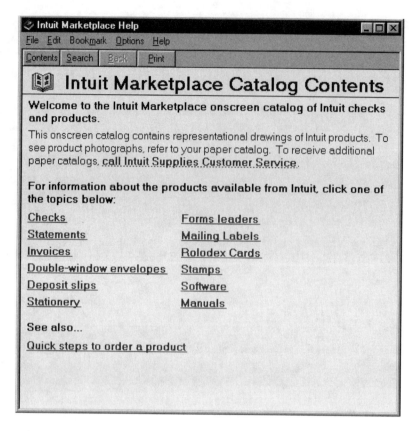

3. When you're ready to choose your first item, select a category by clicking one of the buttons across the top of the Intuit Marketplace dialog box. You have the following choices:

- Checks (standard-, voucher-, and personal-size checks)
- Business Forms (invoices and statements)
- Window Envelopes (designed to match Intuit's checks and invoices)
- Deposit Slips
- Stationery (imprinted letterhead and envelopes)
- Other Products (form leaders, mailing labels, Rolodex cards)
- Stamps (check endorsement stamps, return address stamps, messages such as Past Due)
- Software (Quicken and TurboTax software and manuals)

TIP

Among the software choices you'll find some useful supplemental manuals. For example, the *Quicken Business User's Guide* contains instructions for using Quicken to manage a small business. The *Quicken Deluxe User's Guide* includes additional documentation and tips for users of the Deluxe edition.

4. When you choose a product category, the Intuit Marketplace presents a series of dialog boxes in which you can narrow your selection and enter the specifics for your order. The dialog boxes you will see vary with the item you're ordering. Check orders require you to provide the most information. You must enter (and verify) your bank account number, choose continuous or single-sheet format, indicate what kind of printer you'll use, choose the check size and style, and specify how you want the checks imprinted (see below).

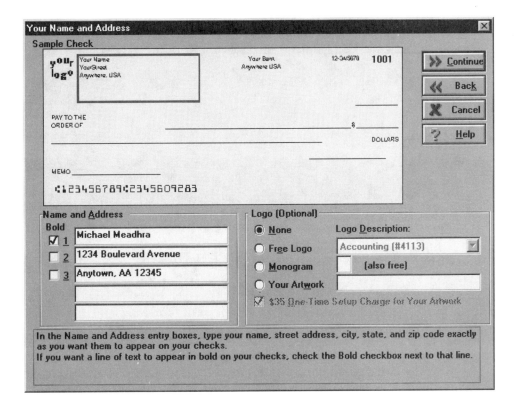

In contrast, to order window envelopes, all you need to do is select the envelope size and quantity in one simple dialog box, as shown below.

5. When you finish specifying the item you want to order, click on the OK button. The program returns to the Intuit Marketplace dialog box where the item is now listed in the Order Summary list, as illustrated below.

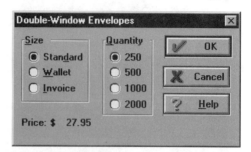

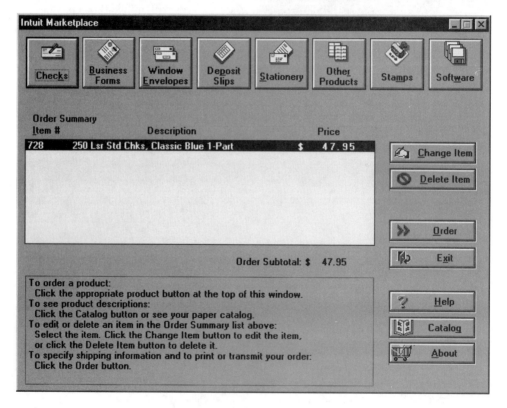

6. Repeat steps 3, 4, and 5 to select additional items for your order. If necessary, you can edit the Order Summary list by changing or deleting items:

- To change an item, select it from the Order Summary list, and click on the Change Item button. The program takes you back through the dialog boxes to redefine the item.

- To remove an item from the Order Summary list, select the item and click on the Delete Item button.

7. Once the Order Summary list is correct, click on the Order button to open the Payment and Delivery dialog box shown below.

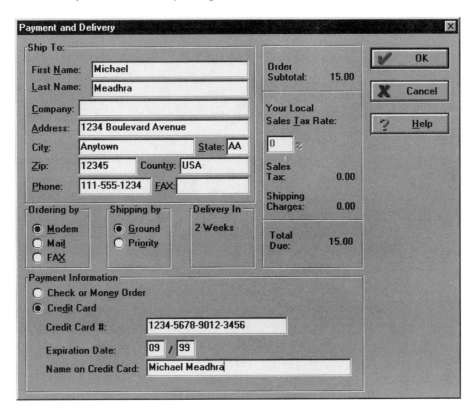

8. Fill in your shipping address, and be sure to enter your local sales tax rate. Choose how you want to submit the order and how you want it shipped. Then supply the payment information: you can pay by check or money order or by credit card (fax and modem orders must be paid by credit card). If you choose the latter option, supply the credit card information. When you've entered all the information, click on the OK button.

9. Review your order in the Preview Order dialog box. If there's a problem, click on the Back button to return to the previous dialog box and make the necessary changes. If the order is correct, click on the Print button. The program will print your order, which you can mail or fax to Intuit, or, if you're ordering by modem, keep in your files for reference.

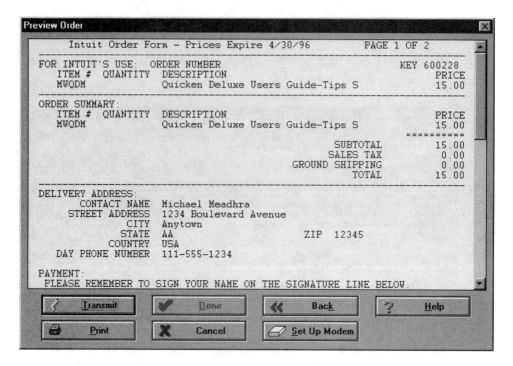

If you plan to mail or fax your order to Intuit, after the order is printed you can click on the Done button to close the dialog box. If you want to send your order to Intuit via modem, continue through the next steps.

10. To send your order to Intuit, click on the Transmit button. The program displays the Online Status dialog box (see below) to keep you informed of its progress as it sets up your modem, dials Intuit's number, logs onto the network, transmits your order, and then disconnects.

11. After the online session, the program displays a confirmation message such as the one shown below. Make a note of the confirmation number, and then click on the OK button to close the dialog box.

12. Click on the Done button to close the Preview Order dialog box, and then click on the Exit button to close the Intuit Marketplace dialog box.

Exploring the Quicken Financial Network

The Quicken Financial Network (QFN) is Intuit's World Wide Web site—its home on the Internet. QFN includes many items of interest to Quicken users—especially those who are interested in online personal finance. Some of the things you'll find on QFN include:

- Information about the latest versions of Quicken
- Technical support
- Articles on personal finance
- Questions and answers about using Quicken
- Information about, and links to, participating financial institutions
- Access to NETworth for information on mutual funds

QFN isn't just for Internet veterans. You don't even have to have an existing Internet access account or Web browser software in order to access QFN; Quicken comes with everything you need (assuming that you have a modem and an available phone line). The software includes a customized version of Netscape Navigator—the popular Web browser program—and offers to install it automatically when you install Quicken. In addition, Intuit has arranged for Quicken users to access QFN via the facilities of Concentric Network Corporation—a nationwide Internet service provider. The combination of the Concentric Network and the Netscape Navigator software lets you browse QFN from within Quicken.

Access to QFN is free. There are no monthly membership fees or connect-time charges when you take advantage of the free access to QFN from within Quicken. However, although you're connected to the Internet, you're restricted to the QFN site; you can't go beyond it to other Web sites, Internet e-mail, or newsgroups. For a fee, you do have the option of upgrading to full Internet access; see the section titled "Internet Access from Quicken" later in this chapter.

WARNING Long-distance tolls and other phone charges may apply when you access QFN from within Quicken. Concentric provides local phone numbers in more than 200 locations across the country. Most, but not all, Quicken users will be able to access one of these numbers without incurring toll charges.

Accessing QFN

Assuming that you elected to install Netscape Navigator Intuit Edition, you can access the Quicken Financial Network from Quicken by following these steps:

1. Pull down the Online menu and choose Quicken Financial Network, or click on the QFNet button on the toolbar.
2. The first time you access QFN, the program will take you through a short registration process. Just fill in the blanks in the dialog boxes to continue. Once you complete the registration, Quicken displays the Connect to Quicken Financial Network dialog box shown below.

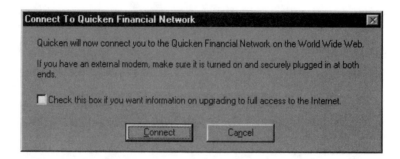

NOTE   You must register for access to QFN from Quicken. The program will automatically take you through the registration process the first time you access QFN. Subsequently, you won't see the registration screens.

3. Click on the Connect button to get things started. Quicken launches Netscape Navigator Intuit Edition and dials the Concentric Network. The Concentric Network message box (see below) keeps you informed of what's happening.

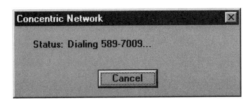

4. Once you're connected to the network, the Quicken home page loads in Netscape Navigator (see Figure 15.1). Notice the small dialog box that stays on top of the Navigator window to monitor the duration of your Internet connection.

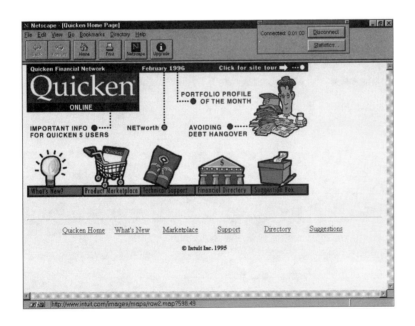

FIGURE 15.1:
This is Quicken's home page on the World Wide Web.

> **TIP**
>
> Accessing QFN from within Quicken takes you directly to Quicken's home page (http://www.intuit.com/quicken/). However, you may also want to check out the information about other Intuit products that's available on the corporate home page (http://www.intuit.com/). To go there, pull down the Directory menu and choose Intuit.

5. Start browsing the QFN Web site with Netscape Navigator Intuit Edition:

- Use the scroll bars to view different portions of the page.
- Click on underlined text (hyperlinks) to jump to another page with more information.
- Move the pointer around the page. When the arrow changes to a pointing hand, you can click on that item to go to another page for more information.

If you need more help using Navigator, pull down the Help menu and choose Handbook to open an online manual.

> **NOTE**
>
> Most of the help files and documentation for Netscape Navigator are available online. You must be logged on to the Internet in order to access them.

6. When you're ready to leave QFN, click on the Disconnect button in the small connection status dialog box (see below). This will break the modem link to the Concentric Network and the Internet.

7. Close the Netscape Navigator window by choosing Exit from the File menu or by clicking on the Close button (Windows 95).

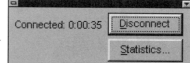

> **WARNING**
>
> Free access to QFN is for users of the current version of Quicken only. After December 31, 1996, you must upgrade to the next version of Quicken to maintain your free access to QFN.

Things to Do on QFN

The Quicken Financial Network Web site is constantly changing. You can expect new and updated information and features to appear on a regular basis. The best way to find things on QFN is to go exploring. When you see something interesting, click on it and see where it leads. If you want to back up a step, click on the Back button. To return to the Quicken home page, click on the Home button.

With all the changes going on at QFN, it's impossible to write precise instructions for finding particular information. But it's safe to say that the Quicken home page serves as a table of contents that can direct you to interesting features elsewhere on QFN. For example, here's a brief summary of the links available on the Quicken home page (refer back to Figure 15.1):

- Important Info—click here to get information about the latest software update.
- NETworth—get prices and information about stocks and mutual funds (more on this feature in the next section).
- Portfolio Profile of the Month—QFN profiles real persons, and financial planners analyze their investment portfolio.
- Avoiding Debt Hangover—another monthly feature article providing financial advice
- What's New—a collection of news and information about Quicken and related personal finance topics.
- Marketplace—news of special offers and the option to order products online
- Support—product updates and frequently asked questions.
- Financial Directory—links to member banks and an updated list of participating financial institutions.
- Suggestions—tell QFN what you think of the service.

Sometime soon (perhaps by the time you read this), Intuit plans to expand the capabilities of QFN to encompass Online Banking and Online BillPay. The plans call for enabling Internet users to access these features on QFN in much the same way you can use them from Quicken. (Don't expect it to replace Quicken, though. At best it'll probably be a subset of Quicken's more comprehensive features.) The built-in encryption capabilities of Netscape Navigator will protect the user's privacy. As this book goes to press, details aren't yet available; you can check QFN for the latest news and developments.

> **NOTE**
>
> Netscape Navigator includes built-in security features to protect your privacy by encrypting data that you enter on-screen and send to QFN. You'll know when this feature is active by the appearance of the key symbol in the lower left corner of the Navigator window. If the key is whole, the data is being encrypted. If the shaft of the key is broken, the encryption feature is inactive.

NETworth

NETworth is a stock and mutual fund information service provided by GALT Technologies (which was recently acquired by Intuit). It's available on QFN and provides yet another way to get online information about stocks and mutual funds.

NETworth serves up more than just recent security prices. You can also get fund prospectuses, performance statistics, and charts of historical prices. Plus, you can search the Morningstar database of more than 6,500 mutual funds.

NETworth is free, but you do have to register to use it. (It's a separate registration from QFN.) The basic service, Mutual Fund Manager, is available to Quicken users with free QFN access. However, you must upgrade to full Internet access (or access QFN from a separate Internet access account) to use the complete NETworth service, which includes these more advanced features:

- Mutual Fund Market Manager—a database containing profiles of mutual funds
- Financial Planner—worksheets and tips to help you plan for retirement or college education
- Equities Center—stock quotes
- The Insider—links to news, analysis, and reports

Like the rest of QFN, NETworth is constantly evolving to meet the needs of its users. Figure 15.2 shows the NETworth main menu page as it appeared during the development of this book. It may look different when you visit it.

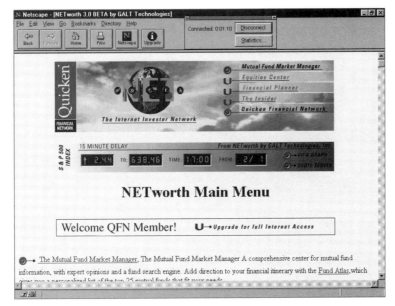

FIGURE 15.2:
The NETworth main menu page serves as your entry point into the service.

You can reach this page by clicking on NETworth on the Quicken home page in QFN. From here, you select the area of NETworth you want to visit by clicking on the underlined text in the menu (scroll down to see more of the menu page). Other pages will appear in turn, where you can make more selections and type in information such as the name or symbol of a mutual fund you're interested in.

You'll have to identify yourself before you can view some information, so don't be surprised when you see a page such as the one shown in Figure 15.3, asking you to log in. If you don't already have a user name and password for the NETworth system, you can jump to another page to register.

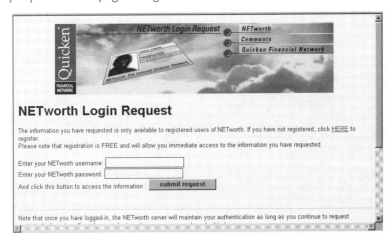

FIGURE 15.3:
NETworth asks you to log in before it will display some information.

As an example of what you can find in NETworth, Figure 15.4 shows just some of the information that's available on a popular mutual fund. There's even a link to the fund family's Web site.

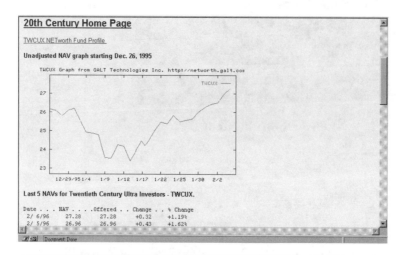

FIGURE 15.4:
This graph is just part of a mutual fund report available from NETworth.

NOTE You'll need to upgrade to full Internet access to get information such as the chart shown in Figure 15.4.

Internet Access from Quicken

By default, Internet access from within Quicken is limited to the QFN Web site. You get Netscape Navigator Intuit Edition and an Internet link provided by Concentric Network Corporation, which you can use for unlimited free access to QFN. However, the system is configured so that your access is restricted to QFN; you don't get any access to Internet e-mail, newsgroups, or Web sites outside of QFN.

If you want to go beyond QFN, you have the option to expand to full Internet access at a very competitive price. Concentric Network Corporation offers a special rate to Quicken users for Internet access:

- $1.95 per hour
- $1.95 per month minimum billing

This is a big difference from most online services and other Internet service providers that normally require at least $5-10 per month minimum billing and often charge higher hourly rates for connect time. If you expect to spend more time surfing the Net, you might want to consider Concentric's frequent user plan:

- 7 hours for $9.95
- $1.95 per additional hour

Concentric's network of more than 200 local access locations in cities across the country means that there's a good chance that you'll be able to access the system with a local phone call.

> **WARNING** Once you upgrade to full Internet access, you lose the free access to QFN. It's an either/or deal: either restricted access for free, or full Internet access (including QFN) for $1.95 per hour. After you switch to full access, Concentric has no way of tracking how much time you spend on QFN and how much time you spend elsewhere on the Net.

If you decide you want to upgrade your free QFN access to full Internet access through the Concentric Network, follow these steps:

1. The next time you start an online session on QFN, do one of the following:
   - Click on the Check this box… option in the Connect to Quicken Financial Network dialog box
   - Click on the Upgrade button in the Netscape Navigator toolbar once you're online
   - Go to the Technical Support area on QFN and click on Internet Account Administration
2. Following the on-screen prompts, fill out the forms with your name, address, and a credit card number for billing, choose your user ID and password, and read the service agreement and instructions.

That's all there is to it. You can get instructions online that will tell you how to connect to the system and use other Internet utilities.

Access to QFN from the Internet

Quicken may come equipped to connect to QFN with its own Web browser and Internet connection, but that doesn't mean you can access QFN only with those tools. You can use your own Internet connection and Web browser software if you like. You can access QFN from an account with an Internet service provider or from an online service such as CompuServe, America Online, or Microsoft Network.

QFN is "open to the public." It makes no significant difference whether you access QFN from within Quicken or from your own Internet account—the content available on QFN is the same either way. If you have the ability to browse the World Wide Web, you can view the Web pages of QFN. All you need is the correct URL or address. Just enter one of the following addresses in your browser:

- Intuit home page (**http://www.intuit.com/**)
- Quicken's home page (**http://www.intuit.com/quicken/**)

WARNING If you already have Netscape Navigator installed on your system, do *not* install the version that comes with Quicken. Installing more than one copy of Netscape on your system can cause problems. If you've already installed Netscape Intuit Edition with Quicken and are experiencing conflicts with your other copy of Netscape, uninstall the Intuit Edition and then, if necessary, reinstall your regular copy of Netscape Navigator to restore the system settings for the proper copy of the program.

TIP As long as your existing Web browser doesn't conflict with Netscape Navigator Intuit Edition, you may want to go ahead and access QFN from Quicken, even though you can access QFN from your regular Internet connection. The reason is that QFN access from within Quicken is free. The time you spend browsing QFN from Quicken won't run up your bill with your regular Internet service provider.

Quicken Information on the Commercial Online Services

Intuit sponsors forums (discussion groups) on the major commercial online services. These forums provide a venue for information exchange among users of Quicken and other Intuit products, on such topics as the Quicken features and issues relating to online personal finance. (See Figure 15.5.) The forums are monitored by Intuit support staff who step in from time to time to offer help and advice. In addition, there are file libraries containing information, utilities, and software update patches.

You can find Quicken forums on the following online services:

- America Online (keyword: **Intuit**)
- CompuServe (**GO INTUIT**)
- Prodigy (**JUMP INTUIT**)

FIGURE 15.5:
Intuit hosts an area on America Online.

You can often get more information about Quicken's online banking features from the online forums than you can by sending e-mail inquiries directly to your bank or Intuit Services Corporation. The reason is that you are getting help directly from other Quicken users. If you have a question about Quicken, the odds are that someone else has had the same question and may be willing to share the answer with you.

Of the major online services, CompuServe seems to have the most active Quicken forum discussions. Intuit sponsors a forum on CompuServe devoted to Quicken and personal finance issues (see Figure 15.6), including sections on Online Banking, Online BillPay, CheckFree, Investor Insight, and more.

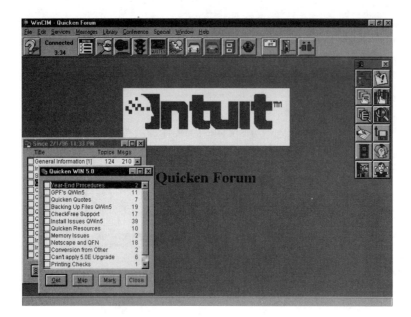

FIGURE 15.6:
You'll find lots of activity on CompuServe's Quicken forum.

Using Quicken Quotes to Get Stock Prices on CompuServe

Quicken Quotes is a separate utility program designed to download stock and mutual fund prices from CompuServe and update the prices in your Quicken investment portfolio. It was discontinued in the latest version of Quicken, replaced by Portfolio Price Update.

Portfolio Price Update is more tightly integrated into the Quicken program, and the service costs less than updating prices with Quicken Quotes by calling a 900 number at $1 per call. However, for CompuServe users, Quicken Quotes is actually cheaper. Instead of calling the 900 number, CompuServe subscribers can configure Quicken Quotes to call the local CompuServe access number, log in using their CompuServe member ID, and download stock prices for the cost of the connect time on the CompuServe system. Unless you're tracking a lot of securities, this option costs much less than using either the 900 number or Portfolio Price Update.

Even though Intuit no longer includes Quicken Quotes with the Quicken software, the utility still works. If you have an existing copy of Quicken Quotes, you can use it with a new version of Quicken. If you'd like to try Quicken Quotes, you can download the utility from the Quicken Forum file library on CompuServe.

Reinstating Quicken Quotes after an Upgrade

If you had Quicken Quotes installed before upgrading to the latest version of Quicken, all the necessary files should still be on your hard disk. To use Quicken Quotes with your new version of Quicken, follow these steps:

1. Use Windows Explorer (Windows 95) or File Manager (Windows 3.1) to locate the Quicken Quotes program file (QQUOTE.EXE) in your Quicken directory (usually C:\QUICKENW).

2. Double-click on the program file to run Quicken Quotes. The first time you run Quicken Quotes, it should update your Quicken configuration file and add Quicken Quotes to Quicken's Add-Ons menu. In the future, you should be able to run Quicken Quotes by choosing it from the Add-Ons menu.

Installing Quicken Quotes

If you are a new Quicken Quotes user, follow these steps to download and install the program:

1. Go to the Quicken Forum on CompuServe and download the file QQUOTES.EXE (note the *S* in the file name). You'll probably find it in Library 4.

2. Place the file in your \QUICKENW directory.

3. Using Windows Explorer or File Manager, double-click on the file to run it. This will expand and extract the component files from the self-extracting archive.

4. Locate the program file—QQUOTE.EXE (no *S* in this filename)—and double-click on it to run Quicken Quotes. When you run the program for the first time, it automatically updates your Quicken configuration file, adding Quicken Quotes to Quicken's Add-Ons menu.

Using Quicken Quotes

Quicken Quotes is a simple utility—it's not complicated to use. You can configure Quicken Quotes and use it to update the security prices in your Quicken investment portfolio by following these steps:

1. In Quicken, pull down the Add-Ons menu and choose Quicken Quotes. When the Quicken Quotes window first appears, the Stock Symbols list box is blank, as shown on the next page.

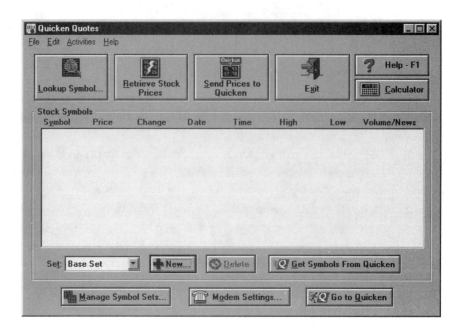

2. Click on the Modem Settings button to open the Modem Settings dialog box (shown below). Enter the appropriate information in the dialog box:

- Choose the correct port and speed for your modem.
- In the Phone text box, enter your local CompuServe access number.
- Enter your CompuServe ID and Password in the corresponding text boxes.

Click on the OK button to record your settings and close the dialog box.

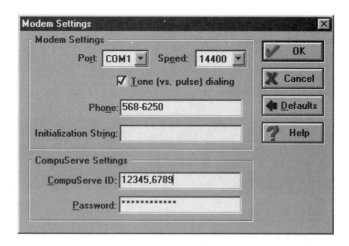

3. Click on the Get Symbols From Quicken button. Quicken Quotes will retrieve the stock symbols for the securities in your Quicken investment portfolio and add them to its list, as shown below.

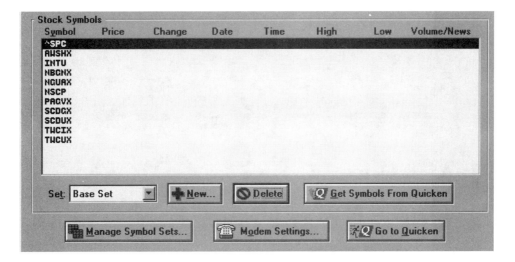

4. Next, click on the Retrieve Stock Prices button. Quicken Quotes will dial your local CompuServe number, log on, and download prices for the stock symbols in its list. A small message box (see below) appears to keep you apprised of the process.

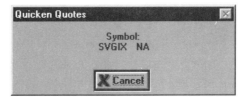

5. After downloading the stock prices you requested, Quicken Quotes displays the results in its Stock Symbols list, as shown on the next page. To update your Quicken investment portfolio with these prices, simply click on the Send Prices to Quicken button.

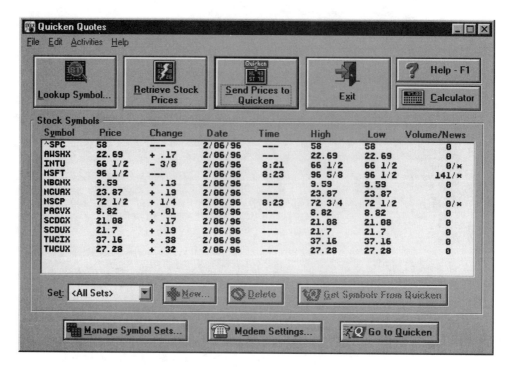

6. When you're through updating stock prices, click on the Exit button to close the window and exit the program.

For routine stock price updates, you can repeat this procedure, skipping steps 2 and 3.

Online Banking on America Online

As this book goes to press, Intuit has announced, but not yet implemented, plans for online banking on America Online. Intuit will offer AOL subscribers the ability to connect to participating financial institutions and get online statements, in much the same way you can get online statements in Quicken. AOL subscribers may get online bill payment capabilities as well. These online banking features are likely to be similar to the features found in Quicken, but without the links to the rest of the Quicken program and its ability to manage your finances.

Online banking on AOL probably won't replace the online personal finance features in a program like Quicken, but it's an interesting development that promises to extend the online banking experience to even more people. If you're interested in keeping up with the latest developments, check AOL's Intuit area (keyword: **Intuit**) for the latest announcements.

Appendix A

WHERE TO FIND HELP

- **On-screen help and manuals**
- **Intuit, Inc. technical support**
- **Intuit Services Corporation**
- **Bank customer service**
- **CheckFree**
- **Online services**

Quicken and its online personal finance features have grown far beyond a simple program for balancing your checkbook. It is now a complex system of programs and services that, when used in combination, can help you manage nearly every aspect of your personal finances.

Unfortunately, no complex system can work flawlessly all the time. Problems, glitches, and a certain amount of confusion and misunderstanding are inevitable. Fortunately, Intuit and its various partners provide a variety of support services to help you deal with the inevitable problems when they occur.

If you have a problem with Quicken or any of its online personal finance features, there's plenty of help available. You can get assistance from Intuit, Inc. (the software folks), from Intuit Services Corporation, from the participating financial institutions, and (if you use their service) from CheckFree. You can ask questions and receive answers via phone, fax, and e-mail. In fact, there are so many help options that it's sometimes hard to know where to turn to get the help you need in the most efficient manner. The descriptions of the various sources of information and assistance in the following pages can help guide you to the right place.

On-Screen Help and Manuals

Often, the most effective help you can get is self-help. It's always available at any time of the day or night, with no waiting. If you have a problem or question, don't reach for the phone until you've tried to resolve the situation yourself. You have some excellent resources right at your fingertips:

- Quicken Help—Quicken's help file is close at hand (choose Quicken Help from the Help menu in Quicken). You can find instructions for Quicken's most common tasks plus background and troubleshooting information.
- Onscreen Manual—available on the Deluxe CD-ROM, the Onscreen Manual is like an expanded and enhanced version of Quicken Help combined with a search utility that helps you find the information you need.
- *Quicken User's Guide*—the standard book that comes in the box with the software is still a valuable reference, although there's surprisingly little coverage of Quicken's online features.
- *Intuit Online Services Guide*—this supplement to the *Quicken User's Guide* fills in the missing information about Quicken's online features.
- This book—of course.

Intuit, Inc. Technical Support

The technical support department of Intuit, Inc. (the software company) is the place to turn for help with using the basic features of the Quicken software. They can help you with installation and configuration problems, as well as program operations that do *not* involve online personal finance features.

Intuit's technical support staff also monitor Intuit's forums on the online services, where they answer questions by e-mail, and you can also contact them via fax, but you're most likely to communicate with them by phone. The first number in the following list works, but you can skip a couple of layers of call routing by dialing the support number for the specific version of the Quicken product you're using:

- Quicken 5 for Windows—505-896-7219
- Quicken Financial Suite—505-896-7239
- Quicken 5 for Windows CD-ROM—505-896-7221
- Quicken 5 for Windows (floppy disk)—505-896-7220

Hours for these support lines are 6 a.m. to 6 p.m. mountain time, Monday through Friday. You pay for the phone call, and you can expect to wait on hold before talking to a representative. My experience has been that the staff is helpful and the hold times are not unreasonable.

Don't waste your time (or long-distance phone call) asking the Intuit, Inc. technical support staff about anything that has to do with online services. All such questions get transferred to Intuit Services Corporation.

Intuit Services Corporation

Intuit Services Corporation has a separate support facility from Intuit, Inc., located in a different state with a different staff and a different mandate. ISC handles everything related to any of Quicken's online services, including:

- Intuit membership
- Modem setup
- Online Banking
- Online BillPay
- Portfolio Price Update
- Quicken Financial Network
- All Quicken operations associated with any of the online features

ISC's support phone numbers are:

- 708-585-8500
- 800-462-6765 (automated response and live support)

Hours are 7 a.m. to 11 p.m. central time weekdays, and 8 a.m. to 5 p.m. on weekends.

When you call ISC, a call-routing system directs you to the appropriate option. Most of the choices you are given are obvious, but the dividing line between customer service and technical support can be a bit fuzzy.

WARNING
As I write this, ISC is suffering severe growing pains. Its support facilities have been overwhelmed by the demands placed on it. As a result, extremely long hold times on the phone lines are all too common, and e-mail messages take weeks to get answered. A call to ISC's support number can test your patience and tax your phone bill. To its credit, ISC is aggressively adding staff and taking other measures to address the problem, so the situation should get better eventually.

ISC's customer service department handles the following:
- Intuit membership setup
- Lost passwords
- Liaison with member banks (except for credit card companies such as American Express and the Quicken Credit Card)
- Setting up Online BillPay at a non-member bank
- Resetting check numbers (for non-member banks)
- Tracking lost or late payments

On the other hand, the technical support department is charged with the following areas:
- Modem problems
- Quicken software operations associated with online services
- Network log-in problems
- Liaison with credit card companies

TIP
For the fastest service, call Intuit Services Corporation early in the day. The earlier you call, the less time you're likely to spend waiting on hold.

Bank Customer Service

If you have an online banking relationship with one of the participating financial institutions, the bank's customer service department can be an excellent source of help. Many of these banks have support staff that specialize in online banking. Contact your bank for questions in the following areas:
- Setting up new bank accounts

- Online Banking
- Online BillPay
- Payments, transactions, or other issues concerning your account
- Forgotten PINs or other access problems

TIP If you have a question or problem and are having trouble getting through to ISC, try contacting the bank where you have your online account. They can often intercede on your behalf and get an answer for you. In some cases, they can transfer your call (on their toll-free line) to ISC and get you a priority position in the on-hold line for ISC support.

CheckFree

If you elect to use CheckFree instead of ISC's Online BillPay, you'll need to contact CheckFree to resolve any problems with the payments sent through its system. (However, if you have a problem that occurs in the Quicken software *before* you transmit the payment, call ISC.)

If you have a technical problem with a transmission, call CheckFree Technical Support:

- 800-297-3180

If you have a problem with a late or lost payment or with your CheckFree account, call CheckFree Customer Support:

- 800-848-6070

Online Services

Intuit and ISC technical support staff monitor Intuit-sponsored forums on the major online services. In addition, you can get invaluable help from other Quicken users on these forums. Here's how to access them:

- America Online—keyword: **Intuit**
- CompuServe—**GO INTUIT**
- Prodigy—**JUMP INTUIT**
- Quicken Financial Network—**http://www.intuit.com/quicken/**

Appendix B

CHECKFREE AND QUICKEN

CheckFree is an online bill payment service that works in much the same way as Intuit Services Corporation's Online BillPay. In fact, CheckFree provided the bill payment service for previous versions of Quicken. Online bill payment for the Macintosh version of Quicken still goes through CheckFree. Like the Online BillPay service from ISC, CheckFree can make payments drawn on just about any U.S. bank account that offers checking privileges.

Now that Intuit Services Corporation is providing online bill payment services, Intuit has structured the Quicken software to steer new online bill payment users to ISC. At the same time, Quicken continues to support connections to CheckFree for existing users. However, even if you are a new user of online bill payment, it's still possible to use CheckFree instead of ISC. You can even keep connections to both services operational and switch between them. Read on to learn how.

Why CheckFree?

Using CheckFree for your online bill payment service has some advantages over using ISC. As mentioned in Chapter 2, CheckFree has been in the business of providing bill payment services for several years—for large corporations as well as individuals. That means that CheckFree has had ample time to work out the glitches in its system and establish a good reputation with merchants across the country. CheckFree is past many of the start-up pains that Intuit Services Corporation is going through now. As a result, CheckFree users seldom report problems with late payments, and the customer support lines (toll-free) aren't swamped with callers.

In addition, CheckFree makes a much larger percentage of its payments by electronic funds transfer (EFT) as opposed to printed checks. CheckFree still makes most payments with paper checks, but EFTs account for a substantial portion (about a third) of its payments. (ISC makes only a tiny percentage of its payments by EFT—even to payees on its standard merchants list.) This is an important distinction, because scheduling EFTs to pay major vendors is so much more reliable than depending on the postal service to deliver paper checks.

NOTE When you send an online bill payment, CheckFree compares your payee against its list of EFT-capable merchants. If it finds a match, CheckFree pays your bill by EFT automatically. You don't have to do anything special (such as select the payee from a list of standard merchants) to take advantage of payment by EFT.

Of course, there are some disadvantages too. For Quicken users, lead times for making payments through CheckFree are longer (five days compared with two to four days with ISC), and you can access only one bank account with each CheckFree membership. Although CheckFree has recently begun to allow shorter lead times for some payees and to support payments from more than one bank account, these new features are available *only* from CheckFree's own software—not from Quicken. Unfortunately, the CheckFree software can't compare to Quicken in other areas.

Quicken documentation and press releases mention lower price as another advantage of using ISC instead of CheckFree. However, CheckFree has introduced a no-frills service at a price that matches what ISC charges for the service at a non-member bank. So the two companies are even on this score. However, if you're banking with one of the participating financial institutions in the Intuit network, you might get a better price for online bill payment from your bank. If you do sign up for Online BillPay through a member bank, ISC will handle the payments—you won't even have the option of using CheckFree.

Continuing to Use CheckFree

You say you've used CheckFree for years with previous versions of Quicken, and now the new version of Quicken works with Intuit Services Corporation instead—but you'd rather fight than switch!

Put away your boxing gloves. You can upgrade to the current version of Quicken *and* continue to use CheckFree if you like.

When you upgrade to the latest version of Quicken from a previous Quicken installation that used CheckFree, you get CheckFree support automatically. The familiar Check-Free commands are all available (albeit on slightly different menus) and operate as they did in previous versions of Quicken. Just click on CheckFree in the Activities menu to see a fly-out menu of CheckFree commands.

Choosing CheckFree Instead of Online BillPay

Although Quicken steers you toward Intuit Services Corporation's Online BillPay service, you can sign up for CheckFree's service instead. You just have to do a little more preparation on your own.

In principal, both services work the same way, and much of the information in Part Three of this book applies to CheckFree as well as to ISC and Online BillPay. (Of course, some implementation details will differ, as you will see in the rest of this appendix.) Check-Free isn't part of Intuit's network of participating financial institutions, so CheckFree makes no distinction between accounts at member banks and those at non-member banks. If you want CheckFree's online bill payment service, you contact CheckFree directly, not your bank.

Like Online BillPay from ISC, signing up for online bill payment from CheckFree is a two-step process:

- Signing up for the bill payment service
- Configuring Quicken to send electronic payments from your Quicken account

Unlike previous versions of Quicken, you won't find any CheckFree information or sign-up forms in the Quicken 5 for Windows package. That's not an obstacle, though. Simply call CheckFree's sales department (800-882-5280) for instructions on signing up for the service. Once you submit the necessary information about the bank account you want to make payments from, CheckFree can set you up to use its bill payment service from Quicken.

Next, you need to configure Quicken to send online payments to CheckFree for processing. The procedure consists of four main steps:

- Enabling CheckFree support in Quicken
- Switching to CheckFree in Quicken
- Setting up your modem to call CheckFree via the CompuServe network
- Activating your Quicken account for online payments with CheckFree

Now, let's look at each of these steps in more detail.

Enabling CheckFree Support in Quicken

Unless you upgraded from a previous version of Quicken in which you were using CheckFree for online bill payment, Quicken leaves its CheckFree support disabled in favor of Online BillPay from ISC. If you want to activate CheckFree support in a new Quicken installation or in an upgrade from a previous version that didn't use CheckFree, you must follow these steps:

1. Make sure Quicken is not running.
2. Open the QUICKEN.INI file (found in your \WINDOWS directory) using Notepad, WordPad, or another text editor. Usually, you can just double-click on the file in File Manager or Windows Explorer to open it with the appropriate text editor.
3. Scroll down through the file and locate the [AFS] section.
4. Add the following line to the [AFS] section. The entry must appear on its own line, but it can usually be anywhere within the [AFS] section (on some systems it must be on the first line):
   - EnableCheckFree=1
5. Save the edited QUICKEN.INI file, and exit the text editor.

Switching to CheckFree in Quicken

After you enable CheckFree support, you can switch Quicken from Online BillPay to CheckFree for electronic payments by following these steps:

1. Start Quicken.

2. From the Activities menu, choose CheckFree. Quicken opens the dialog box shown below.

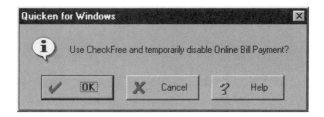

3. Click on the OK button to enable CheckFree.

Setting Up Your Modem to Call CheckFree

Since CheckFree doesn't go through the Intuit network, you'll need to set up your modem separately for CheckFree access via CompuServe by following these steps:

1. Pull down the Activities menu and click on CheckFree. When the fly-out menu appears, choose Set Up Modem to open the Set Up Modem dialog box shown below.

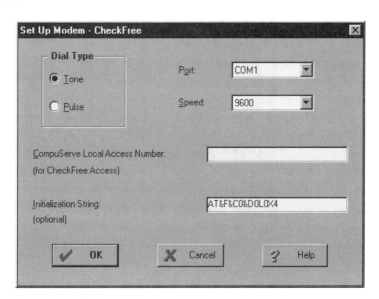

2. Enter the phone number for your local CompuServe access node. If you're a CompuServe subscriber, you can use the same local phone number you use for other CompuServe access. Otherwise, use the phone number recommended by CheckFree when you signed up for the service.

3. Check the other settings in the dialog box and adjust them if necessary; then click on the OK button to record the settings and close the dialog box.

Activating Your Quicken Account

The final preparatory task is to activate one of your Quicken accounts for online bill payments with CheckFree. This is the CheckFree counterpart of the process described in Chapter 10, "Setting Up a Quicken Account for Online BillPay." But for CheckFree, these are the steps to follow:

1. In the Activities menu, click on CheckFree, and then choose Set Up Account from the fly-out menu. Quicken opens the Online Payment Setup dialog box shown below.

2. From the Account List, select the account you want to use for CheckFree payments and then click on the Set Up button to open the Online Payment Account Settings dialog box shown on the next page.

3. Make sure the Enable Online Payments option is checked, and then fill in the Your Information section. In the CheckFree Information area, enter your account number (your Social Security number) and security code (your PIN).

4. Review the information in the dialog box to make sure it's correct, and then click on the OK button. When Quicken returns to the Online Payment Setup dialog box, you'll notice a lightning bolt marking the account as activated for electronic payments, as shown below.

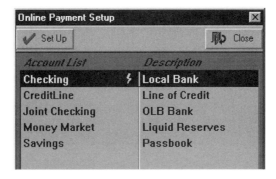

5. Click on the Close button to close the dialog box. Your account is now ready to use for electronic payments via CheckFree.

Switching between CheckFree and Online BillPay

You can have both CheckFree and Online BillPay services set up in the same Quicken file, and you can switch back and forth between them as often as you like. It only takes a few seconds to switch. You can even have both bill payment services set up to pay bills from the same bank account. You just can't have both bill payment services active at the same time.

If you're using CheckFree and want to switch to ISC's Online BillPay, follow these steps:

1. From the Online menu, choose Online Bill Payment. Quicken will display the message box shown below.

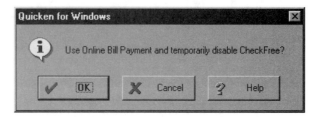

2. Click on the OK button to disable CheckFree and begin using Online BillPay. Quicken will open the Online Bill Payment window.

At this point, the CheckFree features are disabled, and the fly-out menu of CheckFree commands doesn't appear beside the CheckFree command on the Activities menu. Instead, the Online BillPay features are active. When you view your account register (see below), you'll notice the distinctive lightning bolts marking electronic transactions, and you can use Online BillPay features such as Payment Inquiry with those transactions.

2/22/96	130	⚡	Chevron USA		16	00
			[Gas-Chev]			
2/23/96	E-PMT		WIC		118	98
			Auto:Auto Insur			

If you're using Online BillPay and want to switch to CheckFree, follow these steps:

1. From the Activities menu, choose CheckFree. Quicken will display the message box shown below.

2. Click on the OK button to disable Online BillPay and begin using CheckFree.

This time, you've disabled the Online BillPay features and activated CheckFree's. The fly-out menu of CheckFree commands now appears beside the CheckFree command on the Activities menu. You can't open the Online Bill Payment window, the distinctive lightning bolts marking Online BillPay transactions in your account register are gone (see below), and you can't use Online BillPay features such as Payment Inquiry with those transactions.

2/22/96	130	Chevron USA	16	00
		[Gas-Chev]		
2/23/96	E-PMT	WIC	118	98
		Auto:Auto Insur		

Working with CheckFree in Quicken 5

If you used CheckFree in a previous version of Quicken, you'll soon feel right at home using the service in Quicken 5. The differences are minor and mostly cosmetic. It's not much more difficult to switch from Online BillPay to CheckFree, or to adapt the instructions and procedures in Part 3 of this book.

For instance, creating an online payment in the Write Checks window, as shown in Figure B.1, is similar to the same operation in the previous version of Quicken and exactly the same as creating a payment for Online BillPay.

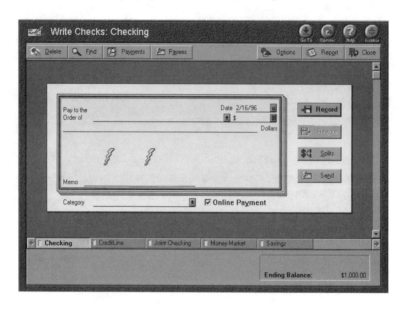

FIGURE B.1: CheckFree or Online BillPay? You can't tell the difference from this window.

When you get to the account register, however, you'll notice a difference between CheckFree and Online BillPay. Electronic payments are designated by "E-PMT," as shown below, instead of by "SEND" or a check number followed by a lightning bolt symbol.

2/23/96	E-PMT	WIC		118	98
		Auto:Auto Insur			

Unlike Online BillPay, CheckFree's Payment Inquiry and Stop Payment commands aren't on the Edit menu or on a pop-up menu that appears when you right-click on an electronic transaction in the account register. Instead, you'll find the equivalent commands by pulling down the Activities menu, clicking on CheckFree, and then selecting the command (Inquiry, Stop Payment, or Online Payment Information) from the fly-out menu.

CheckFree and Online BillPay can share many of the same entries in your Online Payee List, and you still manage the list in the Online Payee List window as described in Chapter 11. About the only differences are that the list of standard merchants isn't available when you're defining a payee for CheckFree, and there's no lead time column in the Online Payee List because the software imposes a uniform five-day lead time on all payments, regardless of payee.

Transmitting Payments to CheckFree

One significant procedural difference between Online BillPay and CheckFree is that you don't work in the Online Bill Payment window to send payments to CheckFree. When you're ready to send payments to CheckFree, follow these steps:

1. Pull down the Activities menu, click on CheckFree, and then choose Transmit from the fly-out menu to open the Transmit Payments dialog box shown below.

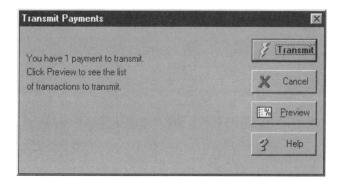

2. Click on the Preview button to open the Preview Transmission to CheckFree dialog box shown below. (This step is optional, but recommended. You can also click on the Transmit button to send the payments immediately.)

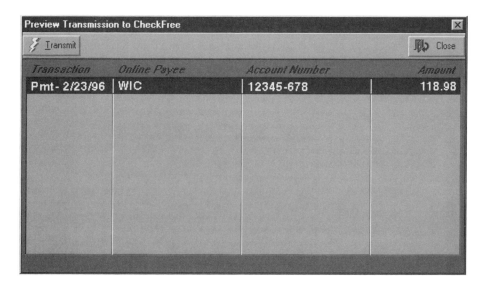

3. Review the transactions in the preview list. When you're ready to send them to CheckFree, click on the Transmit button. Quicken displays the plain, unadorned message box shown below to keep you informed of the progress of the call.

4. After sending your payments to CheckFree, Quicken displays a message confirming that the transmission was successful. Click on the OK button to close the message box.

Making Payment Inquiries and Stopping Payments

Payment inquiries and stop-payment orders for CheckFree transactions are similar to their Online BillPay counterparts described in Chapter 12. However, you use different techniques to access these features.

Payment Inquiries

If you just need to know the date or amount of an online payment you made, or the account it came from, you can view the information by following these steps:

1. Open the account register and select the transaction for which you want to get information.
2. Pull down the Activities menu and click on CheckFree, then choose Online Payment Info from the fly-out menu. Quicken displays a message similar to the one below.

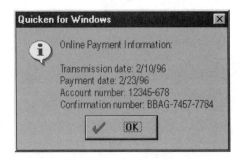

3. After viewing the information, click on the OK button to close the message box.

After a payment has been sent, you can ask CheckFree for additional information or request help in tracing a lost or misapplied payment. To send an online inquiry about a payment, follow these steps:

1. Open the account register and select the transaction for which you want to request help or information.

2. Pull down the Activities menu and click on CheckFree, and then choose Inquiry from the fly-out menu. Quicken displays a message similar to the one below.

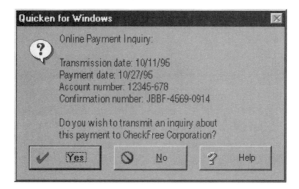

3. When you click on the Yes button, Quicken opens the Transmit Payment Inquiry to CheckFree dialog box shown below.

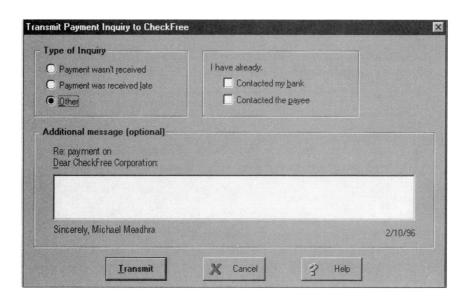

4. Make the appropriate selections to indicate the type of inquiry and whether you have already contacted the bank and the payee. Type any additional message in the large text box.

5. When your message is complete, click on the Transmit button. Quicken immediately calls CheckFree and logs on to transmit your message.

6. When the transmission is complete, Quicken will display a message to that effect. Click on the OK button to close the message box.

Stopping Payments

As with Online BillPay, you can stop a payment you have sent to CheckFree up until the time CheckFree sends it to your payee. When you need to cancel an online payment, follow these steps:

1. Open the account register and select the transaction you want to cancel.

2. Pull down the Activities menu and click on CheckFree, and then choose Stop Payment from the fly-out menu. Quicken displays a message box where you can confirm the action.

3. Click on the OK button in the message box. Quicken immediately calls CheckFree and logs on to transmit your request.

4. When the transmission is complete, Quicken will display a message to that effect. Click on the OK button to close the message box.

Using CheckFree E-Mail

Any time you log onto the CheckFree system, Quicken will automatically download any waiting e-mail messages for you, whether they are general messages to CheckFree subscribers or specific responses to an earlier inquiry. To read and manage your e-mail correspondence with CheckFree, follow these steps:

1. Pull down the Activities menu and click on CheckFree, and then choose E-Mail from the fly-out menu. Quicken opens the Read E-Mail window, as shown in Figure B.2.

2. Select a message header from the list at the top of the window. The message text then appears in the large panel.

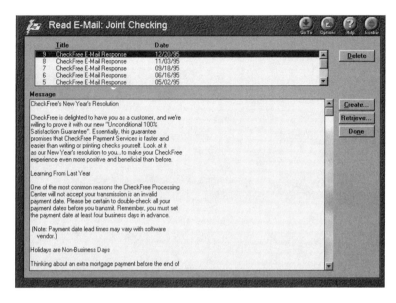

FIGURE B.2:
E-mail from CheckFree gets its own window.

3. After reading the message, you can delete it by clicking on the Delete button.

4. If you want to log onto the CheckFree system and check for new messages, click on the Retrieve button. Quicken will call the system, log in, and download any waiting messages.

On the other hand, if you want to create an e-mail message and send it to CheckFree, follow these steps:

1. Open the Read E-Mail window (refer to step 1 above), and click on the Create button. This will open the Transmit Message to CheckFree dialog box shown below.

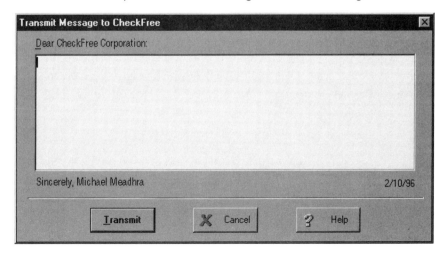

2. Type your message, and then click on the Transmit button. Quicken immediately calls CheckFree and logs on to transmit your message.

> **WARNING**
>
> Initially, the CheckFree e-mail feature didn't work properly in Quicken 5 for Windows. You could create and send a message, but it arrived at CheckFree improperly formatted and would be rejected by the CheckFree system. A software patch for Quicken solves the problem. If you have problems with CheckFree e-mail, make sure you get the latest update for your Quicken software. (The update is available for download from CompuServe or by request from Quicken technical support.) Until you get the update installed, you can still send payment inquires and receive e-mail messages from CheckFree; you just can't create messages in the Read E-Mail window.

How to Discontinue the Service

If, for any reason, you decide to discontinue the CheckFree service, the procedure is very similar to that for discontinuing Online BillPay. It's a two-part process:

- Contacting CheckFree to discontinue the service
- Deactivating CheckFree in Quicken

To discontinue the CheckFree service, you need to submit a written request to CheckFree, either by letter, fax, or e-mail. (If you don't know the address, you can contact CheckFree's customer service department at 800-882-5280.)

To deactivate CheckFree access from your Quicken account, you reverse the process you followed to activate it. Or, you can simply switch to Online BillPay mode by choosing Online Bill Payment from the Online menu and clicking on the OK button in the dialog box that appears.

Appendix C

MEMBER BANK OFFERINGS

The table on the following pages summarizes the online banking services offered by some of Intuit's participating financial institutions. The table is far from comprehensive. All of these banks offer a variety of products and services, and space limitations prevent a complete list here. In addition, banks are constantly changing and expanding their services. For example, some banks that previously served only a limited area can now set up an online relationship with customers anywhere in the United States. Several banks anticipate adding access to credit card accounts over the coming months.

We've done our best to make sure the information in this table is accurate as of the time this book goes to press. However, you'll need to call the financial institutions for current information when you're ready to open an account. In addition, the list of participating financial institutions is constantly growing as Intuit adds more member banks to its online banking network. As of summer 1996, you'll find a periodically updated version of this list on Sybex's World Wide Web site on the Internet (**http://www.sybex.com/**).

Bank Home Area	American Express	Bank of Boston MA	Centura Bank NC	Chase Manhattan Bank NY
Toll-free support	800-AXP-7500 M-F: 9 a.m.-1 a.m. Wknd: 10 a.m.-10 p.m.	800-476-6262 M-F: 7 a.m.-11 p.m. Wknd: 8 a.m.-5 p.m.	800-721-0501 M-F: 8a.m.-8 p.m. Sat: 9 a.m.-1 p.m.	800-CHASE24 24 hrs, 7 days
Area served	US	US	US	US
OB accounts supported	Amer. Express Optima	Checking Savings Balance only: IRA, CD	Checking Savings Money market CD	Checking Saving Money market, CD Equity line Credit cards
OBP accounts supported	None	Checking	Checking	Checking
OB fee	AmEx: free Optima: $1.50/4	$5/mo unlimited access	$3.95/mo unlimited access	$8/mo for 12 $1/ea add.
OBP fee	—	Included with OB	$5/mo unlimited	$15/mo for 20 $5/10 add.
ATM fee	—	Free	Free	Free
Foreign ATM fee	—	5/mo free $1.25/ea add.	Free with Online Checking	$1.50
Least expensive account	—	Direct Checking	Online Checking	Chase Direct
Minimum deposit	—	$10	$100	$0
Minimum balance	—	$0	$5,000	$6,000
Service charge	—	$9/mo includes OB and OPB	$10/mo unlimited OB	$20/mo
Per check fee	—	Unlimited free	OBP free Handwritten: 10 free; $.35/ea add.	Unlimited free
Other	—	$2/mo discount for direct deposit; $4/mo discount for OB	Visa debit card included	Pay by phone
Most popular account	American Express	Eagle Plan	Online Checking	Chase Direct
Minimum deposit	—	—	$100	$0
Minimum balance	—	$5,000 combined in all accounts	$5,000	$6,000
Service charge	$50/yr	Waived OB and OBP	$10/mo includes unlimited OB	$20/mo
Per check fee	—	Unlimited free	OBP free Handwritten: 10 free; $.35/ea add.	Unlimited free
Other	—	—	Visa debit card incl.	Pay by phone

Abbreviations used in the table: OB–Online Banking   OBP–Online BillPay   POS–point of sale

Bank Home area	Chemical Bank NY	Citibank CA, CO, CT, FL, IL, MD, NY	Compass Bank AL	CoreStates Bank PA
Toll-free support	800-CHEM-BANK 24 hrs, 7 days	800-446-5331 24 hrs, 7 days	800-COMPASS M-F: 9 a.m.-9 p.m. Sat: 9 a.m.-1 p.m.	800-562-6382 M-F: 8 a.m.-10 p.m. Sat: 8 a.m.-4 p.m. Sun: 9 a.m.-2 p.m.
Area served	US	US except AK*	AL, FL, TX	US
OB accounts supported	Checking Savings Money market CD	Checking Savings Money market Investments	Checking Savings Money market	Checking Savings Money market Credit card
OBP accounts	Checking	Checking	Checking	Checking
OB fee	$2.95/mo for 12 $.50/ea add.	Free	$3.95/mo unlimited	Free unlimited
OBP fee	Included with OB	Free	$5.95/mo unlimited	Free unlimited
ATM fee	Free	Free	Free	Free
Foreign ATM fee	$1	$1–$1.25	$1–$1.75	$1/MAC $2/Plus or Honor
Least expensive account	Lifeline Checking	Basic Checking	Checker	Simplified Checking
Minimum deposit	$1	$100	$100	$50
Minimum balance	$0	$0	$0	$0
Service charge	$4/mo	$3–$5/mo	$10/yr or $1/mo	$3/mo
Per check fee	10 free/mo $.50/ea add.	6 free/mo $.50/ea add.	Unlimited free	8 free/mo $.50/ea add.
Other	—	—	—	—
Most popular account	Chem Plus	Regular Checking	Checker	Core Check
Minimum deposit	$1	$500	$100	$50
Minimum balance	$3,000 daily or $6,000 average	$2,500 average or $5,000 in all accts.	$0	$0
Service charge	$9.50/mo	$15/mo	$10/yr or $1/mo	$7/mo
Per check fee	$.50/ea.	Unlimited free	Unlimited free	Unlimited free
Other	—	—	—	Free checks

*Fees vary by state

Abbreviations used in the table: OB–Online Banking   OBP–Online BillPay   POS–point of sale

Bank Home area	Crestar Bank DC, MD, VA	First Chicago IL	First Interstate Bank CA	Home Savings of America AR, CA, FL, TX
Toll-free support	800-CRESTAR 24 hrs, 7 days	800-800-8435 M-F: 6 a.m.-Mid Wknd: 9 a.m.-5 p.m.	800-YOU-AND-I 24 hrs, 7 days	800-310-4932 6 a.m.-11 p.m., 7 days
Area served	US	US	AK, AZ, CA, CO, ID, MT, NM, NV, OR, TX, UT, WA*	US
OB accounts supported	Checking Savings	Checking Savings Money market Credit card Some loans	Checking Savings Money market Credit card CD Line of credit	Checking Savings Money market CD IRA
OBP accounts	Checking	Checking Money market	Checking	Checking
OB fee	$3.50/mo for 8 $.45/ea add.	$3.95/mo for 12 $1/ea add.	$9.95/mo for 8 $.25/ea add.	$2.95/mo for 8 $.30/ea add.
OBP fee	$6/mo for 20 $.45/ea add.	$6.95/mo for 20 $3.95/10 add.	20 included with OB $.41/ea add.	$5.95/mo for 20 $.40/ea add.
ATM fee	Free	Free	Free	10 free/mo
Foreign ATM fee	$1.50	$1.50	$2	10 free/mo $1/ea add.
Least expensive account	Budget	Self Service	Basic Check	Convenience Checking
Minimum deposit	$0	$0	$100	$100
Minimum balance	$0	$0	$0	$750
Service charge	$3/mo	$9.95/mo	$4.50/mo	$7/mo
Per check fee	6/mo free $.50/ea add.	Unlimited free	8/mo free	Unlimited free
Other	—	—	—	—
Most popular account	Regular	Preferred Checking	Regular Checking	Any ATM
Minimum deposit	$0	$2,500	$200	$500
Minimum balance	$500	$2,500	$750	$2,000
Service charge	$7/mo	$15/mo	$9/mo	$10/mo
Per check fee	Unlimited free	Unlimited free	Unlimited free	Unlimited free
Other	—	OB free OBP $4.96/mo	—	Free ATM

*Fees vary by state

Abbreviations used in the table: OB—Online Banking   OBP—Online BillPay   POS—point of sale

Bank Home area	M&T Bank NY	Marquette Banks/ E Direct MN	Michigan National Bank MI	Quicken Credit Card (Travelers Bank)
Toll-free support	800-790-9130 M-F: 8 a.m.-Mid Wknd: 9 a.m.-5 p.m.	800-708-8768 M-F: 7 a.m.-8 p.m. Sat 9 a.m.-6 p.m. Sun: 11 a.m.-6 p.m.	800-CALL MNB M-S: 8 a.m.-9 p.m Sun: 8 a.m.-6 p.m	800-772-7889 24 hrs, 7 days
Area served	US	US	US	US
OB accounts supported	Checking Savings Credit card	Checking Savings Money market Line of credit	Checking Savings Money market Line of credit	Visa*
OBP accounts	Checking*	Checking	Checking Money market	None
OB fee	$9.95/mo for 8 $.75/ea add.	$4.95/mo for 8 $.25/ea add.	$2/mo unlimited	$2.95/mo
OBP fee	$5/mo for 20 $4/10 add.	$9.95/mo for 20 $.41/ea add.	$5.25/mo for 20 $4.50/10 add.	–
ATM fee	Free	Free	$.40	–
Foreign ATM fee	$1.25/withdraw $1.00/balance $.35/POS	$1	$1.50	–
Least expensive account	Worry Free	Free	Personal Checking	–
Minimum deposit	$25	$100	$25	–
Minimum balance	$1,000	$0	$750 daily or $1,500 average	–
Service charge	$6/mo	$0	$4/mo	–
Per check fee	Unlimited free	Unlimited free	$.40/ea	–
Other	3/mo OB free trial	6 free ATM/mo	–	–
Most popular account	Money Maker Select	Relationship	Rate Plus	–
Minimum deposit	$100	$0	$25	–
Minimum balance	$10,000 in all accounts	$2,500 in all accounts	$6,000 in all accounts	–
Service charge	$0	$8/mo	$12/mo	–
Per check fee	Unlimited free	Unlimited free	Unlimited free	–
Other	Free OB	Earns interest	Savings, CD	–

*OBP requires OB   *Personal
accounts only

Abbreviations used in the table: OB–Online Banking OBP–Online BillPay POS–point of sale

Bank Home area	Sanwa Bank California CA	Smith Barney NY	SunTrust Bank FL, GA, TN, AL	Texas Commerce Bank TX
Toll-free support	800-23SANWA M-F: 7 a.m.-Mid Wknd: 9 a.m.-Mid	800-221-3636 M-F: 8 a.m.-11 p.m. Sat: 8 a.m.-5 p.m.	800-382-3232 24 hrs, 7 days	800-235-8522
Area served	US	US	US*	Not yet available
OB accounts supported	Checking Savings	Brokerage	Checking Savings Money market Credit cards	Not yet available
OBP accounts	Checking	Brokerage	Checking Money market	Not yet available
OB fee	$4.95/mo for 8 $.30/ea add.	$3/mo for 8 $.25/ea add.	$5.95/mo for 8 $.75/ea add.	–
OBP fee	20 free with OB $.45/ea add.	$5.95/mo for 20 $.60/ea add.	$4.00/mo for 20 $.75/ea add.	–
ATM fee	Free	$1	Free	–
Foreign ATM fee	ATM: $1 POS: $.20	$1	$1.25	–
Least expensive account	One Market	Financial Management Account	Basic	–
Minimum deposit	$100	$10,000	$100	–
Minimum balance	$3,500 average	$0	$750 daily or $1,500 average	–
Service charge	$7/mo*	$50/yr	$5/mo	–
Per check fee	Unlimited free	Unlimited free	$.35/item	–
Other	Free checks	Margin buying	–	–
Most popular account	One Market	FMA Plus	All In One	–
Minimum deposit	$100	$10,000	$100 and qualify for credit	–
Minimum balance	$3,500 average	$0	$1,500 average	–
Service charge	$7/mo*	$125/yr	$12/mo	–
Per check fee	Unlimited free	Unlimited free	Unlimited free	–
Other	Free checks Free ATM	Free IRA Free ATM Free reports	Overdraft protection, credit card	–

*Special: 12 mo free *Fees and accounts vary by state

Abbreviations used in the table: OB–Online Banking OBP–Online BillPay POS–point of sale

Bank Home area	Union Bank CA	U.S. Bank CA, ID, NV, OR, WA	Wells Fargo CA	Intuit Online BillPay IL
Toll-free support	800-796-5656 6 a.m.-Mid, 7 days	800-422-8762 M-F: 7 a.m.-9 p.m. Wknd: 8 a.m.-7 p.m.	800-423-3362 ext. Q 24 hrs, 7 days	708-585-8500 M-F: 7 a.m.-11 p.m. Wknd: 8 a.m.-5 p.m.
Area served	US	US*	US	US
OB accounts supported	Checking Savings CD Money market Credit card Line of credit	Checking Savings Money market Credit card Line of credit	Checking Savings Money market Credit card Line of credit and more...	–
OBP accounts	Checking	Checking	Checking Money market	Checking
OB fee	$4.95/mo for 10 $.25/ea add.	$7.95/mo unlimited	Free unlimited	–
OBP fee	$5.95/mo for 25 $.40/ea add.	$9.95/mo for 20 $3.50/10 add.	$5/mo for 25 $.40/ea add.	$5.95/mo for 20 $2.95/10 add.
ATM fee	Free	Free	Free	–
Foreign ATM fee	$1.25*	$1.25	Free for out-of- state users	–
Least expensive account	Per Item	U Bank	Custom Assets	–
Minimum deposit	$100	$50	$25	–
Minimum balance	$750 daily or $1,500 average	$300	$0	–
Service charge	$3/mo	$3/mo	$0	–
Per check fee	$.35/ea	Free unlimited	Free unlimited	–
Other	Special: 5 yr free	–	Requires direct deposit	–
Most popular account	Direct Check	Variety of other accounts	Custom Asset	–
Minimum deposit	$100	–	$25	–
Minimum balance	$1	–	$0	–
Service charge	$0	–	$0	–
Per check fee	Unlimited free	–	Unlimited free	–
Other	Requires direct deposit	–	Requires direct deposit	–
	*Free ATM at Star or Cirrus	*Fees and accounts vary by state		

Abbreviations used in the table: OB–Online Banking   OBP–Online BillPay   POS–point of sale

Glossary

account, bank This definition includes any account at your bank or financial institution, such as checking, savings, credit card, money market, or brokerage accounts.

account, Quicken The collection of Quicken data that records transactions pertaining to a specific bank account or charge account with a merchant.

America Online The largest and fastest-growing of the commercial online services. America Online is known for its rich graphics, ease of use, and active chat rooms. AOL also popularized access to the Internet among many newcomers.

American Stock Exchange The second-largest stock exchange in America, specializing in trading stocks of small to medium-size companies.

AOL The common abbreviation for America Online.

ATM A common abbreviation for an automated teller machine.

automated teller machines Those ubiquitous machines that let you insert a card, punch a few numbers, and get cash. They go by cute names such as Tammy the Anytime Teller, but most people just call them cash machines. The machines can perform most of the routine functions of a teller at a bank branch, with the added advantage of giving you access to your bank account 24 hours a day, 7 days a week.

availability of deposits When you deposit a check into your bank account, the bank has the right to delay your access to those funds to allow time for the check to be paid by the bank on which it was drawn. As a result, the funds may not be available until several days after you deposit the check. Each bank has its own policies regarding how long you must wait for your deposits to become available.

bank As used in this book, the term includes banks and other financial institutions (including savings and loans or credit unions) that provide banking services such as checking and savings accounts.

bank holiday A day when the banks are not in operation, usually in observance of a national or state holiday. Banks seem to observe more holidays than most of us ever knew existed.

bank statement The report you get from your bank detailing your account balance. It usually includes a list of the transactions affecting the account.

Barons A highly respected financial magazine.

bill payment service A service that makes payments according to your instructions (usually transmitted online) by printing and mailing checks or initiating EFTs drawn on your bank account. Intuit Services Corporation and CheckFree are both examples of bill payment services.

broker, stock A person who facilitates the buying and selling of stocks and other securities for clients, usually in exchange for a commission on the sale. Stock brokers typically advise their clients on investment strategies and specific security purchases.

brokerage A financial institution that, for a fee, facilitates the buying and selling of stocks and other securities. A brokerage firm may provide other services such as checking accounts and administration of retirement accounts.

brokerage, discount A brokerage firm that executes security trades at discounted commissions. Usually, a discount brokerage provides little or no investment advice.

canceled check A check that has made the rounds from you to the payee, the payee's bank, and finally to your bank and has been paid from funds in your account. Traditionally, banks returned your canceled checks to you for your records. Increasingly, however, banks are discontinuing this practice; instead, banks may provide copies of your canceled checks upon request. It's all an effort to save on postage and handling costs.

certified check A check that is guaranteed by the issuing bank and is therefore as good as cash. Before issuing a certified check, the bank will verify that the signature is valid and that there are enough funds available to cover the check. Certified checks are sometimes called cashier's checks.

check A paper document instructing your bank to pay a designated amount to the payee from your account at the bank.

CheckFree An independent company that provides online bill payment services for corporations and individuals. Quicken users have had access to CheckFree's services for several years. However, Intuit Services Corporation is now the default provider of online bill payment services for Quicken users.

checking account In the broadest sense, a checking account is any bank account on which you can make withdrawals by writing checks to a third party. However, most people use the term to refer to accounts opened primarily for the purpose of making payments by writing checks and exclude those accounts which offer checking privileges as an ancillary feature.

CompuServe This is the respected elder of the commercial online services, and the favorite haunt of the more advanced users. It's not quite as easy to navigate as America Online, but there's more depth to the service. Although AOL does have slightly more users, CompuServe is running a close second. There's a very active community of Quicken users on CompuServe.

credit card You know what a credit card is: it's that dangerous piece of plastic that makes it all too convenient to make purchases without laying down cash. At the end of the month, you get a bill and must pay for the purchases you made with the card. You can pay the bill in full, or pay only a portion of it and pay the credit card company interest for the privilege of making your purchases on credit.

debit card A plastic card that looks similar to a credit card (and may even carry the same logos). You can use a debit card to make purchases in much the same way you purchase items with a credit card. The difference is that debit card transactions are deducted from your checking account immediately—just like a paper check or ATM withdrawal—instead of being billed at the end of the month.

demand-deposit A type of bank account that allows you to withdraw the funds you have deposited on demand, as opposed to the funds being held by the bank for a fixed (or minimum) term. For example, checking and savings accounts are demand-deposit accounts, but a CD is not.

direct deposit A form of electronic funds transfer in which funds (usually from your paycheck) are deposited directly into your bank account. You don't have to take a paper check to the bank; the deposit happens automatically. If your employer offers you the option of getting your paycheck by direct deposit, take it—it's great!

Dow Jones The parent company that owns and publishes the *Wall Street Journal,* and also the name of a leading stock market index.

download To copy information (files, messages, or transactions) from another computer to your hard disk via a modem connection or network.

e-mail Short for electronic mail, it's a typed message sent via a modem connection or network.

EFT The common abbreviation for an electronic funds transfer.

electronic funds transfer A way of moving funds from one bank to another that uses electronic communications between the banks' computers instead of paper checks. Electronic funds transfers are commonly used for transactions between banks and for payments to or from large corporations and government agencies. You've probably encountered electronic funds transfers in the form of automatic withdrawals to pay insurance premiums or utility bills.

encryption Scrambling data in such a way that it is unintelligible until it is decoded using a secret key. Quicken uses powerful encryption technology to ensure that the online communications between Quicken and Intuit Services Corporation remain private. Even if an unauthorized party manages to intercept a message, he or she can't read the encrypted data to get any information about your online financial transactions.

Federal Deposit Insurance Corporation (FDIC) This government agency insures individual bank deposits up to $100,000.

Federal Reserve Regulates banking and credit in the United States and provides much of the infrastructure for bank-to-bank transactions.

financial institution A generic term that includes banks, credit card companies, savings and loans, and brokerages.

401k A retirement account in which you set aside a portion of your current income for your retirement. Taxes on your contributions and accumulated interest and dividends are deferred until the funds are withdrawn after retirement. A 401k plan must be set up and made available by your employer.

individual retirement account A special savings account in which an individual can set aside money for retirement. If you meet the eligibility requirements, the funds you contribute to the IRA (up to $2,000 per year for most people) as well as the interest the account earns will receive favorable tax treatment.

initialization string A sequence of characters that your computer program sends to your modem to give it configuration information.

IntelliCharge The original name for Quicken's credit card, now simply called the Quicken Credit Card. With this card you can download information about your transactions into Quicken.

Internet This is the highly publicized "information superhighway." It's not a single online service or network, but many interconnected networks.

Internet service provider A company that, for a fee, provides individuals and companies access to the Internet. With a computer and modem, you can dial into the Internet service provider's facility and, from there, link up with the rest of the Internet.

Intuit banking network The partnership of Intuit Services Corporation and the participating financial institutions that have joined to provide Online Banking for Quicken users.

Intuit, Inc. The company that designs and markets the Quicken software and also owns and operates Intuit Services Corporation to provide online services for Quicken users.

Intuit Services Corporation The subsidiary of Intuit, Inc. that provides such online services as Online BillPay, Online Banking, and Portfolio Price Update. Intuit Services Corporation acts as the intermediary between Quicken users and the participating financial institutions.

Investor Insight A powerful Windows program for serious investors, Investor Insight is included with the Deluxe version of Quicken. It not only downloads stock prices, but also gives you access to news reports and historical data for the securities you specify.

IRA When you see IRA in this book, it's an abbreviation for individual retirement account, not Irish Republican Army.

ISC An abbreviation for Intuit Services Corporation.

joint account A bank account owned jointly by two or more people.

late charge A fee imposed by a merchant or lender for a payment made later than the date on which it was due.

lead time The time you must allow between submitting a payment request and the effective payment date. Usually, the lead time includes processing time at the bill payment service plus time for the check to travel through the U.S. Postal Service.

local bank A bank operating within a relatively small geographic area such as an individual city, county, or state.

log on/log off The procedure of connecting to or disconnecting from a network. For security reasons, the log-on process usually requires the user to provide a valid ID and password in order to gain access to the system. On the other hand, the log-off procedure simply ensures an orderly disconnection.

member bank One of the participating financial institutions that have joined with Intuit Services Corporation to provide Online Banking for Quicken users.

modem The piece of hardware that enables your computer to communicate with other computers over normal telephone lines. The term is short for modulation/demodulation device. The modem may be installed inside your computer or it may be housed in a small, separate box connected to your computer with a cable.

money market account A bank account that is tied to money market investments in some way. The details vary from bank to bank, but a money market account is typically a hybrid savings account with limited checking privileges. It usually earns higher interest rates than other interest-bearing, demand-deposit accounts, but it is not insured by the FDIC.

NASDAQ The computer-based stock exchange that provides an alternative or supplement to the traditional trading floors of the New York Stock Exchange and American Stock Exchange.

Netscape Navigator The most popular Web browser software for viewing documents (called Web pages) on the Internet's World Wide Web. A specially modified version of Netscape Navigator is included with the latest version of Quicken.

New York Stock Exchange America's largest stock exchange; this is where stocks of the country's largest corporations are traded.

non-member bank Any bank that is *not* one of the participating financial institutions that have joined with Intuit Services Corporation to provide Online Banking for Quicken users.

Online Banking The Quicken feature that allows you to get online bank statements and download transaction details from your bank. (Note the capitalization when the term refers to the Quicken feature.)

online banking Conducting banking-related activities online. (Note that the term appears in lowercase when it is used to describe the generic activity instead of the specific Quicken feature.)

Online Bill Payment Essentially, this is another term for Online BillPay, the Quicken feature that allows you to pay bills online by instructing Intuit Services Corporation to print a check or initiate an electronic funds transfer on your behalf. You'll see this term in various Quicken windows and menus that access the Online BillPay feature. (Note the capitalization when the term refers to the Quicken feature.)

online bill payment Paying your bills online by instructing a bill payment service such as Intuit Services Corporation or CheckFree to make the payment on your behalf. (Note that the term appears in lowercase when it is used to describe the generic activity instead of a specific Quicken feature.)

Online BillPay The name of the Quicken feature that allows you to pay bills online by instructing Intuit Services Corporation to print a check or initiate an electronic funds transfer on your behalf. Also the name of the service provided by Intuit Services Corporation.

online payee A payee for which you have supplied all the information Quicken needs (full address, phone number, and account number) in order to make an online bill payment to that payee.

online personal finance This is my inclusive term for Online Banking, Online BillPay, and other online financial services such as Portfolio Price Update and Investor Insight—in short, all the personal finance services you can find online.

online service Any service that is provided over a modem connection or network. However, the term usually refers to the commercial services such as CompuServe and America Online that host discussion groups and provide libraries of downloadable files in exchange for a monthly subscription and hourly connect-time fees.

online session A single instance of connecting to a network or online service, exchanging data, and then disconnecting.

overdraft This is what happens if you write a check for more money than you have in your checking account. It's an embarrassing and costly mistake to make. Both the bank and the merchant will probably charge stiff penalties for handling a check that is not paid because of insufficient funds in your account.

overdraft protection Some banks offer a service whereby the bank will pay a check even though it will create an overdraft. Usually, overdraft protection is accomplished by transferring funds from a credit card account or line of credit into your checking account.

password A secret code word (or string of characters) used for identification and to gain access to a protected area. In Quicken, your Intuit membership password is your electronic key that unlocks access to the services provided by Intuit Services Corporation.

payee The person or company you designate as the recipient of a check or other payment; in other words, the party you are making the payment to.

payment inquiry A request for more information about a specific online payment. For example, you can find out the date the payment was processed as well as the date it was scheduled to reach the payee. If the payee has no record of the payment, you can request the bill payment service to trace the lost payment for you.

personal identification number A secret code number that you are required to enter in order to verify that you are authorized to use an online banking feature. Your PIN is your electronic access key which proves that you are who you say you are. No doubt you're accustomed to using a PIN with your ATM card; you'll also use a PIN to access online banking services from Quicken.

PIN The common abbreviation for your personal identification number.

portfolio A collection of investments. In Quicken, the term encompasses all your investment accounts. In Investor Insight, on the other hand, a portfolio is simply a group of securities that you want to track together. You can define multiple portfolios in Investor Insight.

Portfolio Price Update A service that lets you download stock prices and update the value of your Quicken investment portfolio. Portfolio Price Update is a built-in feature of Quicken, but there is a monthly fee for using the service.

processing center The facility where your online bill payments and other electronic transactions are processed. In most cases, this will be Intuit Services Corporation, although some users may contract with CheckFree for bill payment services.

Prodigy One of the major commercial online services. Originally developed by IBM and Sears, Prodigy was a very popular service for a while. However, it hasn't kept up with the times or the growth of the larger online services.

proprietary software Software designed for the exclusive use of a limited group, such as the customers of one financial institution.

QFN An abbreviation for the Quicken Financial Network.

Quicken The most popular personal finance software on the market today.

Quicken Financial Network Intuit's home on the Internet. You can use your World

Wide Web browser to locate and view information about Quicken and other Intuit products, plus lots of other information about online personal finance, mutual funds, and more. Quicken includes the necessary software and a link to an Internet service provider to give you free access to the Quicken Financial Network from within Quicken.

reconcile an account To reconcile an account is to compare your records to those of the bank to make sure they agree. During reconciliation, you verify the account balance, determine which transactions have cleared and which are still outstanding, and check each transaction for accuracy.

recurring payments Fixed payments that occur on a regular basis, such as rent and loan payments. You can automate recurring payments by using Scheduled Transactions in Quicken by or instructing your bill payment service to make repeating payments.

regional bank A bank that operates throughout a larger geographic area than a local bank. The bank's operating area may include several states. Some regional banks can serve customers nationwide via online banking, but they can provide full service only within their native region.

repeating payments Payments that will be made by your bill payment service on a regular basis to pay recurring bills automatically. You need to send instructions for a repeating payment to your bill payment service only once; from then on, the service will make the payments automatically without further word from you.

routing number A bank identification number that appears on checks and other similar documents and transactions. The routing number enables the banking system to get your check back to your bank for payment from anywhere in the country.

safe-deposit box A small, locked box or drawer in a bank vault which you can rent to provide safekeeping for important papers and other valuables.

Scheduled Transactions A Quicken feature that allows you to set the program to automatically enter (or prompt you to enter) recurring transactions.

securities A general term for stocks, bonds, and related financial instruments.

Standard & Poors A rating service for securities.

standard merchant One of a list of payees with which Intuit Services Corporation has made special arrangements for the delivery of online bill payments from Quicken users. In most cases, the arrangements consist of a special address where payment checks will be sent, and perhaps some expedited handling. With a few standard merchants, Intuit Services Corporation has made arrangements to pay them by electronic funds transfer.

stop payment When used in the context of online bill payments, *stop payment* means to cancel an online payment after it has been submitted to the bill payment service, but before it has been processed and sent to the payee. On the other hand, issuing a stop-payment order at your bank instructs the bank not to honor a check that you have written (or had printed by a bill payment service).

transaction A single financial item or activity such as a check, deposit, online bill payment, transfer, stock purchase, or credit card charge.

URL Universal Resource Locator—a fancy term for an Internet address.

wire transfer Banks (and certain companies such as American Express and Western Union) can use wire transfers to move funds from one location to another almost instantaneously. Wire transfers are fast and reliable, but expensive.

World Wide Web The multimedia portion of the Internet. It's a system for publishing electronic documents that may contain graphics, text, and links to other similar documents. You need special software—called a Web browser—to view these documents. Quicken includes a copy of Netscape Navigator for this purpose.

Index

Note to the Reader: Throughout this index, main entries are highlighted in **boldface**. **Boldface** page numbers indicate primary discussions of a topic. *Italic* page numbers indicate illustrations.

E

F

U

V